VIETNAM STUDIES

FIELD ARTILLERY, 1954–1973

by
Major General David Ewing Ott

DEPARTMENT OF THE ARMY
WASHINGTON, D.C., 1975

Library of Congress Cataloging in Publication Data
Ott, David Ewing
　Field artillery, 1954–73.

　(Vietnam studies)
　Includes index.
　Supt. of Docs.: D 101.74:F45/954–73
　1. Vietnamese Conflict, 1961–1975.　2. United States. Army. Field artillery—History. I. Title. II. Series.
U742.O87　　　959.704'342　　　75–619336

First Printing

For sale by the Superintendent of Documents, U.S. Government Printing Office
Washington, D.C. 20402 – Price $3.10 (paper cover)

Stock Number 008–020–00556–8

Foreword

The United States Army met an unusually complex challenge in Southeast Asia. In conjunction with the other services, the Army fought in support of a national policy of assisting an emerging nation to develop governmental processes of its own choosing, free of outside coercion. In addition to the usual problems of waging armed conflict, the assignment in Southeast Asia required superimposing the immensely sophisticated tasks of a modern army upon an underdeveloped environment and adapting them to demands covering a wide spectrum. These involved helping to fulfill the basic needs of an agrarian population, dealing with the frustrations of antiguerrilla operations, and conducting conventional campaigns against well-trained and determined regular units.

It is still necessary for the Army to continue to prepare for other challenges that may lie ahead. While cognizant that history never repeats itself exactly and that no army ever profited from trying to meet a new challenge in terms of the old one, the Army nevertheless stands to benefit immensely from a study of its experience, its shortcomings no less than its achievements.

Aware that some years must elapse before the official histories will provide a detailed and objective analysis of the experience in Southeast Asia, we have sought a forum whereby some of the more salient aspects of that experience can be made available now. At the request of the Chief of Staff, a representative group of senior officers who served in important posts in Vietnam and who still carry a heavy burden of day-to-day responsibilities have prepared a series of monographs. These studies should be of great value in helping the Army develop future operational concepts while at the same time contributing to the historical record and providing the American public with an interim report on the performance of men and officers who have responded, as others have through our history, to exacting and trying demands.

The reader should be reminded that most of the writing was accomplished while the war in Vietnam was at its peak, and the monographs frequently refer to events of the past as if they were taking place in the present.

All monographs in the series are based primarily on official records, with additional material from published and unpublished secondary works, from debriefing reports and interviews with key participants, and from the personal experience of the author. To facilitate security clearance, annotation and detailed bibliography have been omitted from the published version; a fully documented account with bibliography is filed with the U.S. Army Center of Military History.

The qualifications of Major General David Ewing Ott to write *Field Artillery, 1954–1973,* are considerable. He served in combat with field artillery units in World War II, Korea, and Vietnam. In World War II he was a forward observer with the 868th Field Artillery Battalion of the 65th Infantry Division, and during the Korean War he was executive officer and operations officer of the 64th Field Artillery Battalion of the 25th Infantry Division. In Vietnam he served as executive officer of II Field Force Artillery in 1966 and as commander of the 25th Infantry Division Artillery in 1967. Other assignments that make him particularly qualified to write the monograph include instructor of field artillery gunnery at the Field Artillery School from 1948 to 1951; S–3, 82d Airborne Division Artillery, 1957 to 1959; commander of the 2d Howitzer Battalion of the 83d Artillery from 1959 to 1960; Chief, Artillery Branch, Officer Personnel Directorate, Office of Personnel Operations, Department of the Army; and Director, Vietnam Task Force, International Security Affairs, Office of the Assistant Secretary of Defense. General Ott is presently the Commanding General, U.S. Army Field Artillery Center, and Commandant, U.S. Army Field Artillery School, at Fort Sill, Oklahoma. He is thus the Army's senior field artilleryman.

Washington, D.C.
15 March 1975

VERNE L. BOWERS
Major General, USA
The Adjutant General

Preface

This monograph will illuminate some of the more important activities—with attendant problems, shortcomings, and achievements—of the U.S. Army Field Artillery in Vietnam. The wide variations in terrain, supported forces, density of cannon, friendly population, and enemy activity which prevailed throughout South Vietnam tend to make every action and every locale singular.

Though based largely upon documents of an historical nature and organized in a generally chronological manner, this study does not purport to provide the precise detail of history. Its purpose is to present an objective review of the near past in order to assure current awareness, on the part of the Army, of the lessons we should have learned and to foster the positive consideration of those lessons in the formulation of appropriate operational concepts. My hope is that this monograph will give the reader an insight into the immense complexity of our operations in Vietnam. I believe it cannot help but reflect also the unsurpassed professionalism of the junior officers and noncommissioned officers of the Field Artillery and the outstanding morale and esprit de corps of the young citizen-soldiers with whom they served.

I would like to express my appreciation to the following people who assisted in this effort:

Major General Roderick Wetherill, as commandant of the Field Artillery School, authored the monograph from November 1972 until his retirement in May 1973, when authorship was transferred to me. To General Wetherill go my sincere thanks for getting this project off the ground. Under his direction the initial outline was developed, a research team formed, and initial research conducted.

Major General Gordon Sumner, Jr., presently with the Office of the Assistant Secretary of Defense (International Security Affairs), must be credited with conceiving this project and finding support for its accomplishment.

Major General W. D. Crittenberger, Jr., presently Deputy Director, Plans and Policy Directorate, J–5, Joint Chiefs of Staff, sponsored this project and helped to lay the initial groundwork. During the research and writing of the monograph his advice, based on his experiences as II Field Force Artillery commander in Vietnam, has been invaluable.

Brigadier General Robert J. Koch, assistant commandant of the

Field Artillery School, has been my principal assistant in this effort (as he was for General Wetherill before me). He has helped me to steer the activities of all those who participated in producing the monograph. Beyond that, he has provided valuable input to the monograph based on his experiences as the commander of the 23d Artillery Group and the XXIV Corps Artillery in Vietnam.

Colonel Vincent G. Oberg, director of the Army-Wide Training Support Department of the Field Artillery School, with the help of two of his division chiefs, Lieutenant Colonels Ray K. Casteel and Carl W. Sullinger, co-ordinated this effort within the Field Artillery School. He developed a plan of work, sought out source material, and formed the monograph research team.

The monograph research team consisted of officers and clerks assigned to various field artillery activities on post and of officers who had recently completed the field artillery officer advance course and were on casual, or "blackbird," status awaiting further assignment. The monograph team must be credited with accomplishing the leg work—researching the topic and expanding into more detail the general guidance they received. Members of the team were Lieutenant Colonel Calvin DeWitt III, Major Bob W. Garner, Major Ronald N. Funderburk, Major Craig H. Mandeville, Captain Richard L. Murphy, Captain Fred R. Franzoni, Captain Richard H. Reed, Captain Nicholas A. Radvanczy, First Lieutenant Melvin M. Yazawa, Mrs Pamela K. Morales, and Private First Class C. Foster Deen.

Last, I extend my sincere thanks to all field artillerymen who contributed much of the source material for the monograph either by relating to us their personal experiences and observations or by lending us their personal files.

Fort Sill, Oklahoma
15 March 1975

DAVID E. OTT
Major General, U.S. Army

Contents

Chapter	Page
I. THE VIETNAM ENVIRONMENT	3
Geography	3
The Enemy	7
Political-Military Considerations	18
II. THE ADVISORY EFFORT, 1950–1965	21
Background—Military Assistance Advisory Group, Vietnam, Organized	21
The Field Artillery Adviser	22
The Adviser's Challenge	24
The Adviser Learns, Too	31
III. IN ORDER TO WIN	38
The Impact of Vietnam on Field Artillery Organizations	39
Fire Support Co-ordination	47
Field Artillery Weapons	49
Field Artillery Mobility	51
The Fire Base	55
Base Camp Defense	73
Riverine Artillery	75
IV. THE BUILDUP (1965–1967)	81
The Buildup Begins and Early Actions Around Saigon	81
New Arrivals	86
The Pleiku (Ia Drang) Campaign	87
The Buildup and Major Combat Operations During 1966	96
The Buildup and Major Combat Operations During 1967	110
Overview: 1965 to Pre-Tet 1968	129
V. THE HOT WAR (1968–OCTOBER 1969)	137
Tet 1968	137
Khe Sanh	148
A Shau	157
Actions at Fire Bases and Lessons Learned	161
Peak Strength and Beginning of Redeployment	167
Artillery Organizations	168

Chapter	Page
Safety	173
Target Acquisition	179
Artillery Raids	184
Harassing and Interdiction Fires	187
Civic Action	188
VI. VIETNAMIZATION, NOVEMBER 1969–FEBRUARY 1973	190
Field Artillery Assistance Programs	190
Operations Into Cambodia	205
Toward Vietnamese Self-Sufficiency	215
1972 Enemy Offensive	220
Problems During Phase-Down of U.S. Forces	225
VII. AN OVERVIEW	231
Work To Be Done	231
The Field Artilleryman's Performance	236
INDEX	241

Charts

No.		
1.	Characteristic Sapper Organization	16
2.	Field Artillery Task Organization, January 1968	170
3.	Field Artillery Task Organization, July 1969	171

Maps

1.	Administrative Divisions, South Vietnam	2
2.	Vietnam Topographic Regions	4
3.	Enemy Activity, 1954–1965	36
4.	Ia Drang Valley	88
5.	Area of Operations: MASHER/WHITE WING	99
6.	Landing Zone BIRD	109
7.	Operation JUNCTION CITY, 22 February–14 May 1967	114
8.	Battle of Suoi Cut, FSB BURT	119
9.	Fire Support Base CUDGEL	126
10.	The *Tet* Offensive, 1968	139
11.	The Battle of Hue: Enemy Attack, 30–31 January 1968	140
12.	The Battle of Hue: Friendly Situation, 24–25 February 1968	141
13.	III Corps Tactical Zone	144
14.	North Quang Tri Province	149
15.	Khe Sanh Valley	150
16.	I Corps Tactical Zone	158
17.	Fire Support Base MAURY I	162

No.		Page
18.	Fire Support Base PIKE VI	164
19.	FSB CROOK: Enemy Situation, Friendly Fires, 6–7 June 1969	183
20.	Enemy Base Areas	208
21.	III ARVN Corps Operations	210
22.	1st Cavalry Division Operations, May–June 1970	211

Diagrams

1.	M101 105-mm. Artillery Field Position	63
2.	M102 105-mm. Emplacement	64
3.	Semipermanent 105-mm. Self-Propelled Howitzer Emplacement	65
4.	Towed 155-mm. Howitzer Emplacement	66
5.	Self-Propelled 155-mm. Howitzer Emplacement	67
6.	Heavy (8-inch or 175-mm.) Artillery Emplacement	68
7.	Battery A, 2d Battalion (Airborne), 320th Artillery, Fire Base	121
8.	Artillery Box	152

Illustrations

ARVN Outpost	26
ARVN Gun Section	28
155-mm. Howitzer in Tuy An District Headquarters	33
Early Movement of Artillery by Air	34
CH–47 With M102 Howitzer	51
CH–54 Lifting 155-mm. Howitzer	52
Fire Support Base J. J. CARROLL	53
Star Formation	54
Building Parapets	56
1st Battalion, 40th Field Artillery, in Position Along Demilitarized Zone	57
Typical Towed 155-mm. Position	57
Battery C, 2d Battalion, 138th Field Artillery, on Hill 88	58
Battery D, 3d Battalion, 13th Field Artillery, at Fire Support Base STUART	59
155-mm. Howitzer Position Using Speedjack and Collimator	60
6,400-Mil Chart	62
Artillery Hill at Pleiku	69
AN/MPQ–4 Countermortar Radar	71
TPS–25 Ground Surveillance Radar	72
30-Inch Xenon Searchlight	74
CH–47 Emplacing Airmobile Firing Platform	76

	Page
Riverine Field Artillery Battalion Command Post	77
Riverine Battery Position	78
Riverine Platoon Moored to Canal Bank	79
Riverine Gun Section in Traveling Configuration	80
105-mm. Battery Firing From Hasty Position	82
Aerial Rocket Artillery UH–1B with XM3 Weapons System	85
Field Force Artillery	97
175-mm. Gun	98
CH–54 Emplacing 155-mm. Howitzer	102
M102 Firing High-Angle	103
Battery A, 2d Battalion, 320th Field Artillery, in Position on Operation WHEELER	123
Aerial Field Artillery Cobra in Flight	131
Aerial Field Artillery Cobra and Light Observation Helicopter	132
Major General David E. Ott Demonstrates FADAC	135
1st Battalion, 8th Field Artillery, Fire Direction Center	176
FADAC Computer	177
Ammunition Resupply by CH–54	187
Formal Fire Direction Center Class for ARVN Field Artillerymen	203
ARVN 155-mm. Howitzer Static Position	206
ARVN 103d Field Artillery Battalion in Training	207

Illustrations on front and back covers of softback edition are the work of Specialist 6 Jim Gardner.

FIELD ARTILLERY

MAP 1

CHAPTER I

The Vietnam Environment

The environment of Southeast Asia, and more specifically of Vietnam, posed particular problems that plagued all military activities. The U.S. Military Assistance Advisory Group (MAAG), Vietnam, began the publication of a series of "lessons learned" reports in March 1962. *Lessons Learned Number 31*, on artillery organization and employment, appeared in September 1963. Observations made in this report were prophetic. Artillery must be organized and employed in counterinsurgency to meet new requirements, for "there are no well defined battle areas." Indeed, the report of the American advisers continued, "The entire republic of Vietnam can be considered an area of operations." (*Map 1*) Moreover, the terrain in Vietnam was such that it became a major concern along with the tactics and techniques of the enemy. The artillery, especially, must adapt to the physical environment because, the report concluded, even "if time to displace were available the road net or terrain would frequently prohibit displacement."

These early observations foreshadowed some of the fundamental problems that American forces would encounter in succeeding years. The Vietnam environment—the human challenge as well as the elemental implications—determined the character of the conflict in terms of geography, the enemy, and the government of Vietnam.

Geography

The coastline of Vietnam, which extends for more than 1,200 miles, forms an S-curve that reaches from the southern border of China to the tip of the Indochina peninsula. The length of the coastline almost equals that of the Pacific coast of the continental United States. The total land area of Vietnam, some 127,000 square miles, is approximately the same as that of New Mexico. To the north, the country widens irregularly to a maximum of 300 miles; to the south, it reaches a maximum width of 130 miles.

Vietnam may be divided into five distinct geographic regions: (1) the Northern Mountains, (2) the Northern Plains, (3) the

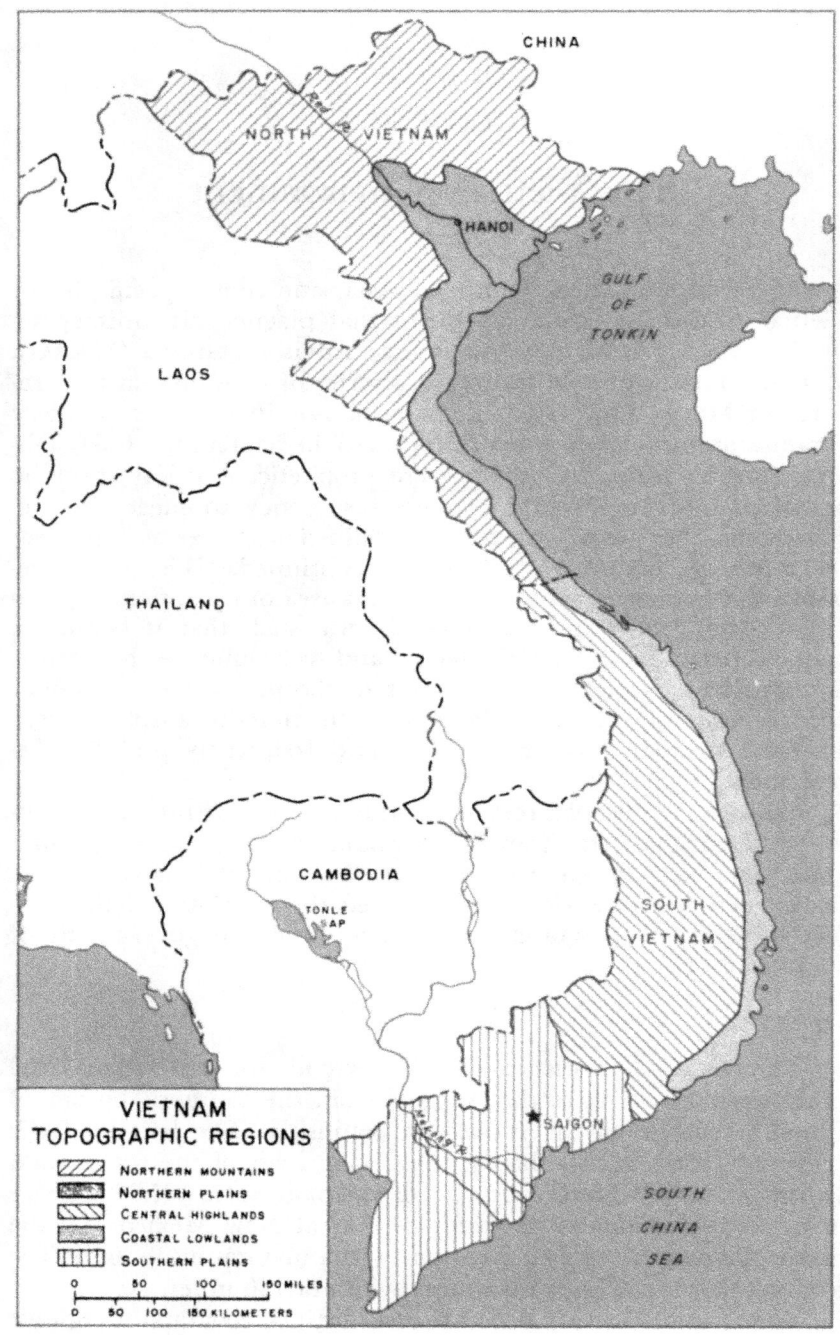

MAP 2

Central Highlands, (4) the Coastal Lowlands, and (5) the Southern Plains. *(Map 2)*

The Northern Mountains region encompasses about 40,000 square miles of rugged terrain in what is part of the Annamite Mountains. The peaks are higher in the north, northwest, and west, where they range from 4,000 feet to about 8,000 feet. The southernmost spur of the Annamite Mountains, over 750 miles long, originates in Laos and stretches southeastward to the Vietnamese-Laotian border and thereafter generally parallels the coast. To the east, the slopes fall off steeply to the narrow coastal plains; to the west, the Annamite spur slopes more gradually to the valley of the Mekong in Laos and Cambodia.

The Northern Plains region includes the Red River Delta and the narrow coastal lowlands of North Vietnam. The area is well cultivated and densely populated. The delta proper, about 5,700 square miles, is indented by the many small mouths of the Red River. Levees, some up to 35 feet high, are built along the major river and stream networks and divide the land into a series of saucer-shaped basins. Most of the land is not over 10 feet above sea level, and much of it is 3 feet or less. Hence, the whole area is subject to frequent flooding.

The Central Highlands region is the 18,600-square-mile region of central South Vietnam. The northernmost portion of the highlands is adjacent to the Northern Mountains region and is largely a continuation of the Annamite Mountains. The ranges are rugged, with elevations near 7,000 feet. Farther south the region is dominated by gently rolling volcanic plateaus with elevations between 2,600 and 5,000 feet.

The Coastal Lowlands region is the narrow belt of plains extending from the Mekong Delta to the Northern Plains region. The region, enclosed on the landward side by the Central Highlands, is never more than 40 miles wide. The entire coastal strip is segmented by mountain spurs that extend to the sea. The region is in varying degrees of cultivation and is interspersed throughout with sand dunes.

The Southern Plains region takes in the intermediate lowlands and the fertile Mekong Delta. The intermediate lowlands constitute the transitional zone between the Central Highlands and the delta proper. Basically an undulating plain interrupted occasionally by marshland, this transitional zone slopes southward. Elevations range from 300 feet in the northern sector to sea level near the delta. Dense rain forests cover large areas of the region; however, dry field crops such as corn, sweet potatoes, and beans, in addition to the rubber plantations and the less extensive rice fields, are scattered throughout. The Mekong Delta is the most fertile plain in Vietnam and is its largest rice-producing area. Almost the entire delta is covered with rice fields situated within an interlacing network of rivers, streams, and irrigation canals. The plain is low and level; nowhere is it more than 10 feet above sea level. Gradients vary as little as one-fifth foot per mile. The dominant relief features are the rice paddy dikes. The drainage network is irregular and, because of poor runoff conditions, the northern edge of the delta is marshland. Yet the Mekong, unlike the Red River, has a moderating element whenever the river is in flood. The Tonle Sap, a large freshwater lake in central Cambodia, serves as a regulating reservoir to stabilize the flow of water through the lower Mekong. During flood stage the silted delta outlets cannot carry off the flood waters. The swollen Mekong then backs up into the Tonle Sap and expands the lake so that it covers as much as four times its low-water area. As the flood subsides, the water reverts to its original flow from the lake to the sea. The regulating reservoir thus significantly reduces the danger of serious floods.

All five major geographical regions contain several basic types of vegetation. Vegetation areas fall into six general categories: (1) rain forest, (2) open forest, (3) swampland, (4) marshland, (5) grassland, and (6) cultivated areas. The rain forest, predominant in the Northern Mountains, Central Highlands, and intermediate lowlands regions, consists of a continuous, multilevel canopy of numerous species of trees—primarily broadleaf evergreens. Secondary growth rain forests tend to contain small, closely spaced trees and dense undergrowth. The open forests of the plateau region of the Central Highlands and areas of the Northern Mountains and the transitional zone of the Southern Plains include widely spaced trees above a floor of tall, sharp-edged thatch grass. The primarily deciduous trees shed their leaves during the dry season. Swampland is characteristic of the coastal sectors of the Northern Mountains, the Red River Delta, and the Mekong Delta. Primary vegetation in these areas is the mangrove, a variety of evergreen that thrives in brackish water and muddy soil. The tree crowns form a dense canopy and the prop roots constitute an almost impenetrable ground barrier. Marshland fringes the northern edge of the Mekong Delta near the Cambodian border. Reclamation projects have lessened its extent. In the marshland areas, sharp-bladed reeds and rushes grow to heights of seven feet. Grassland is most prevalent in the Northern Mountains, near the Chinese border, but sections of grassland are dispersed throughout Vietnam. Thatch grass is the most common vegetation in these locations. The vegetation and crops of the cultivated areas, particularly in the Northern and Southern Plains and Coastal Lowlands regions, include corn, beans, potatoes, and other dry field crops, as well as coconut, sugar cane, rubber, and rice. The deltas in particular are covered with rice paddies.

As important as topography and vegetation in a geographical survey of Vietnam is a consideration of its climate. Paramount in climatic changes are the seasonal monsoons. During the southwest, or summer, monsoon, the heat of central Asia rises and causes humid air to flow inland from the ocean, usually from mid-May to early October. The humid airflow brings heavy rains to the plateau area and the western slopes of the mountain regions. Average rainfall during these months ranges from 55 to 110 inches in the north and 40 to 95 inches in the south. However, sections along the eastern slopes and the coastal plains receive relatively little moisture. Except for local variations, high humidity, tropical temperature, and cloudiness prevail during these months. The northeast, or winter, monsoon results from the high pressure in the Asian interior forcing dry, cool air out toward the sea. This flow generally begins in early November and continues until mid-March. The coastal region receives relatively heavy precipitation, whereas across the mountains in Laos the weather is hot and dry. During January, February, and early March, the coastal areas, especially along the Gulf of Tonkin, experience the "crachin"—a period of intermittent drizzle and low cloud overcast. The periods between these monsoons are known as the spring and autumn transitions. The spring transition, from mid-March until mid-May, is a period of very high temperatures and high humidity and a number of cloudy, overcast days. The autumn transition includes the weeks from early October until early November. For the central portion of the coastal plains, the heaviest amount of precipitation and cloud cover occurs during this transitional phase.

The Enemy

The requirements for countering insurgency in South Vietnam were considerably different from those experienced by U.S. artillery in past combat operations. First, the enemy could attack ground forces or the local populace at times and places of his choosing. Second, he was indistinguishable from the populace and even from some of the irregular friendly paramilitary forces. There could be little progress toward identifying and finding this elusive enemy without first acquiring detailed knowledge of his organizations and methods.

The Indochinese Communist Party (ICP) in 1941 formed the Viet Minh, or League for the Independence of Vietnam. A decade later, the Viet Minh had grown unwieldy and and was reorganized, following the March 1951 Congress of Unification of the Lien-Viet and Viet-Minh Fronts, into the Vietnam Dang Lao Dong, or Vietnam Workers' Party. Ho Chi Minh and the other leaders of the Viet Minh hoped ultimately to reconstruct, within this broad national front, a hard inner core around which a well-disciplined following could be organized. The Central Executive Committee of the new Lao Dong Party was headed by Ho Chi Minh and included the former Viet Minh leadership. The Indochinese Communist Party meanwhile had been dissolved in 1945 after fifteen years of operation and was succeeded by the Marxist Study Club. The Lao Dong Party was, in effect, a less ostentatious recreation of the Indochinese Communist Party. "We may tell the party adherents that the new party is basically the Communist Party under a new form," a confidential executive committee circular pointed out, "but to those that are outside of the party, we will say that it is a newly-created party merely continuing the revolutionary work of the preceding parties."

In the years after the 1954 Geneva Accords, as it became apparent that the agreement for national elections would not be honored and that the Diem government would soon collapse, Lao Dong Party cadres went south and began organizing the dissidents in South Vietnam. By December 1960 the National Liberation Front (NLF) of South Vietnam had been formed. The organization of the Front, according to Douglas Pike, was a "phantom edifice." Lao Dong cadres first conceived the front on paper and then applied it to the grievances of the south. Organizational impetus, in other words, came from the Lao Dong Party, whereas the support, primarily an anti-Diem coalition, was indigenous. Lao Dong participation in the National Liberation Front, never seriously concealed, became apparent with the formation in January 1962 of the People's Revolutionary Party (PRP), which replaced the southern branch of the Lao Dong Party. Communist domination marked the end of the phase of intensive organization building. Membership in the National Liberation Front had reached approximately 300,000, and the creation of the People's Revolutionary Party initiated a period of internal NLF solidification which eventually culminated in Northern control of the Front. By 1964, relocated northerners made up about one-half of the Front's 40,000 civilian cadres.

The military arm of the National Liberation Front was the People's Liberation Armed Force (PLAF), which was known before 1966 as the Liberation Army of the Front. Allied forces referred to the Force simply as Viet Cong—a nebulous term for Vietnamese Communists that nevertheless persisted. The army was made up of main force regulars and paramilitary units. The regulars (*Chu-Luc-Quan*), stationed mainly in secret bases and secured areas, were professional, well trained, disciplined, and thoroughly indoctrinated soldiers. They were chosen from battle-experienced regional units or infiltrated from North Vietnam. The organizational plan called for the incorporation of party commissars from the company level up and for a party cell in each platoon that worked with the company commissar.

Until 1956, Communist forces in the south were mostly guerrilla units supplemented by a few regulars. The number of regular forces increased continuously in the succeeding years, so that by 1963 the estimated strength of main force regulars was between 25,000 and 30,000 and by 1965 about 35,000 men. The missions of the PLAF main force regulars resembled those of the armed forces of North Vietnam—the People's Army of Vietnam (PAVN), more commonly known as the North Vietnamese Army (NVA). Coordination and efficiency were essential. "They have the capacity," North Vietnam Defense Minister General Vo Nuyen Giap observed, "to annihilate major units or command posts of the enemy."

The paramilitary forces of the People's Liberation Armed Force, made up primarily of indigenous personnel, consisted of regional units and local militia. The regional units were guerrilla bands that operated mainly in their home provinces and districts. Their primary responsibilities were to (1) train and assist the local militia, emphasizing not only military doctrine but also political activities, (2) screen the operations of the main force regulars, and (3) serve as reserves and reinforcements to the regulars. These activities kept the government forces off balance. In 1965, the regional forces contained an estimated 60,000 to 80,000 men. The local militia (*Dan Quan Du Kich*) were largely untrained, poorly equipped, and inadequately indoctrinated. However, as an integral part of the population, they filled an important logistical role for the regional and regular forces. Their social role was perhaps even more critical than their military potential. Proselyting the local populace called for nonmilitary indoctrination. It has been estimated that militia training, conducted by regional units or regular forces, included 70 percent political and only 30 percent military subjects.

After 1959 Communist troop infiltration south was continuous.

The majority of the infiltrators were former Viet Minh who had regrouped to the north after the Geneva agreement. Until 1960 the North Vietnamese Army assisted the insurgency in the south mainly by providing specialists to the National Liberation Front and the People's Liberation Armed Force. By late 1964, the demand for more NVA units in the south forced changes in the makeup of infiltrators. North Vietnam began recalling former enlisted men in 1964 and officers in 1965. The new need also altered draft requirements. The draft formerly affected those between 18 and 25 years old; it expanded to include persons between ages 17 and 35. Also, by mid-1966 the semiannual call had become a quarterly call and the term of service, once 3 years, had been extended to the duration of the war.

The enlarged numbers of infiltrators soon exceeded the capabilities of the North Vietnamese training units. The 338th Brigade until 1964 had been responsible for infiltration training, but additional training commands were now needed to cope with the buildup. The 22d Training Group, 250th Training Division, 320th Training Division, and 350th Division joined the training efforts of the 338th. Together these units could train between 78,000 and 96,000 men per year.

The tempo of activity picked up in 1968 and inflated the manpower requirements of the military. Consequently, the People's Liberation Armed Force as well as the North Vietnamese Army underwent further modifications. The PLAF main force and regional units faced the dilemma of enlarged needs and diminished manpower resources. In 1968, approximately 60,500 men were recruited; in 1969, about 57,000. Of these, it has been estimated that 50 percent were recruited through the use or threat of force. Large numbers of these recruits were under 17 years old. The North Vietnamese Army, in turn, was forced not only to aid the PLAF main force but also to send some of its own elements to the regional units. The burden on manpower resources, though heavy, was not critical for the North Vietnamese. An estimate of the number of males of military age (15 to 49 years) in January 1969 showed that of a total of 4,607,000 approximately 2,700,000 were fit for military duty and that another 100,000 men would become eligible each year.

The tactics of the North Vietnamese Army, and especially of the People's Liberation Armed Force, emphasized security, silence, and speed. The carefully detailed plans, the rehearsals whenever feasible, the speedy execution, and the equally quick and cautious withdrawals were forced upon them because of the preponderant firepower of the U.S. forces. Offensive activities had to be maintained, the positional defense avoided; NVA and PLAF artillery support adapted to these prerequisites.

Until 1967 the North Vietnamese Army and the People's Liberation Armed Force used primarily mortars and recoilless rifles in standoff attacks against allied military installations and outposts. The limited destructive capability of these weapons and the tightened installation security of the allies, which came to include those areas within medium mortar range, forced the enemy to lessen the frequency of his attacks.

In early 1966 enemy use of Soviet cannon artillery became more common. The 85-mm. Soviet divisional gun, the 122-mm. Soviet M1938 howitzer, the 122-mm. Soviet D14 gun, and the 152-mm. Soviet M1939 gun-howitzer, as well as captured U.S. 75-mm. and 105-mm. howitzers, increased the NVA and PLAF long-range destructive capability. However, allied firepower placed restrictions on their use. A survey conducted by the U.S. Army XXIV Corps Artillery over a seven-month period in 1968 concluded that the hours most preferred by the NVA for firing were from 1000 to 1300, from 1400 to 1500, and from 1600 to 1900. The frequency rose steadily during the morning hours, peaked around 1130, and then dropped off considerably. Artillery fire peaked again around 1430 and 1830 and decreased significantly following each peak period. The preference for daylight hours, according to the survey, was probably determined by a desire to avoid counterbattery fire. Frequent nighttime moves from position to position were mandatory to avoid detection, and firing was limited to a few rounds per gun from several widely scattered positions.

By late 1966 Soviet and Chinese Communist rockets were in the enemy inventory. These rockets were not only more suitable than cannon artillery for attacking larger targets but also lighter and more adaptable. And because of their low trajectory, rockets often escaped location by the U.S. AN/MPQ-4 (Q-4) countermortar radar. The 140-mm. rocket attack on Da Nang air base on 27 February 1967 commenced a new phase in the war in terms of enemy capabilities by extending the attack range by about 3,500 yards beyond the maximum range of the 120-mm. mortar and more than doubling the warhead payload. Moreover, rockets were more mobile than conventional artillery. A captured enemy training document explained that the "main purposes of the rockets are objectives having a large area, usually 400 x 400 m, such as enemy strongholds, air fields, storage points, or towns." The rockets could also be used "to support the infantry and to attack distant objectives that may affect the combat mission of the infantry."

All the rockets could be employed from improvised launchers.

The 140-mm. rockets used in the attack on Da Nang air base were fired from 134 crudely mounted launching positions consisting of single metal tubes mounted on wooden boards, with elementary elevation and deflection devices. The enemy accomplished simultaneous launchings by wiring several weapons to two ignition wires and then to a battery. A modified Soviet 122-mm. rocket was used during the 6 March 1967 attack on Camp Carroll. The launcher was a single tube taken from the Soviet multiple rocket launcher, the 40-round BM–21, shortened by 18 inches from the original 9.6 feet, fitted with a tripod mount, and equipped with a modified optical sight taken from the Soviet 82-mm. recoilless gun. In this form the weapon could be broken down into five manageable loads for jungle mobility. But the enemy was even able to launch the 122-mm. rocket by propping it against sandbag mounts or wooden stakes. Although errors increased, only three manpacks were sufficient to transport the weapon when it was used in this fashion. The 122-mm. rocket soon became the standard rocket of the North Vietnamese Army and the People's Liberation Armed Force.

The Chinese Communist 107-mm. rocket, used in February 1968 against the U.S. base camp at Quan Loi plantation, added another dimension to the NVA and PLAF arsenals. The 107-mm. rocket packed a smaller warhead and had a shorter range than the 122-mm. rocket. However, because they were relatively light, three 107-mm. rockets could be transported as easily as one 122-mm. round. And like the 140-mm. and 122-mm. rockets, the 107-mm. could be launched from improvised pads. An enemy training document pointed out that 107-mm. rocket firing pads could be made of dirt, bamboo frames, or crossed stakes. The rocket could be launched from "road embankments, a dike between two rice fields, the brim of a combat trench, an earth mound, a bomb crater, or an ant hill." In the summer of 1968, reports mentioned the possible enemy use of multiple rocket launchers. U.S. forces had encountered twin-tubed 107-mm. launchers fitted as if they were intended to be attached to other tubes. These rather sophisticated launchers were obvious contrasts to the crudely improvised 140-mm. and 120-mm. assemblies. On 16 September 1968, the Americans captured a Chinese Communist-manufactured 12-round launcher for the 107-mm. rocket. Broken down, the launchers were easily transportable and delivered the 107-mm. rocket against separate targets; assembled, the multiple launcher massed 12 rounds on a single target area.

Enemy units continued to make the most of their weapons by adapting available resources to prevailing requirements. For example, they created the 107-mm., 120-mm., and 140-mm. overcaliber rockets by attaching larger warheads to the original assemblies. Modification lessened accuracy, but the overcaliber rockets provided effective harassing and saturation fires.

Enemy company commanders, like their counterparts in the cannon artillery units, were conscious of U.S. firepower. A captured company commander explained in December 1968 that U.S. air observers could follow the rocket exhaust and pinpoint launch sites for air strikes. Hence it was necessary to employ "hit and run tactics in accordance with the principles of guerrilla warfare." Fire control and co-ordination was primary. "No more than five rounds are fired from any single tripod-type launcher. This takes about 20 minutes." No more than two salvos were fired in about ten minutes time from improvised launchers. Displacement involved "the immediate pickup of all equipment and leaving the area with all possible speed, which takes about 5 minutes."

By late 1969 the rocket, because of its advantages in terms of payload and mobility, had become the prime weapon of the NVA and PLAF artillery. The rocket units were organized into regiments, battalions, companies, and platoons. The regiment included a headquarters squadron, a signal and reconnaissance company, and three rocket companies. The number of rockets and launchers per company varied with the caliber of the weapons. A 107-mm. rocket company normally consisted of twelve launchers and twenty-four rockets; a 122-mm. company, six launchers and eighteen rockets; and a 140-mm. company, sixteen launchers and sixteen rockets.

The makeup of the cannon artillery units varied according to their location. Medium artillery pieces were prevalent only in the Demilitarized Zone, where regiments usually contained 36 tubes—24 of 105-mm. and 12 of 130-mm. and 152-mm. In addition, a few 85-mm. and 100-mm. pieces were sometimes incorporated. Elsewhere, conventional NVA and PLAF units normally included weapons not considered artillery pieces in American units. The 60-mm., 81-mm., 82-mm., and 120-mm. mortars and the 57-mm., 75-mm., and 82-mm. recoilless rifles, along with the 12.7-mm antiaircraft machine gun, were commonly parts of their artillery arsenal. Less common, though still available, were the 70-mm. Japanese and 75-mm. U.S. howitzers. Artillery training, in fact, envisioned the use of captured American artillery pieces. Assembly and disassembly of the 105-mm. howitzer and the use of U.S. aiming devices in laying the 75-mm. and 105-mm. tubes were included in the NVA and PLAF artillery curriculum.

No description of the North Vietnamese Army and the People's Liberation Armed Force and their effect on allied forces would be complete without mention of the ubiquitous sapper. During the first half of 1969, sapper attacks inflicted an average of over $1 million damage per raid. However, the role of the sapper was often misunderstood. Before 1967, the enemy had not grasped the significance of the sapper as an assault soldier. The allies, on the other hand, sometimes erroneously categorized the sapper as a guerrilla simply because some guerrillas employed sapper tactics. The fusion blurred identification. The development of the sapper and his employment before and after the creation of a separate sapper combat arm, equivalent to the infantry and artillery, must be traced before his impact on the war can be appreciated.

The term sapper originated in Europe and traditionally identified a combat engineer. In Vietnam this conventional association remained, but a more particular connotation increasingly qualified the sapper. The sapper signified a raider–ranger unit and gained notoriety as the lead element in an assault on a fixed installation or military field position. Armed primarily with explosives charges, the sapper breached the defensive perimeter and neutralized tactical and strategic positions and thus prepared for the attack of the main body.

Before 1967, however, the sappers were often misused. As late as 1964, the People's Liberation Armed Force envisioned the use of sappers only during the first phase of guerrilla warfare, before the government of Vietnam could establish strongpoints and improve defensive positions. Sapper units remained subordinate to the infantry and served as reinforcements in assaults. Deep penetrations were disallowed. Sapper units were constrained in their operations until the artillery had fired. And sappers themselves were occasionally deficient when employed in raids. Inadequate preparation, incomplete reconnaissance, and inexperience of the demolition men used as penetrators all contributed to the poor execution of these missions. Nevertheless, the number of sapper units in South Vietnam increased steadily after 1965, and by 1967 the enemy recognized the misemployment but also the potential of these forces. The North Vietnamese Army upgraded the entire organization and, in late April or early May 1967, created the Sapper Headquarters, Sapper Department, Joint General Staff.

The sapper force, as an independent combat arm equivalent to the infantry or the artillery, operated (1) in the assault without infantry, (2) in the assault with infantry, (3) in special action group activities, and (4) in "water sapper" operations. Sappers in special action groups operated essentially in the cities, proselyting the population and maintaining pressure, while water sappers mined ships, bridges, and other water-associated targets. Special action groups and water sappers were of less immediate importance to the artillery in Vietnam than were sappers employed in the first two modes.

Sapper assaults, with or without the infantry, depended on stealth and secrecy. Their primary method of attack called for making deep thrusts into allied positions from different directions and hitting several targets simultaneously. Organization was determined by the specific mission and the location and strength of the allied forces. Characteristically, however, the sapper force included assault, security, fire support, and reserve elements. (*Chart 1*)

Assaults without the infantry required fullest use of the fire support or reserve elements, either separately or in combination. The sappers disguised their attacks as attacks by fire through the use of mortars by the fire support elements or as infantry assaults through employment of the reserve elements, which were the equivalent of infantry squads. If the deception worked, the opposing forces would deploy to their bunkers or to the defensive perimeter and leave the center of the installation vulnerable to assault teams.

Sapper attacks with the infantry were either with the sappers in support of the infantry or the infantry in support of the sappers. Sapper units considered supporting the infantry a misuse of their tactical abilities. Attached to a large unit, they tended to lose the advantages of secrecy and surprise. Nevertheless, sappers continued to be employed as reinforcements to the infantry. The second mode of sapper operation—using the infantry as a reserve, security, or secondary assault element—seemed more effective. The greatest threat to allied positions was an attack spearheaded by sappers with explosive charges, followed by the infantry some 100 to 200 meters behind.

During 1968, after the sapper organization had been made a separate combat arm, attacks by sappers or by units employing sapper tactics occurred on a larger scale and often were accompanied by indirect fire support. By the end of that year, heavy Communist losses resulting from large-scale offensives made the sapper and his techniques empirical necessities. Minimum manpower expenditure was imperative, yet military pressure had to be maintained. The sapper was well suited to these dual demands. A captured enemy document explained that considerable damage could be inflicted by a relatively slight force through the cautious application of sapper tactics: small numbers of men could "inflict extensive damage on enemy installations." The sapper should con-

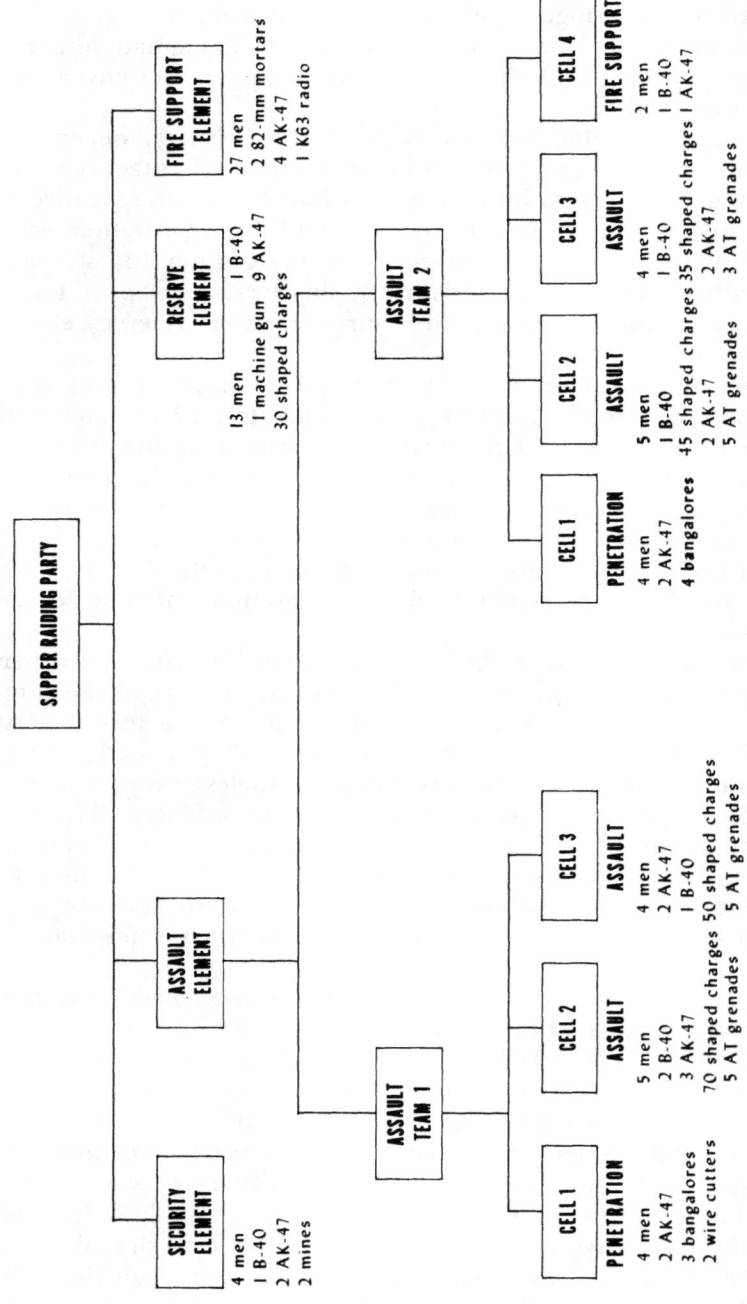

Chart 1—Characteristic Sapper Organization

centrate on strategic structures "located deep within enemy-controlled areas" rather than concern himself with inflicting casualties. The ability to penetrate, and not the preponderance of firepower or men, was crucial. But, the document warned, sapper attacks should "not normally last over 30 minutes after the enemy is aware of the sapper presence."

From the beginning of 1968 until mid-1969, sappers were essential to the enemy's effort. Although they participated in only 4 percent of all assaults, these made up 12 percent of all significant assaults—those which inflicted serious damage. From January 1968 until May 1969, the frequency of sapper raids remained at about five per month, but their effectiveness greatly improved. The average raid during 1968 resulted in approximately $300,000 damage. In 1969, the average raid inflicted more than $1,000,000 damage and accounted for more allied casualties. The selection of targets testified to the increasing boldness of the sapper units. In 1965 the use of sappers against allied combat positions such as outposts, fire support bases, and landing zones was still debated, but in 1967 training for this type of attack was rapidly progressing. During 1968 and 1969 these field positions made up 43 percent of the sapper targets; fixed military installations such as storage depots, base camps, and Air Force installations accounted for 32 percent of the sapper raids; and population centers accounted for 18 percent of the total. More than 51 percent of the raids occurred between 0100 and 0300. General Giap showed the increasing confidence in sapper units when he exclaimed, "Regardless of how strongly the US or puppet troops are defended, they can be easily destroyed by our crack and special troops with their special combat tactic."

The creation of the Sapper Headquarters in 1967, the need for troop conservation, especially after 1968, and the demonstrated effectiveness of the sapper during 1969 contributed to the growing emphasis placed upon these forces. The expansion of the sapper combat arm mirrored this emphasis. In July of 1967 the V–25 Infantry Battalion, a PLAF regional unit in Quang Nam Province, was scheduled to be upgraded to main force status and retained as a sapper force. Here was the first clear indication that large infantry units were being converted into sapper units. By June of 1968, nine main force and regional force battalions and sixteen companies of sappers were in existence. In early 1969, the sapper force had grown to nineteen battalions and thirty-six companies. And by mid-1969, this force had increased to twenty-seven battalions and thirty-nine companies.

Political-Military Considerations

The peculiarities of terrain and enemy operations fundamentally affected the employment of artillery in Vietnam. Gunnery errors in the past seldom had resulted in friendly casualties. Rounds that cleared friendly lines were usually safe. In Vietnam, however, front lines were nonexistent and the enemy operated among the local population. Hence, as one study has estimated, about 50 percent of all artillery missions were fired very close to friendly positions. If response was to be effective, such areas as no-fire zones, specified strike zones, and free-fire zones had to be designated. Otherwise, co-ordination and clearance with the lowest echelon of the central government, the district, was mandatory (the district chiefs presumably could account for the location of friendly elements within the immediate vicinity). In May of 1970 *Lessons Learned Number 77*, on fire support co-ordination, stated, "The requirement for military and political clearances for artillery fire on or near populated areas has an adverse effect on the responsiveness of artillery fire." The goal of responding within two minutes after receiving a fire request was "seldom met for targets near any populated areas." Clearance requirements commonly delayed missions up to ten minutes. In fact, the report continued, it was "not uncommon for the artillery to be unable to fire at all because of lack of clearances." To reduce the time lost in firing, liaison with local government agencies and with allied forces was established. The creation of combined fire support co-ordination centers in some areas minimized the delays. But, the report concluded, the "lack of responsiveness is a source of constant concern and frustration at all echelons of command."

The governmental and the military organizations in South Vietnam were parallel structures that, especially since the 1963 overthrow of the Diem regime, had become closely indentified. The civil government faced the basic problem of central authority versus local autonomy, a predicament not peculiar to Vietnam but pronounced there because of the cultural importance of the village and its kinship relations. The central government extended into four regions—South, Center, North, and Highlands—which formerly were supervised through regional governors but which since 1955 had been directed by four governmental delegates, one for each of the regions. These regions were subdivided into 44 provinces from 540 to 10,000 square kilometers in size and with populations ranging from 33,000 to 850,000. In addition, there were six autonomous cities that occupied positions equivalent to provinces in the governmental hierarchy: Saigon, Hue, Da Nang, Da Lat,

Cam Ranh, and Vung Tau. The provinces were subdivided further into some 236 districts with 2 to 10 districts per province. The districts took in anywhere from 2 to 57 villages but averaged about 10 villages per district. The villages encompassed 3 to 12 hamlets.

Since the ordinance of 24 October 1956, the provinces have possessed a substantial amount of legal autonomy. Province chiefs, appointed by the central government, managed all provincial services. They controlled their own budgets, regulated public property, and dealt directly with the ministries at the national level.

The districts were not legal political entities and hence possessed no autonomous budgetary or fiscal powers. Traditionally, the central government appointed the district chiefs upon the recommendation of the province chiefs. District chiefs thus represented the lowest territorial echelon of the central authority.

The province and district chiefs functioned in military roles. The province chiefs co-ordinated all local security through the Regional Forces (RF) and could, in emergencies, call upon regular army units. Similarly, the district chiefs regulated the actions of the Popular Forces (PF). The Regional and Popular Forces were security forces drawn from the local population and usually confined themselves to their province or district areas. In a strictly military sense, their performance was often erratic. A unit might distinguish itself on one day, yet fail miserably the next because its local leader had been killed. Moreover, these forces complicated the problems of command and control and thus enhanced the need for co-ordination. The paramilitary units were, according to Major General Charles P. Brown, "a mixed bag." Some were consistently good, others consistently poor. "The majority would have to be categorized as mediocre."

The villages ostensibly contained a legislative Village Citizen's Council (VCC) and an executive Village Administrative Committee (VAC). The village chief headed the Administrative Committee, and the Citizen's Council, in principle, included representatives from each hamlet. In the hamlet, the hamlet chief and his deputies administered domestic needs.

The chain of command of the Republic of Vietnam Armed Forces (RVNAF), headed by the Joint General Staff (JGS), encroached upon the basically civilian government structure. The Joint General Staff commanded the four military corps tactical zones (CTZ's) into which Vietnam had been divided. These zones corresponded to the four regions which had been presided over by governmental delegates since the elimination of the regional governors in 1955. The delegates in turn were superseded by the corps commanders, who functioned as assistants to the chief executive. In the aftermath of the 1963 coup, military men increasingly replaced civilian authorities. Not only did the corps commanders oversee the four regions, many military officers became province chiefs and divisional tactical areas generally followed provincial boundaries. In addition, more military men served as district chiefs.

Finally, the villages and hamlets, already part of the military panorama, were further highlighted in the early 1960's not only through the action of the Regional Forces and the Popular Forces but also by the implementation of the government's plans to create "strategic hamlets." Since insurgents ranged from the higher echelons of the People's Revolutionary Party down to the basic three-man cells within the hamlets, the government attempted to cope with the insurgent challenge through its own proselyting program. In early 1962 the Diem government, with the strong support of the United States, initiated the strategic hamlet counterinsurgency program. Patterned after the British experience in Malaya in 1948, the strategic hamlet program attempted to isolate the rural population from the insurgent force in order to deny the latter any popular support and at the same time to enlarge the government's popular base through social reforms. The programs, scheduled for completion by early 1964, envisioned the construction of 11,864 strategic hamlets.

Diem, in February 1963, expressed confidence in winning the war because the strategic hamlet program, he said, had separated the population from the Communists "physically and morally" and thus had undermined the fundamental principle of "Communist subversive war." The insurgents, according to Diem, were "becoming more and more a foreign expeditionary corps reduced to fighting a conventional war." In October 1963, Diem announced that 8,600 strategic hamlets incorporating some 10.5 million persons had been completed. It soon became obvious, however, that the program was a mere facade of what had been visualized. Social reforms were not realized; instead, governmental control often became more intense within the reorganized and relocated hamlets. Coupled with the forced transfer of formerly indifferent peasants, these shortcomings gave credence to the Communist charge that the government had created "concentration camps."

Thus, while the terrain and the enemy forced new and unusual demands on all military activity, the development of an indistinguishable military-political structure in Vietnam posed further problems in the conduct of the war. Dealing with these demands and problems propelled the U.S. effort in general, and that of the artillery in particular, in new directions.

CHAPTER II

The Advisory Effort, 1950–1965

*Background—Military Assistance
Advisory Group, Vietnam, Organized*

The U.S. military advisory effort in Vietnam had a modest beginning in September 1950, when the United States Military Assistance Advisory Group (MAAG), Vietnam, was established in Saigon. Its mission was to supervise the issuance and employment of $10 million of military equipment to support French legionnaires in their effort to combat Viet Minh forces. By 1953 the amount of U.S. military aid had jumped to over $350 million and was used to replace the badly worn World War II vintage equipment that France, still suffering economically from the devastation of that war, was still using.

From the outset, French forces were happy to receive the new material but refused American advice on how to employ it. The U.S. desire was that all Vietnamese units be organized and trained to provide internal defense of their own country and that aid be used to equip those units. Such a desire was at odds with existing French policy. The French Army was employed not only to counter enemy forces but also to assert France as a colonial power. A purely Vietnamese army would not be dependable in this latter role. Accordingly, major units were filled totally by French officers and noncommissioned officers with the ranks made up of Vietnamese. Senior French commanders were so loath to accept advice that would weaken their traditional colonial role that they effectively hampered various attempts by MAAG personnel to observe where the equipment was being sent and how it was being used.

Slowly, however, the French were forced to change their policies. As they steadily lost their grip on the country, they saw that their days as a colonial power were numbered and that, if the country was to be saved from a Communist takeover, a strong, effective Vietnamese force would have to be provided. In 1954 the commanding general of French forces in Indochina, General Navarre, permitted the United States to send liaison officers to Vietnamese forces. But it was too late, as evidenced by daily worldwide news accounts of the seige and fall of Dien Bien Phu in the spring of that year. Under the Geneva Accords, France was forced to surrender the northern half of Vietnam and to withdraw from South Vietnam by April of 1956. On 12 February 1955 at a conference in Washington, D.C., between officials of the U.S. State Department and the French Minister of Overseas Affairs, it was agreed that all U.S. aid would be funneled directly to South Vietnam and that all major military responsibilities would be transferred from the French to the Military Assistance Advisory Group mission under the command of Lieutenant General John O'Daniel. Because there were only 342 U.S. military personnel assigned to the group, not enough to accomplish the advisory mission, it was decided to make the training effort a joint U.S. and French mission under the title of Training Relations and Instruction Mission (TRIM). The mission was short lived, since the French Expeditionary Force formally departed South Vietnam in April of 1956 as directed by the Accords and upon the insistence of President Diem. To fill the void, the MAAG mission was increased to 740 men by the end of June.

During this reorganization period, General O'Daniel had stated a need for assigning military advisers down to the battalion level rather than concentrating them at the higher headquarters levels, but Military Assistance Advisory Group at that time did not have enough personnel. Further, President Diem was reluctant to allow advisers with tactical units. He was fearful that the United States would gain control or influence over his forces if Americans permeated the ranks of the army. It might be surmised that Diem wanted to maintain complete control of his armed forces, which constituted a major political tool to keep his opponents at bay. By 1961, however, conditions had changed. Communist guerrillas were becoming stronger and more active, and enemy contacts increased in size and intensity throughout South Vietnam.

It was evident that the Hanoi government had little intention of abiding by the Geneva agreements to honor the south's territorial integrity. President John F. Kennedy, during late spring of 1961, further increased the U.S. military commitment in both equipment and men. Aid had been averaging $50 million per year for the past several years but was sharply increased to $144 million for 1961. At the same time President Diem agreed to the assignment of advisers to battalion level. Accordingly, the adviser strength jumped from 850 in 1959 to over 2,000 in 1961. By 1964 the advisory force numbered 23,000 officers and men.

The Field Artillery Adviser

The U.S. advisory buildup during the early 1960's included the assignment of field artillery advisory teams down to battalion level as quickly as they could be trained and sent. Each team included an artillery officer, usually a captain, and a senior noncommissioned officer. In most cases both had attended the six-week Military Assistance Training Agency (MATA) course taught at the U.S. Army Special Warfare School at Fort Bragg, North Carolina. The course was established to prepare students for future duties as advisers in Vietnam—to teach them both what to expect and what was expected of them. The curriculum included, among other subjects, a profile of the country, its people, government, history, and geography; the organization and employment of its military and paramilitary forces; and basic language instruction. The "Redleg" (an artilleryman) advisers were given additional instruction concerning Vietnamese artillery and methods of employing field artillery effectively in Vietnam. In addition to the MATA course, artillerymen attending resident courses at Fort Sill after fiscal year 1962 were to receive orientations on counterinsurgency operations. Officers attending the field artillery career course participated in practical exercises in the employment of artillery in support of jungle operations.

Field artillery advisory teams were assigned to battalions of both divisional and corps artillery. Each Vietnamese division in 1961 had a division artillery consisting of one 4.2-inch mortar battalion and one 105-mm. howitzer battalion. Each battalion had three subordinate firing batteries. In 1961 the mortar batteries had nine weapons and the cannon batteries had four weapons each. In 1963 mortar battery weapons were reduced to six and cannon battery weapons increased to six. From late 1964 to early 1965, 4.2-inch mortar batteries were replaced by 105-mm. batteries; 105-mm. weapons, with their longer ranges, had proved to be more valuable in accomplishing the mission of area coverage. Each of the four Vietnamese army corps also had its own artillery, usually two or three battalions, depending on the need. Corps artillery consisted of 105- and 155-mm. howitzer battalions. The 155-mm. howitzer was the heaviest artillery in Vietnam during this period. Like division artillery, the battalions of corps artillery each had three batteries. Each battery initially had four weapons, increased to six by early 1965.

The artillery advisory team was assigned to assist the Vietnamese unit commander and his staff in such areas as administrative procedures, personnel managment, logistics, operations, training, maintenance, and communications, with particular emphasis on the tactical employment of artillery. The officer of the team, whose title was artillery officer adviser, proffered advice on all matters concerned with enhancing unit effectiveness. His noncommissioned assistant, the firing battery adviser, concentrated on assisting the battalion S–3 and operations sergeant in planning, organizing, and supervising training of the firing batteries and individual gun sections. In addition to the battalion advisory teams, an artillery officer, normally a major, was assigned to each corps and division to advise the senior Vietnamese artillery commanders at those levels. This adviser had the additional task of co-ordinating the efforts of the advisory teams with the subordinate battalions.

The young officers and noncommissioned officers who served as battalion advisers were of the highest caliber. They were at once professional, knowledgeable, and aggressive. Yet they were soon to learn that as advisers they could not "get things done" as they had in the American units in which they had served. Now they could only advise, not lead. Their advice could be accepted or rejected as the Vietnamese commander saw fit. Though often frustrating, this exclusively advisory status was necessary if the Vietnamese were to learn without the United States being accused of attempting to grab control of the military with intentions of making Vietnam a puppet state. Accordingly, advisers in the field were specifically directed to avoid any action that might be construed as leading a Vietnamese military organization in combat against the enemy.

To add to their frustrations, advisers were often fearful that their effectiveness would be judged by their superiors in relation to the effectiveness of the unit they advised. Unhappily, in some cases their fears were justified. An outstanding officer might be assigned to advise a mediocre unit which he was powerless to improve if the unit commander was indifferent to his suggestions. Though expressed humorously in this first verse of a rather lengthy poem, the dilemma was a very real one:

> I can't pull the throttle,
> I can't ring the bell,
> But if this goddamn train should stop,
> I'm the one that catches hell.
>
> (an adviser's lament—anonymous)

The Adviser's Challenge

Even when an adviser's suggestion was accepted by his counterpart, it often seemed that the suggestion was executed in a painstakingly slow and inefficient manner. There were several reasons for this.

First, advisers were faced with helping an army whose soldiers came from a culture with a set of values and philosophy far different from their own. The American believed that anything could be accomplished with hard work, and he considered the year he would be in Vietnam' ample time to get the job done. The Vietnamese, on the other hand, believed that one must work hard to live but that progress came about slowly. He had fought an enemy all his life and could not comprehend why Americans felt that they could end the fighting overnight. Many other values held by Americans and Vietnamese clashed. Suffice it to say that it was often difficult for an adviser and his counterpart to understand one another. What was viewed as a reasonable approach to a problem by one was often viewed as inane by the other. Other than making a sincere effort to understand one another's views, little could be done to close this cultural gap.

Another reason for apparent ineffectiveness of Vietnamese units was a void of trained and experienced leaders. Correcting this weakness was somewhat easier than overcoming cultural differences but was still a prodigious task. The French had purposely denied a majority of the leadership positions within their army to Vietnamese. There was evidence, however, of token acceptance of Vietnamese leaders as early as 1948. At that time, the French established an artillery training center forty kilometers northwest of Saigon to train noncommissioned officers as well as enlisted cannoneers for the French Expeditionary Force. In 1951 the school accepted Vietnamese officers for attendance in the basic courses and in 1953 presented the first battery commander's course. After the reorganization of the Vietnamese Army the artillery school was relocated, first at the engineer school near Thu Dau Mot and then on 25 July 1961 at Duc My, approximately fifty kilometers northwest of Nha Trang. At each location activities were expanded to train artillery officers and noncommissioned officers as well as artillerymen with specialized duties. Among other artillery-related courses, the first battery commander's course was offered in 1961 and the first advanced course in 1965. Vietnamese artillerymen could take some pride in their branch being the first in the Vietnamese military to offer an advanced course.

At unit level, advisers pressed their counterparts to provide training of junior officers. Some battalions developed aggressive training programs which brought officers in from the field to present classes and practical training on various aspects of the employment of field artillery.

Many of the most promising young Vietnamese artillery officers and noncommissioned officers received further training at the U.S. Army Artillery School at Fort Sill, Oklahoma, where they were exposed to the latest thinking on field artillery employment and

ARVN Outpost. *Large French-style outpost with a platoon of howitzers.*

developments. From fiscal year 1953 to fiscal year 1973, 663 Vietnamese artillery officers alone were sent to Fort Sill. Peak attendance was during the early years of the expanded advisory effort, 1960 to 1964, when yearly attendance exceeded 60 officers.

Vietnamese field artillery leaders could not be effective if they were not knowledgeable in all aspects of the employment of their weapons. Formal training served that purpose. But an even more important factor in developing leaders was encouraging the Vietnamese to take command themselves. American advisers could not command Vietnamese units, and although the Vietnamese might make mistakes and perform awkwardly initially, they would be challenged to perform and to develop into outstanding leaders. Thus, any frustrations that an adviser might feel in not being given a firmer hand to control the situation were well worth the end result of effective Vietnamese leadership.

A third reason for ineffectiveness was poor operational practices, some inherited from the French and others developed by the Vietnamese over a period of years. Perhaps the most noteworthy of these practices was the use of the field artillery primarily as a defensive weapon. The French had unavoidably set a poor example for the Vietnamese. They had been forced to use their artillery defensively in the face of too few soldiers, poor communications, limited road networks, and insufficient equipment. Since the road network was so vital to their operations and the Viet Minh tactics centered on cutting this network, the French developed a series of small outposts along the roads, each with one or two guns and mutually supporting wherever possible. For this purpose they used approximately 400 weapons of mixed calibers, including U.S. 105-mm. and 155-mm. howitzers and UK 3.7-inch and 25-pound guns. These weapons were manned by crews of seven to eight men and usually were located in an outpost occupied by one or two infantry platoons. From these positions, artillery supported squad-size outposts positioned along roads and canals. As a result of this type of employment, the war was often known as the war of the "firing lieutenant." Each platoon of two guns was commanded by a French lieutenant who, because of his isolated location, actually conducted his own little war. Artillery employed in this static role was not organized into batteries or battalions. Thirty to forty guns were grouped under a small headquarters staff responsible for their administrative and logistical support.

Though the French employed their artillery primarily in a static role, they also had regular artillery battalions organized as division artillery. In early 1951, as Viet Minh operations approached conventional proportions, the French emphasized employment of these battalions in a conventional manner. But this offensive application of artillery was too little and too late to have any effect on the outcome of the war.

The defensive posture that the French adopted for their guns was readily copied by the South Vietnamese. Weapons were placed in static positions throughout the countryside, where they often remained for years at a time, and seldom were used to support offensive operations. A purely defensive role was disheartening; one could never win on the defensive but could only hold off an attack or lose. A defensive attitude came to permeate the ranks at all levels and resulted in operating procedures that would seem ridiculous to anyone who seriously intended to win. Mortars were withheld from outposts where they might do some good because of the illogical reasoning that the outposts might be overrun and the weapons seized. Certain types of special ammunition and mines were withheld for the same reasons. It could only be unsettling to the morale of the defenders that they were denied weapons that might save their lives.

This is not to deny that a system of scattered artillery outposts to provide area coverage was valid in itself. Hamlets, government compounds, and lines of communication required continuous ar-

ARVN GUN SECTION. *Typical 105-mm. position within a hamlet in Kontum Province, September 1963.*

tillery protection. Still, after years of occupying static positions, methods of effectively employing artillery offensively were all but forgotten. Artillery not placed in static outposts was often held in unit motor pools when it should have been used to support ongoing operations or to relieve other artillery that could be so used. Artillery advisers relentlessly pushed their counterparts to move their howitzers out of the motor pools and their mortars out of arms rooms and, wherever possible, to move their guns out of the static outposts to support ground operations.

From 1961 to 1965 there were some changes toward a more offensive spirit on the part of the Vietnamese artillery. Major General Charles J. Timmes, Chief MAAG, Vietnam, noted in June 1964 that there was less hoarding of weapons in motor pools and more of a tendency toward employing all available weapons in the field. He gave much of the credit for the improvement to field artillery advisers. In addition, a U.S. Army contact team noted in a report written in early 1965 that artillery weapons were being used frequently to support South Vietnamese Army operations and that there was little hesitation to move weapons in support of those operations. However, the same report noted that most often only two guns were used to support a battalion-size operation. The report was also critical of the fact that once a platoon of two guns was moved and emplaced to support an operation, it was seldom moved again throughout the duration of the operation.

Another poor operational practice was overcontrol of the artillery commander by the supported maneuver commander. The Vietnamese followed the strictest interpretation of the French artillery commander's relationship to the ground commanders. At regimental level, the infantry commander actually commanded artillery assigned to his support. This alone was not necessarily a bad practice. U.S. artillery doctrine permits it, particularly, as was often the case in Vietnam, when both maneuver and supporting forces are some distance from their parent units on semi-independent operations. Given the command of his supporting artillery, however, the Vietnamese ground commander had a tendency to over-involve himself in the details of its employment. He often selected weapon positions and required that the artillery obtain permission from him before firing. As a result, corps and division artillery commanders were powerless to influence the action through their subordinate artillery headquarters, which were controlled by the supported commanders. They could only make recommendations on the employment of their weapons to their respective corps or division commanders. If the recommendations were accepted, they were passed on as orders through ground command channels. Subordinate maneuver commanders were then responsible for the execution of the orders. Artillery battalion commanders had no more power than their superiors to influence the action of their batteries other than to make recommendations to their supported ground commanders. A more efficient use of the system would have been for the infantry commander to give only general guidance to his artillery on how best to support his maneuver plan. The artillery commander, the more knowlegeable of the two on fire support matters, then would have the freedom and flexibility necessary to deliver the most responsive support. Unfortunately, Vietnamese infantry commanders were leary of giving their subordinates such leeway.

Artillery advisers were justifiably critical of Vietnamese firing procedures. Again, Vietnamese ideas reflected past exposure to French techniques. The French forward observer computed firing data mentally and sent them directly to the guns. The data were not accurate but the system was speedy. The U.S. observer sent his request for a fire mission to a fire direction center, where more accurate data could be computed and sent to the guns. Whereas French procedures were fast, U.S. procedures were accurate. Arguments could be made for either system, but accuracy would appear to be preferable in a situation in which targets were small, only two or three guns were likely to be within range, and the enemy was on foot. The U.S. fire direction center was adopted, but the information required to give accuracy to firing data was not available. The required registrations, surveys, and calibrations were not conducted and meteorological information was not available. The result was that Vietnamese procedures were neither fast nor accurate.

But Vietnamese artillery was not completely ineffective. Prisoner interrogations revealed that the enemy grudgingly respected ARVN artillery and intentionally planned attacks in areas that were beyond its range. Then, too, there were hopeful, though isolated, examples of South Vietnamese artillery operating aggressively and achieving outstanding results. One such example was Operation DAN THANG 106 during the period 15–22 April 1963. Field artillery supporting the operation moved 110 times and fired 1,007 missions. One artillery concentration was credited with killing 60 Viet Cong.

Vietnamese artillery nonetheless had a long way to go, and to the advisers there were as many disquieting signs as there were hopeful ones. The ARVN operation at Ap Bac, a small village in the Mekong Delta, was bitter evidence of the weakness of the artillery. Too long in static positions and dependent on slipshod firing procedures, the artillery in this case showed itself to be unequal to the task of providing responsive support to offensive ground operations.

The attack against Ap Bac in January 1963 was well conceived but poorly executed. It was to be a three-pronged attack, including mechanized infantry, and was designed not only to surprise the Viet Cong but also to trap him and pin him down. Once the enemy was surrounded, government forces would tighten the circle and destroy him with all available fire support from small arms to tactical air power. Open rice land to the east of Ap Bac was left unguarded. The decision was that if the enemy attempted to escape in that direction, he would make an excellent target for aircraft and artillery. As the joint ground and air assault was launched, the Viet Cong 514th Battalion reinforced by local guerrilla forces made attempts to escape the closing trap but was checked in every case. With all avenues of escape closed, the Viet Cong withdrew into the village, dug in, and prepared to fight even though they were outnumbered and outgunned.

Problems started when areas near helicopter landing zones were not cleared by preparatory artillery fire. Enemy gunners shot down five helicopters with intensive automatic small-arms fire, which could have been neutralized by an adequate artillery preparation. Poor leadership, lack of aggressiveness by the South Vietnamese, incorrect and unco-ordinated use of the armored personnel carriers, and the unwillingness of the Vietnamese commanders to listen to their advisers caused the assault to slow and halt. Reinforcements were parachuted in but were not employed correctly. Night set in, and the Viet Cong picked up their weapons and casualties and escaped through the leaky trap set by the ground forces. Artillery was not fired during the night to hold the enemy in position; instead, the next morning the Vietnamese cut loose with an unobserved artillery barrage into the village and killed government soldiers. When the battlefield was searched, only three enemy bodies were found. Reports from the field attempted to declare this controversial battle a victory for the South Vietnamese. It was not.

The Adviser Learns, Too

Although the Vietnamese displayed significant weaknesses in certain aspects of the employment of their artillery, at the same time they demonstrated a considerable degree of ingenuity. They had been fighting essentially the same enemy for several decades and had developed or copied from the French various employment concepts that were particularly well suited to the peculiarities of their situation. Their country and the enemy presented a situation the likes of which the U.S. Army had not faced since the Indian wars. Artillery advisers were in a position to learn from their counterparts as much as if not more than their counterparts could learn from them. What advisers learned and reported to their superiors was later invaluable in the employment of U.S. artillery.

Advisers learned, for instance—as their counterparts knew all along, that artillery could not be responsive if it had to be moved into supporting distance after a hamlet was attacked. A majority of the enemy's attacks were of small scale and lasted for only a short time. They normally terminated before artillery could be positioned. Even worse, the enemy could easily plan an effective ambush of any artillery convoy that was rushing to the relief of a hamlet. The artillery had to be pre-positioned throughout the countryside so that the maximum number of hamlets would be under the protective umbrella of one or more weapons. The amount of artillery available and the number of positions to be occupied dictated that only two or three weapons, rather than a full battery, could occupy a single position. This piecemeal application of artillery was contrary to everything U.S. artillerymen had learned relative to the employment of field artillery; past wars had shown that artillery was most effective when the fires of entire battalions could be massed against the enemy. But in the past area coverage was not important.

Cannons in this environment could be called on to fire in any direction. Artillerymen were quick to term this a "6,400" mil environment, the mil being the angular measurement used by the artillery with 6,400 mils in a complete circle. Procedures to shift fires quickly from one direction to another had been developed by the French and passed on to the Vietnamese, who made further refinements. The French routinely constructed in their outposts circular gun pits and protective parapets, which allowed the guns to be swung in all directions while providing protection for their crews. Sufficient markers of known azimuth were located around the gun emplacements to provide convenient reference points no matter in what direction the guns were to fire. The Vietnamese adopted in their fire direction centers a circular firing chart that was several times the size of a normal chart but permitted the computation of fire missions in any direction.

The adviser also learned that the use of scattered outposts required a host of changes to what he had considered normal operating procedures. Wire communications could be cut or tapped easily and could be used only within outpost perimeters. Radio, previously considered a backup system, became predominant. Another change was that infantry was required to protect artillery positions. This placed restrictions on the artillery that American advisers had not experienced. Artillery commanders, at best, were required to consider the availability of infantry protection in planning each of their moves. At worst, artillery movements could be totally controlled by an unwise infantry commander, who could deny protection if artillery did not move when and where he desired. Still another change was that each outpost had to be able to direct its own fire. U.S. Army doctrine said that fires would be directed from battalion fire direction centers, with backup provided by the firing battery. With his batteries spread over wide areas, the battalion commander was too far removed from the action to have a full appreciation of each local situation. Commanders of batteries or their platoons were in the best position to establish priorities and decide what targets to engage.

Advisers could not but be impressed with the innovative techniques devised by the Vietnamese that enabled a hamlet to call for artillery fire. In the initial years of the American advisory buildup, hamlets and villages were not equipped with radios but requested

155-MM. HOWITZER IN TUY AN DISTRICT HEADQUARTERS. *Typical emplacement to defend local populace.*

fires by prearranged signals such as colored flares. A hamlet was given four flares of different colors, each color representing a cardinal point. Red might represent north; green, south. If the hamlet was attacked, its defenders fired a flare of the color that indicated the direction of the enemy attack. From the outposts, data were computed and guns fired at various preplotted points on the appropriate side of the hamlet. Another signal was a large wooden arrow lit with kerosene at night and swung horizontally to point in the direction of an enemy attack. This procedure required that the supporting artillery outpost be at a higher elevation than the hamlet and in a position to see the arrow. As radios became available, they were issued to hamlet officials. An artillery target indicator was then devised. This was a simple circular board containing the outline of the hamlet and the relative locations of preplanned numbered concentration points. The operator pointed a rotating arrow in the direction of the enemy attack to find the azimuth and identify the point nearest the activity. With a radio the operator could request fires by concentration numbers and make subsequent corrections.

EARLY MOVEMENT OF ARTILLERY BY AIR. *CH–34 with 105-mm. carriage.*

The Vietnamese had moved their fire support weapons by helicopter to support combat operations several years before U.S. combat units were committed in Vietnam. True, procedures for such movement had been developed and rehearsed by U.S. Army troops stationed in the United States, and it was largely American advisers who taught the procedures; further, the Vietnamese used U.S. helicopters and pilots. Even so, this was the airmobility concept in its infancy and advisers could only profit from the experience. The CH–34 (then called the H–34) helicopter could lift the 105-mm. howitzer under normal conditions. Unfortunately, atmospheric conditions and mountainous terrain in Vietnam greatly restricted lifting capacity. The solution was to strip the 580-pound shield from the weapon and leave it behind. Then the weapon was dismantled into two separate helicopter loads—the tube and the carriage. Both parts were lifted by sling from an external hook on the bottom of the aircraft.

The 4.2-inch mortar, being considerably lighter than the 105-mm. howitzer, was easier to move by helicopter and probably was moved at least as often, though there are no records to support this assumption. One such move of particular significance was made on 5 May 1963. Three mortars of the South Vietnamese 25th Battalion (advised by Captain Theodore F. Smith) were moved by H–21 helicopters north of Bong Son into a landing zone well beyond the range of friendly artillery. Believing they were safe from artillery, the Viet Cong were caught by surprise and suffered "numerous" casualties.

American advisers regained a respect for lightweight towed artillery weapons in Vietnam. All but forgotten in scenarios pitting our forces against a sophisticated enemy in Europe, where the punch of heavier artillery was required, the 105-mm. howitzer again came to the forefront as the principal Army combat artillery piece. Although the 105-mm. projectile was much smaller and thus had less destructive power than the 155-mm. projectile, the 105-mm. howitzer was easy to manhandle, was helicopter transportable, and had a high rate of fire. It therefore proved to be the most desirable U.S. artillery weapon in counterguerrilla operations.

One of the most important lessons learned by field artillery advisers was that efficient clearance procedures were absolutely neccessary if artillery was to be at all effective. The necessity for obtaining clearance was peculiar to a counterguerrilla operation in which the enemy operated in and around populated areas. Clearance was often agonizingly slow in coming. The reasons for delay could be completely valid. For instance, the ground commander might be unsure of the location of one of his patrols or the responsible government official might have reason to believe that civilians were in the target area. On the other hand, the delay could be totally inexcusable and caused by inefficient clearance procedures or indifference of the responsible official.

The above are only the more important of countless lessons learned from the Vietnamese by U.S. artillery advisers. Those advisers who were career soldiers would find themselves returning to Vietnam before the conclusion of hostilities. Many would be assigned to U.S. artillery units and could use profitably much that they had learned as advisers.

How effective was this early advisory effort? If we judge results against the established goal of providing assistance necessary for the South Vietnamese Army to defend its country, we must admit failure. Throughout the period the army continued to lose its hold on the country until, in 1965, it was in so tenuous a position that the United States was forced to intercede with combat troops. (*Map 3*)

But was the goal a realistic one? Only four years passed from the time the U.S. advisory commitment was significantly expanded in

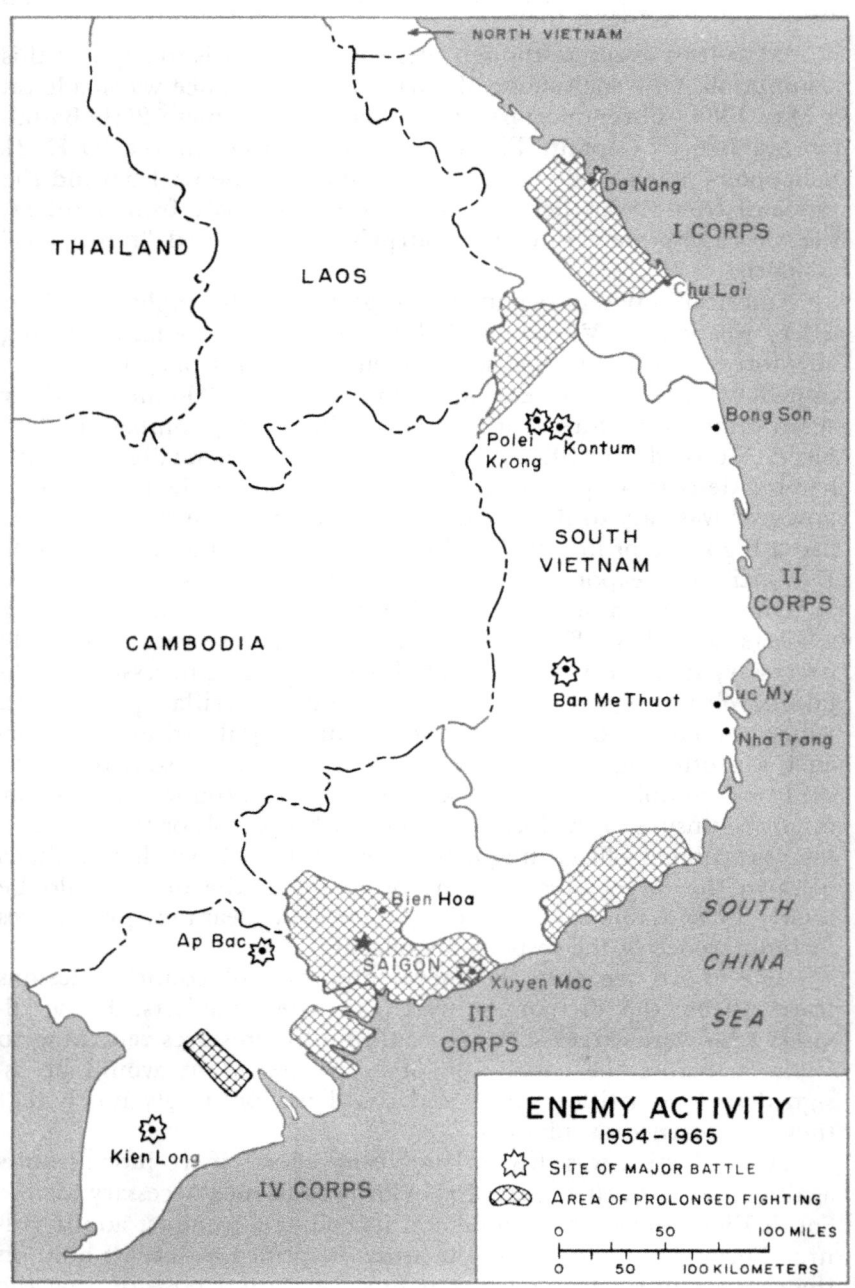

MAP 3

1961 until American combat forces were engaged. Such a short time can hardly be considered adequate to prepare an army to face an adversary that would prove itself capable of giving even American forces a difficult time.

Aside from problems of geography, cultural differences, and Vietnamese military experience and practices, it must also be stressed that the overthrow of President Diem on 1 November 1963 occurred in the midst of the advisory effort. His government had been slow and plodding, reflecting the many checks he had built into the government machinery to keep ambitious subordinates in rein. But Diem had kept a firm grip on the country that had contributed to cohesiveness and unity of purpose. In the aftermath of the coup, however, came a series of military and civil power grabs that for the better part of a year disrupted the government to the point that only the most routine matters could be concluded. Unity of purpose was sacrificed to personal advancement and gain.

But regardless of these problems, the advisory period was useful. It ended with a better led and better trained South Vietnamese fighting force, although room for improvement remained. The U.S. advisers can also be credited with having helped the South Vietnamese Army ride out the aftermath of the coup. The advisory organization remained functional even when the Vietnamese military or government organizations were not; in emergencies, for example, advisers could appeal to their superiors to help cut red tape and effect the release of needed supplies or reinforcements.[1] And in general, what the advisers learned and reported over the four years gave U.S. combat commanders an advance appreciation of the situation as well as insights into the tactics, organizations, and weapons most appropriate to defeat the enemy.

The advisory effort continued after U.S. combat troops were committed. Indeed, the success of these troops gave advisers more time to help the Vietnamese defend their country.

---

[1] Interestingly enough, the Vietnamese field artillery played a significant role in Diem's overthrow. Apparently the artillery was directed to tie down the palace guards and not to damage the U.S. Embassy across the street from where the guards were billeted. Field artillery was positioned some 10,000 meters northwest of Saigon and a forward observer was positioned down the street from the palace guard quarters. The battalion commander had no accurate plot of their quarters; he used a tourist map to establish a grid location. The first round fired was smoke and was a target hit. The battery continued to fire the one gun with high-explosive projectiles and destroyed the top of the structure. No one was killed, yet the guards were neutralized and forced to withdraw to the cellar for protection. The field artillery had been employed with surgical precision. Not even a window was shattered in the U.S. Embassy. (The division commander was then General Nguyen Van Thieu.)

CHAPTER III

In Order To Win

By late 1964 it was apparent that the South Vietnamese could not win the war alone despite heavy infusions of U.S. equipment and advisers. Most of the country was either firmly controlled or hotly contested by the enemy. The South Vietnamese Army weekly casualty rate was equivalent to a full battalion, a rate that could not be long sustained. To complicate matters further, the enemy was concentrating forces in II Corps Tactical Zone in preparation for a major offensive to cut the country in half at National Highway 19. Accordingly, President Lyndon B. Johnson, acting under authority of the Gulf of Tonkin Resolution, ordered U.S. combat forces to South Vietnam. The first troops, U.S. Marines represented by the 9th Marine Expeditionary Brigade, arrived on 8 March 1965. They were followed two months later by the 173d Airborne Brigade. Combat troops would continue to arrive over the next three years until the total commitment was equivalent to over ten divisions—two Marine divisions, seven Army divisions, three separate brigades, and an armored cavalry regiment plus requisite control headquarters and support.

More than two battalions of field artillery would arrive in Vietnam for each combat brigade. One battalion would be in direct support of each brigade, and the remainder would provide augmenting fires or area protection. The very size of the field artillery indicated that it was being counted on heavily to provide a major portion of the combat power required to win. Artillerymen at all levels were challenged to insure that so large and important a force be employed to its maximum effectiveness.

If field artillery units were to be effective from the outset of their introduction to the war, they had to arrive in Vietnam well trained. In the United States, commanders of field artillery units alerted for deployment to Vietnam carefully planned and executed intensive training programs for their troops. There was little time and much to be done.

A minor part of the total training of all units consisted of instruction in subjects applicable to all branches. Headquarters, United States Continental Army Command, directed that a sixteen-

hour block of instruction consisting of the following subjects be given to all Vietnam-bound units:
- Orientation—2 hours
- Perimeter defense—1 hour
- Duties of sentries—1 hour
- Ambush drill, mounted and dismounted—8 hours
- Field sanitation—1 hour
- Jungle survival—1 hour
- Lessons learned—1 hour
- Miscellaneous—1 hour

The remaining training time was devoted to artillery-related subjects. All field artillery headquarters, from division artillery and artillery group down, underwent intensive training centered on employing their units against irregular forces. Battalions conducted section, battery, and battalion training which culminated, when possible, in field training exercises to test unit proficiency. Battery commanders emphasized platoon operations and gunnery and fire direction procedures in the 6,400-mil environment. They foresaw the need for additional fire direction center personnel in the event their battery weapons were split among several locations. As a result, time permitting, survey and howitzer crews were cross-trained in fire direction center procedures.

Because of leaves, reassignments, and last-minute arrival of replacements, classes and practical exercises often had to be conducted several times to insure that all personnel received the necessary training. Training for all units then continued aboard troop transports. Classes were presented for two hours daily. They were followed by twenty to thirty minutes of physical training, conducted during the warmest part of the day in order to acclimatize soldiers to tropical heat.

The Impact of Vietnam on Field Artillery Organizations

Not in recent history had the U.S. Army faced an insurgent force of such significance on terrain that so favored the enemy as in Vietnam. Since the enemy largely dictated how the war would be fought, it was necessary for the Army to modify established operational doctrine considerably to be successful against him. These modifications had a tremendous impact at all organizational levels. The impact on field artillery organizations is most readily explained by comparing the tactics used in fighting a conventional war with the tactics developed in Vietnam.

In a conventional ground war, U.S. maneuver forces are disposed along a line facing the enemy. To the front, security forces are positioned to warn of the enemy's approach and to delay him while inflicting maximum punishment. To the rear, additional maneuver forces are held in reserve by all ground commanders above company level, and each is committed by its commander when needed.

Also to the rear are the combat support activities, including the field artillery, as well as combat service support activities. For the most part the rear area contains no large enemy forces, so units operating there are considered sufficiently strong to defend themselves. With little enemy ground activity, wire communications are used extensively in the rear area. Radio is considered a secondary means of communication, for the most part used by units on the move. The main threat to the survival of a unit is the enemy's fire power from aircraft and artillery that can reach behind the front lines.

Most of the available field artillery is used to engage the enemy forward of front-line maneuver forces; therefore, most artillery units, though as scattered and dispersed as possible, are disposed laterally behind the front line. Each maneuver division has artillery to support its ground forces, the composition depending on the type of division. In most cases the division artillery has three similar battalions of light or medium cannon artillery, sufficient to support each of the three brigades of the division, and one or more additional battalions of heavier artillery to provide augmenting fires.

The division artillery commander supports the division commander's maneuver plan by assigning missions to his artillery battalions and by co-ordinating the employment of all available fire support, including nondivisional field artillery and fire support from other branches and services. A field artillery unit can be assigned to support a single maneuver unit (it is then said to be in direct support), or it can be employed to augment the fires of other artillery units. In the latter case, a unit can have a reinforcing mission, augmenting the fires of a single designated field artillery unit; a general support mission, augmenting the fires of all field artillery units of the division; or a general support-reinforcing mission. A unit on this last mission again augments the fires of all field artillery units but gives priority to reinforcing the fires of a single designated artillery unit of the division.

Mission assignment has proved to be an extremely effective method of weighting the main effort of the division and economizing combat power elsewhere. It has provided the flexibility required for adjusting fire support to the ever-changing needs of the battlefield. Mission assignment has been particularly effective in conventional operations, in which units can displace virtually at will to give maximum support to the ground forces.

In assigning missions to subordinate battalions, the division artillery commander first places one of his three light battalions in direct support of each committed brigade. Thus, if the division has two brigades on line and one in reserve, only the two brigades on line receive direct support artillery. The division artillery commander than assigns an augmenting mission to the third of this three similar battalions. Perhaps the most common mission for this battalion is to reinforce the direct support battalion covering the area of greatest effort or largest threat. At the same time, the reinforcing battalion is instructed to revert to direct support of the brigade in reserve when that brigade is committed to battle. The division artillery commander most commonly places his heavy artillery battalion in general support of the division or in general support-reinforcing of the fires of a specific direct support battalion. However the division artillery commander employs his battalions at the beginning of an operation, he is free to adjust them at any time to meet unforeseen developments.

In conventional operations, missions seldom are assigned to artillery units smaller than battalion. A battalion in direct support of a brigade supports the entire brigade rather than assigning one of its batteries to each of the brigade's battalions. To control the fires of its three batteries, the battalion establishes a centralized fire direction center. Centralized control permits the battalion to bring all the fires of its batteries to bear at any point in the brigade sector. This massing of fires is possible because all batteries are likely to be well within range of the entire brigade front. In fact, combat power might be so highly concentrated in some instances that all the artillery of a division can be massed on a single target.

Even so, there are occasions on the conventional battlefield where firing batteries or battalions are widely separated; for example, artillery units might be sent forward to support long-range screening or covering force operations, or units might be sent to support a force on an independent operation. Artillery organizations and doctrine have provided for such contingencies. Firing batteries have fire direction centers which under normal conditions provide backup support of the battalion fire direction center but act independently where the battery is too distant for its parent unit to control or support it. When a battery or battalion is distant from its parent unit, it is normally attached to its supported maneuver unit.

In a conventional battle plan before the Vietnam era, field artillery doctrine was that sizable amounts of field artillery, in addition to that organic to division artilleries, are available to support ground operations. This artillery is organic to a field army and is organized into separate battalions or groups. (A group controls two or more battalions.) The field army commander provides additional combat power to his subordinate corps by assigning his field artillery to them. He can thus effectively weight the combat power of the corps that he considers to have the highest priority, based on the mission he has given it. The corps commander receiving artillery from field army in turn assigns the artillery to augment his subordinate divisions. He also gives primary consideration to that division with the most critical mission.

The war in Vietnam was anything but conventional. The enemy was not contained by a line of friendly forces. Instead, he operated throughout the country, mostly in small units, but massing formidable strength when and where he chose. Accordingly, military ground operations were characterized by numerous, concurrent, widely dispersed small-unit operations. These tactics permitted continuous pursuit of the widely scattered enemy. To insure that the maximum area was defended by available troops, a section of terrain called an area of operations (AO) was assigned to each ground unit from the highest level down. A ground force commander conducted operations throughout his assigned area. The two field force commanders divided their areas, each corresponding to one of the four South Vietnamese military regions, among their divisions. The divisions in turn divided their territory into brigade areas of operations. Brigades split their areas among their battalions; battalions, among their companies.

The wide dispersal of maneuver forces required significant changes in the employment tactics of supporting artillery. The size of brigade areas of operations and range limitations of the cannons prevented a direct support battalion from massing the fires of its batteries in support of an entire brigade. Instead, artillery was disposed to provide the maximum area coverage, with each of the three batteries of a battalion in direct support of one of the three maneuver battalions of the brigade. The infantry battalion commander and the supporting battery commander were jointly responsible for insuring that the battery was always positioned to cover adequately all maneuver forces of the battalion.

Fire direction was no longer centralized at field artillery battalion but was decentralized to battery level or, when the battery was forced to occupy two positions, to platoon level. The primary justification for centralizing fire direction was the ability to mass fires. Now that that ability no longer existed, the best place to control fires was at the battery, where the commander could best appreciate the needs of the supported infantry battalion. Firing batteries were isolated with their supported battalions. They did not have the freedom of movement they would have on the conventional battlefield but moved with their supported infantry battalions and were protected by these battalions. Wire communications were vulnerable, and radios were used exclusively for communicating beyond defensive positions. Because of the distances involved, a battery, without freedom of movement, could do little to support itself administratively or logistically without increased assistance from its parent battalion.

Small friendly units operating throughout the area of operations were difficult to pinpoint and added to the difficulties of providing supporting fires to ground forces. Artillery forward observers with maneuver companies continuously transmitted position locations to the battery, but the terrain made land navigation difficult and there was always the possibility of a mistake by the forward observer. Any mistakes could have resulted in friendly casualties. Out of respect for that danger, an infantry battalion commander rightfully restricted the activities of his direct support battery until its men had demonstrated their competence to his satisfaction. This took several weeks at best. Once his confidence was won, the commander loosened restrictions and the total combat system worked as it had been designed to work. Fires were planned and executed within general guidance from the ground commander, who was then free to devote his attention to the maneuver plan.

The artillery and infantry have always had a close working relationship, a requirement if maneuver and fire support are to be completely complementary. This relationship was never closer or more important than in Vietnam. The artillery battery was isolated with its supported infantry battalion. Each was dependent on the other for survival—the artillery for protection, the infantry for supporting fires. The relationship was further strengthened by a policy of "habitual association" of a direct support battalion with a specific brigade and each battery of the battalion with a specific maneuver battalion.

The policy of habitual association was logical and easily executed. Every maneuver brigade was committed to the defense of an area of operations; none was placed in reserve. For that reason, each of the three light battalions of division artillery was always in direct support of a brigade. So rigidly was the policy of habitual association enforced that an artillery battalion and its associated brigade often entered the country at the same time, remained together throughout their involvement there, and withdrew from Vietnam or stood down together.

Vietnam also had its impact on the activities of the division artillery. With each of his light battalions in direct support of a maneuver brigade, the division artillery commander was powerless to vary their tactical mission or otherwise rearrange the support they provided. The only unit remaining with which he could influence the action was his heavy battalion, which generally consisted of three 155-mm. batteries and an 8-inch battery. He would direct the batteries of the heavy battalion to provide additional fires where he thought they were most needed. Often one of his 155-mm. batteries was committed to the direct support of the division cavalry squadron, reducing his flexibility to influence the action even more. Furthermore, distances and the situation prevented the division artillery commander from utilizing his remaining artillery as responsively as he could in conventional operations. Heavy artillery was positioned in advance of an operation and moved only infrequently, if at all.

Since the capability to influence the battle at division artillery level was reduced, the work load normally associated with the capability was also reduced. Yet as the responsibilities of the division artillery commander were lessened in one area, they were increased in others. The wide dispersal of artillery units increased the problems of supply and maintenance, and staff officers were kept busy seeking ways to increase the support the battalions could provide to their batteries. Trucks and helicopters for hauling supplies were sought out and requested. Needed maintenance and administrative support was arranged for battalions to send to isolated batteries. In addition, the division artillery commander was responsible for contributing forces, weapons, and equipment to the defense of the division base camp or for directing the entire base camp defense. Also, because winning the support of the population was so important to the success of a counterguerrilla war, added emphasis was placed on civil affairs and the work load in that area expanded considerably. Division artillery staffs were augmented with an officer to plan and direct civil affairs activities and to co-ordinate those of subordinate battalions.

The work load of the division artillery commander in other areas was much the same as it had always been. He was still the adviser to the division commander on fire support matters. Intelligence had to be gathered and collated continuously and actions of division maneuver forces and artillery updated. A fire support element at division had to be established to support ongoing maneuver operations. And the use of nondivisional fire support means, including field artillery, Air Force tactical air and strategic bombers, and naval air and naval gunfire, had to be planned, requested, and co-ordinated.

As in conventional operations, there were large amounts of field artillery in addition to that organic to divisions; however, the manner in which it was organized and employed was vastly different. In a conventional operation, nondivisional field artillery normally is at the field army level and is apportioned to corps on the basis of their needs. United States Army, Vietnam (USARV), was organized into two field forces and a separate corps. The field force, a new organization to the Army, was roughly equivalent in level of command to a corps but had greatly expanded supply and administrative responsibilities. The corps, on the other hand, was a tactical headquarters and its lean staff could only co-ordinate logistical activities. In Vietnam, field artillery was assigned on a permanent basis to each of the field forces and the separate corps. This practice recognized that the requirements of each command tended to remain stable and that the long distances involved precluded continuous shifting of artillery from one field force to another. The stability of artillery requirements of the two field forces and the separate corps was a result of the mission assigned to nondivisional artillery. Whereas divisional artillery supported specific U.S. maneuver operations, nondivisional artillery served in an area support role, a role that was new to the field artillery yet vital under the circumstances.

Of overriding importance in Vietnam, as in any counterguerrilla action, was winning the support of the people for their government. They had to be shown that the government could improve their lot as well as protect them from the insurgent. Field force artillery firing units were positioned to provide maximum coverage of population centers, lines of communication, and government installations. Firing units answered calls for fire support from any friendly party, civil or military, within range. The position location of each unit had to be carefully planned in relation to the position locations of all others. This planning was done at field force level. In past wars commanders at such high levels were not concerned with the positioning of individual firing units; subordinate artillery commanders had the authority to decide within liberal territorial limitations where units could best be placed to perform their mission. But in Vietnam much of the responsibility for positioning their units was taken from them.

As was true of division artillery, commanders of groups and battalions in field force artillery had increased work loads in other areas as a result of added logistical support problems and civil affairs and position defense responsibilities. Also, the role of nondivisional artillery created a requirement for continuous dialogue with local government representatives and supported military and paramilitary forces. Such dialogue was necessary not only for the artillery to do its job but also for its survival. Firing units providing area cover were often far from U.S. maneuver forces and had to turn to the Vietnamese for protection.

Commanders of both division and field force artillery in Vietnam continued the practice of providing fire support through mission assignment, though the meanings applied to the missions were somewhat changed. Since units were so widely dispersed, a single artillery unit normally could not be positioned to augment the fires of several other artillery units. Instead, general support became area coverage. For units of divisional artillery, area coverage placed primary importance on plugging gaps in the coverage of direct support units. For units of field force artillery, area coverage placed primary importance on supporting all friendly forces within range of their positions. Thus, quite contrary to its normal meaning, the mission of general support was often given to a unit that had no other field artillery within range. The meaning of the reinforcing mission changed little. Reinforcing artillery still augmented the fires of a specific artillery unit. General support-reinforcing artillery was positioned to augment the fires of a specific field artillery unit but otherwise provided area coverage.

Another change occurred in respect to batteries too distant from their parent battalions to receive control or support. Practice in the past had been to attach such batteries to their supported maneuver battalions, but in Vietnam such an arrangement was not fully satisfactory. Maneuver commanders had neither the equipment nor the expertise to support artillery units adequately, particularly for lengthy operations. And field artillery commanders, who were schooled and experienced in the employment of artillery to serve the maneuver forces best, were unable to influence the situation. Instead of attachment, the status of operational control (OPCON) was most often used. For example, if a firing battery was to be separated from its parent headquarters, it was placed under the operational control of another artillery battalion headquarters in the area in which the battery was employed. A battery that was under the operational control of a field artillery battalion was controlled by that battalion but continued to receive support from its parent battalion. Maneuver commanders could then receive the best possible fire support without being burdened with additional support requirements.

Though operational control served a useful purpose, its use complicated operations of battalions with both divisional and nondivisional artillery. At any one time, one battalion might be controlling its own three batteries plus several others that were under its operational control. Another battalion might have lost the operational control of all its organic batteries to another battalion. Artillery battalions had to be flexible enough to direct the operations of a varying number of batteries.

On numerous occasions artillery units were employed in ways quite contrary to the general practice that had been developed in Vietnam. Division artillery normally supported divisional maneuver forces whereas field force artillery served in an area support role. Yet on any one day during the height of the U.S. commitment, one could point out numerous cases in which roles were reversed. For example, when division artillery supported divisional maneuver units in such rugged terrain that its organic 155-mm. self-propelled howitzers could not follow, the division artillery commander might be provided with airmobile 155-mm. towed howitzers from field force artillery for the duration of the operation. There were also frequent occasions when field force artillery units were placed in direct support of maneuver units, and many times division artillery units provided area support.

Fire Support Co-ordination

The responsibility for co-ordinating the various types of fires available to the maneuver commander falls largely on the field artillery. At all maneuver headquarters above company level, an artillery fire support co-ordinator (FSCOORD) is responsible for co-ordinating all available fire power—field artillery, armed helicopters, Air Force and Naval tactical air, air defense weapons in the ground support role, and naval gunfire. In addition, an infantry battalion commander often delegates responsibility for co-ordinating the battalion heavy mortar fire to his co-ordinator. At maneuver company, the company commander is the fire support co-ordinator though a field artillery forward observer is available to aid and advise him. At maneuver battalion the co-ordinator is a liaison officer from the direct support field artillery battalion. At higher levels he is the commander of the artillery supporting the force; however, in practice he delegates the detailed co-ordination activities to a subordinate. The artillery battalion commander delegates the duty to the artillery liaison officer with the brigade. The division and corps (or field force) artillery commanders delegate the duty to an assistant co-ordinator. Within each of the operation centers of maneuver forces, a co-ordinator establishes and supervises a fire support co-ordination activity, called a fire support co-ordination center (FSCC) at battalion and brigade level and a fire support element (FSE) at division and higher. In the center are representatives of all available fire support units. Some representatives are not included in the fire support element, being normally found elsewhere in the tactical operations center; but their presence in the center still allows efficient co-ordination.

The field artillery liaison officer (now titled the fire support officer) with either a maneuver battalion or brigade was tasked in Vietnam as never before. Because of advances in weapon technology, more types of fire support were available. To complicate matters, each type of fire support could deliver a host of different munitions, each designed for a different job. The field artillery liaison officer was the one who insured that the most appropriate ordnance available arrived at the right targets at a specified time and that all the fires delivered complemented one another. Besides having more weapons to co-ordinate, he often had to support not only U.S. Army forces but also Vietnamese military and paramilitary, Korean, Australian, Thai, New Zealand, Philippine, and U.S. Marine forces during joint operations. That task required more than processing and passing requests to the appropriate support means; it required establishing priorities as well as insuring that the organic fires of the other force were co-ordinated with the support being requested. This frequently called for him or an Army forward observer to be on the scene to request and direct or co-ordinate the fires. His efforts were further complicated by differences in language and in operating procedures.

As if such complications were not enough, he was required to obtain clearance to insure that no civilians were in the area before employing weapons. Clearance was most often obtained from the government district in which the supported force was operating, and arrangements had to be made to open and maintain the necessary radio nets in advance of an operation. Clearance had not been required in past U.S. wars, in which the enemy was engaged forward of a battle line and was not operating among the friendly population. Another responsibility of the liaison officer that was peculiar to Vietnam was the co-ordination of air space usage. Artillery warning control centers (AWCC's) were established, normally at maneuver battalion and brigade levels, to advise the numerous aircraft over the area of operation of current supporting fires. All support means were required to notify the warning center before firing. Aircraft entering the area would, in turn, contact the center and receive current information plus a flight path to follow to avoid firings.

Field Artillery Weapons

The wide variances in the types of field artillery weapons sent to Vietnam gave senior artillery commanders great flexibility in tailoring fire support to satisfy best the needs of the situation.

The 105-mm. towed howitzer most often served in the direct support role. Its light weight, dependability, and high rate of fire made it the ideal weapon for moving with light infantry forces and responding quickly with high volumes of close-in fire. Units were initially equipped with the M101A1 howitzer, virtually the same 105-mm. howitzer that had been used to support U.S. forces since World War II. In 1966 a new 105-mm. towed howitzer, the M102, was received in Vietnam. The first M102's were issued to the 1st Battalion, 21st Field Artillery, in March 1966. Replacement of the old howitzers continued steadily over the next four years.

Many of the more seasoned artillerymen did not want the old cannon replaced. Over the years they had become familiar with its every detail and were confident that it would not disappoint them in the clutch. Old Redlegs could offer some seemingly convincing reasons why the M101 was still the superior weapon: its waist-high breech made it easier to load; it had higher ground clearance when in tow; but most important, it was considerably less expensive than the M102. Their arguments, however, were futile. The new M102 was by far the better weapon. It weighed little more than $1\frac{1}{2}$ tons whereas the M101A1 weighed approximately $2\frac{1}{2}$ tons; as a result, more ammunition could be carried during heliborne operations, and a $\frac{3}{4}$-ton truck rather than a $2\frac{1}{2}$-ton truck was its prime mover for ground operations. Another major advantage of the M102 was that it could be traversed a full 6,400 mils. The M101A1 had a limited on-carriage traverse, which required its trails (stabilizing legs) to be shifted if further traverse was necessary. A low silhouette made the new weapon a more difficult target for the enemy, an advantage that far outweighed the disadvantage of being somewhat less convenient to load.

Certain field force artillery units were equipped with the M108, a 105-mm. self-propelled weapon. The weapon was obsolescent but was still in the U.S. field artillery inventory. In Germany, it had been replaced by the 155-mm. self-propelled howitzer as the direct support artillery for U.S. armored and mechanized divisions. The M108 was too heavy to be lifted by helicopter, so its support of highly mobile light infantry forces in Vietnam was restricted. Still, the M108 was employed effectively in the area support role and, if the terrain permitted, in support of ground operations.

The next larger caliber artillery weapons were the 155-mm. howitzers. Firing units were equipped with either the towed M114A1 or the self-propelled M109. Both weapons normally provided area coverage or augmented direct support artillery. Occasionally, however, the 155-mm. self-propelled howitzer was used in direct support of maneuver units, as with the 1st Brigade, 5th Mechanized Division. Or when a divisional cavalry squadron operated as an entity, it was often provided a 155-mm. battery for direct support. Like the M108, the towed M114A1 was considered obsolescent. It was no match for the 155-mm. self-propelled weapon for supporting conventional ground operations against a highly mobile, armor-heavy enemy. In Vietnam, however, the M114A1 proved invaluable because it was light enough to be displaced by helicopter and so could provide medium artillery support to infantry forces even where roads were nonexistent. The 155-mm. howitzers, whether towed or self-propelled, had a maximum range of 14,600 meters, over 3,000 meters greater than that of the 105-mm. howitzer. The weight of the 105-mm. projectile—95 pounds—was almost three times the weight of the 105-mm. projectile. For these reasons, the 155-mm. howitzers could provide a welcome additional punch to existing direct support weapons.

The M107 self-propelled 175-mm. gun and the M110 8-inch howitzer had identical carriages but different tubes. The 175-mm. gun fired a 174-pound projectile almost 33 kilometers. This impressive range made it a valuable weapon for providing an umbrella of protection over large areas. The 8-inch howitzer fired a 200-pound projectile almost 17 kilometers, plus being the most accurate weapon in the field artillery. The 8-inch howitzer was found with most division artilleries, and both the 8-inch howitzer and 175-mm. gun were with field force artillery. At field force the proportion of 8-inch and 175-mm. weapons varied. Since the weapons had identical carriages, the common practice was to install those tubes that best met the current tactical needs. One day a battery might be 175-mm.; a few days later it might be half 175-mm. and half 8-inch.

Aerial rocket artillery (ARA) proved to be extremely effective in augmenting and extending the range of the cannon artillery of the airmobile divisions. Aerial rocket artillery units initially employed the UH–1B or UH–1C (Huey) helicopter equipped with a weapon system that could carry and fire forty-eight 2.75-inch rockets. In early 1968 the improved AH–1G (Huey Cobra) was outfitted as an aerial rocket artillery aircraft. Its maximum speed of

CH–47 WITH M102 HOWITZER

130 knots was some 30 knots faster than that of the Huey. In addition, it carried a larger payload of 76 rockets. In early 1970 the designation of aerial rocket artillery was changed to aerial field artillery (AFA). By either name, it was in every sense a field artillery weapon system, organized as such and controlled by artillerymen through artillery fire support channels.

Field Artillery Mobility

The importance of mobility in insurgency operations cannot be too highly stressed. From experience in past guerrilla actions in Malaya and the Philippines, the conclusion was that at least ten soldiers are required to counter every enemy soldier. The ratio is high because the enemy has the initiative. He can hit wherever he desires and thus require that friendly forces be ready in sufficient numbers at all locations likely to be contested. Once the enemy has attacked and withdrawn, sizable forces are needed to sweep the countryside if there is to be any hope of finding him. Superior mobility allows the available friendly units to be more widely deployed and permits planners to reduce the ratio of friendly to

CH–54 Lifting 155-mm. Howitzer

enemy troops. For example, a highly mobile infantry battalion and its supporting battery could complete an operation in one area and in a matter of hours be moved to another some distance away.

Mobility in Vietnam for ground troops and artillery alike was provided by ground vehicles, Air Force assault aircraft, watercraft, and helicopters. More artillery was moved by road than by any other means. When a landing zone could be conveniently reached by road, it was to a unit's benefit to move in this fashion if operational considerations did not dictate otherwise. The unit could be moved in convoy by its own vehicles and in its entirety, whereas movement by helicopter usually required several lifts. Because of its weight, all self-propelled artillery was moved in convoy. The Air Force, usually employing C–130's, supported long-distance moves between improved or unimproved airstrips. Watercraft transported both infantry and artillery in the delta areas, where a network of rivers, rivulets, and canals favored such movement.

The Vietnam war saw the first large-scale use of helicopters by the U.S. Army to transport troops, artillery, and supplies. Helicopters added a new dimension to the battlefield by providing the

Fire Support Base J. J. Carroll in Military Region I. *A large fire support base, J. J. Carroll contained four firing units.*

commander a more responsive and flexible means to concentrate his combat power where it was needed.

Before 1962, the helicopter had been used sparingly, but through the imagination and drive of several key officers, notably Generals James M. Gavin and Hamilton H. Howze, the airmobile concept was developed. They envisioned the deployment of lightly equipped troops by lift helicopters, with fire support to and within the objective area provided by light tube artillery and armed helicopters. What airmobile troops lacked in weight they would compensate for with mobility. They were planned for use against a sophisticated enemy where highly mobile forces have always been needed. Covering force and screening operations, economy-of-force missions, flank and rear area security, and securing of key terrain, bridges, and installations behind enemy lines were a few possible applications. In 1962 the Airmobility Requirement Board (commonly known as the Howze Board) was formed to develop organizational requirements for an airmobile brigade. The efforts of the board resulted in the activation of the 11th Air Assault Division, which was redesignated the 1st Cavalry Division (Airmobile) in June 1965 and programed for deployment to Vietnam. Though the division was initially configured for use in a sophisticated environ-

STAR FORMATION. *Battery B, 1st Battalion, 77th Field Artillery, in well-prepared base camp.*

ment, it proved to be extremely effective in Vietnam against an unsophisticated enemy.

The airmobile division artillery was equipped with 105-mm. towed howitzers and UH–1B (Huey) helicopters armed with rockets. Howitzers were lifted by the division's own CH–47A (Chinook) medium-lift helicopters. The Chinook could carry 33 combat troops and internal cargo up to 78 inches high, 90 inches wide, and 366 inches long or external cargo of 6,000 to 8,000 pounds, depending on atmospheric conditions. A 105-mm. howitzer battery with a basic load of ammunition could be moved in as few as 11 CH–47A sorties. Other maneuver units that followed the 1st Cavalry Division also used Chinooks extensively to move their howitzers; however, with the exception of the 101st Airborne Division these helicopters were not part of the divisions but were provided by aviation groups supporting the military regions. Every infantry unit in Vietnam was, in fact if not in name, airmobile infantry and its direct support artillery was airmobile artillery.

The CH–54 (Tarhe), nicknamed the Crane for its lifting ability, followed the Chinook to Vietnam. It could lift up to 18,000 pounds either by sling or by an attachable pod, but sling loads were by far the more common in Vietnam. Of special importance to the field artillery was the Crane's capacity to lift the 155-mm. towed howitzer without breaking it down into two separate loads as was required for the CH-47 helicopter. This would expedite the positioning of medium artillery in areas not accessible by road.

The Fire Base

Cannon artillery is the only nonorganic fire support serving maneuver forces that is immediately responsive, always available, and totally reliable. It is immediately responsive because it is positioned to be always within range of the supported force, whereas other fire support means most often must be brought to the battle area or moved within range. It is always available because it is organized to provide field artillery in direct support of every committed maneuver force. A maneuver commander may not always receive other fire power because it is apportioned according to the needs of all commanders. It is totally reliable because it can function in any weather and in poor visibility, when helicopters and planes are grounded or their effectiveness is reduced.

Infantry commanders fully appreciated the value of field artillery support. In developing their maneuver plans, they worked closely with their supporting artillery commanders to insure that the plans could be fully supported by the artillery. If plans envisioned that maneuver battalions would be so widely dispersed that they could not be supported by direct support batteries operating from single battery positions, additional artillery was requested. If additional artillery was unavailable, the direct support batteries were split to occupy several positions and thereby increase area coverage even though fire power was reduced. Only on rare occaisons did maneuver forces in Vietnam operate beyond the range of friendly artillery.

Use of available mobility allowed direct support artillery to follow supported ground forces virtually anywhere. But once field artillery was displaced to a preplanned position to provide supporting fires, it was extremely vulnerable to the enemy, who could attack in mass from any direction. Firing batteries had neither the personnel nor the expertise to defend their positions against determined enemy attacks. Accordingly, infantry units provided defensive troops. The position jointly occupied by supporting artillery and defending infantry was referred to as a fire base or fire support base. It was commanded by either an infantryman or an artilleryman, usually whoever was the senior. From its fire base an artillery fire

MEN FROM BATTERY A, 2D BATTALION, 319TH FIELD ARTILLERY, BUILDING PARAPETS

unit could shoot in any direction to its maximum range and would answer calls for fire support from maneuver forces operating under its protective umbrella.

The position for a fire base was selected jointly by the artillery and infantry commanders. The primary concern of the artillery commander was that the position be adequate to support maneuver elements throughout the area of operation. An important consideration was the availability of other artillery within range of the position that, if required, could be called on to provide indirect fire in defense of the fire base. Other important considerations were the type of soil to support the howitzers and how readily the position could be defended and supplied by air. The primary concern of the infantry commander was defense of the position unless he intended to establish his headquarters on the fire base to take advantage of the available security. In that event, he was concerned that the fire base be central to his maneuver forces so they could be effectively controlled. This priority was generally agreeable to the artillery commander, who could provide better all-round coverage from such a location.

1st Battalion, 40th Field Artillery, in Position Along Demilitarized Zone

Typical Towed 155-mm. Position. *Note trail blocks.*

Battery C, 2d Battalion, 138th Field Artillery, on Hill 88, *March 1969.*

Because of the manpower drain on maneuver units had they been required to defend all artillery positions, fire bases were constructed almost exclusively for direct support artillery. When such a fire base was established, it was usually to support a large operation of at least divisional size or to provide a position when no available one was even marginally acceptable. Division or field force artillery generally chose the best positions for their firing units not in direct support from among defensive positions already established. As a result, such a unit might occupy a fire base with one or more other artillery units or, for that matter, might occupy any other type of defensive position belonging to either American or allied forces. Any commander was happy to have the additional fire power that a battery would bring to his position.

The organization of a fire base was a reflection of the flexibility and ingenuity of the American soldier. Terrain, area available, and number and caliber of weapons, plus numerous other variables, made it impossible to standardize procedures for occupying such positions. Still, some generalities can be cited.

The formation of artillery pieces on the ground varied with the

Battery D, 3d Battalion, 13th Field Artillery, at Fire Support Base Stuart, June 1969. *Chain link fence has been installed for protection against B40 rockets.*

terrain and the caliber and number of weapons. Insofar as possible, weapons were arranged in a pattern with as much depth as width to eliminate the need for adjusting the pattern of effects on the ground. Six-gun batteries, which included all 105-mm. and 155-mm. batteries, were emplaced in a star formation, with five guns describing the points of the star and the sixth gun in the center. This configuration provided for an effective pattern of ground bursts and for all-round defense. At night the center piece could effectively fire illumination while the other pieces supported with direct fire. Firing units with only three or four guns arranged their pieces in a triangular or square pattern, if terrain permitted. The diamond formation was most commonly used by composite 8-inch and 175-mm. batteries. The 175-mm. guns were positioned farthest from the center of the battery, where the fire direction center and administrative elements were located, thus reducing the effects of blast on personnel, equipment, and buildings.

The infantry established a perimeter as tight as feasible around the guns. The desired configuration was a perfect circle, but this was seldom possible because of the varied terrain to be defended. Perimeter defensive positions were dug in and bunkered where possible. To the front, barbed wire was strung and claymore mines and trip flares were emplaced. Infantry soldiers defended the fire

155-MM. HOWITZER POSITION USING SPEEDJACK AND COLLIMATOR. *Speedjack is under center of howitzer, collimator to the rear of howitzer on sandbags.*

base perimeter with their individual rifles and grenade launchers and with crew-served machine guns and recoilless rifles. In addition, the infantry was equipped with both 81-mm. and 4.2-inch mortars. Mortars were invaluable for fire base defense, not only for their heavy volumes of high-explosive fires but also for close-in illumination during enemy night attacks. A fire base was fortunate if it had air defense weapons on its perimeter. Both the M42A1 "Duster," a dual 40-mm. weapon, and the M55 (quad), four .50-caliber machine guns fired simultaneously, provided impressive ground fires, though neither weapon had been designed for that role. These weapons were organic only to nondivisional air defense battalions and were not available in sufficient numbers to provide protection to all fire bases.

The defense responsibilities of the infantry did not end with the establishment of a strong defensive perimeter. Just as important was aggressive and continuous patrolling around the fire base to frustrate enemy attempts to reconnoiter the base and prepare for an attack. Usually, a single-battery fire base was provided a rifle company to man the perimeter and conduct necessary patrols. This provision was recognized in the organization of infantry battalions in Vietnam, where each battalion was assigned four rifle companies instead of only three.

The field artillery on the fire base also contributed to its defense. In fact, the contribution of the artillery was often the deciding factor in staving off a determined attack. Artillery defensive fires included direct fire, countermortar fire, and mutually supporting fire.

Direct fire, as its name implies, required line of sight between weapon and target. It involved the use of special antipersonnel munitions and techniques. The XM546 antipersonnel projectile, called the Beehive round, was particularly effective in the direct fire role. The projectile was filled with over 8,000 flechettes, or small metal darts. The field artillery direct fire capability was integrated with the infantry defense to cover likely avenues of approach and the most vulnerable areas. It was imperative that the infantry bunkers be built up in the rear so that the infantrymen were protected from the effects of the Beehive ammunition. Beehive was fired in combat for the first time on 7 November 1966 by Battery A, 2d Battalion, 320th Field Artillery. A single round killed nine attacking enemy and stopped the attack. The round was employed on many occasions with similar success, perhaps the best known being during the enemy attack on Landing Zone BIRD.

Another effective direct fire technique was "Killer Junior," perfected by Lieutenant Colonel Robert Dean, commander of the 1st Battalion, 8th Field Artillery, of the 25th Infantry Division Artillery. The technique was designed to defend fire bases against enemy ground attack and used mechanical time-fused projectiles set to burst approximately 30 feet off the ground at ranges of 200 to 1,000 meters. The name Killer Junior applied to light and medium artillery (105-mm. and 155-mm.), whereas "Killer Senior" referred to the same system used with the 8-inch howitzer. This technique proved more effective in many instances than direct fire with Beehive ammunition because the enemy could avoid Beehive by lying prone or crawling. Another successful application of the Killer technique was in clearing snipers from around base areas. The name Killer came from the radio call sign of the battalion that perfected the technique. To speed the delivery of fire, the crew of each weapon used a firing table containing the quadrant, fuze settings, and charge appropriate for each range at which direct fire targets could be acquired.

Countermortar (or counterbattery) fires, the second type of artillery defensive fire, were preplanned, unobserved fires that were

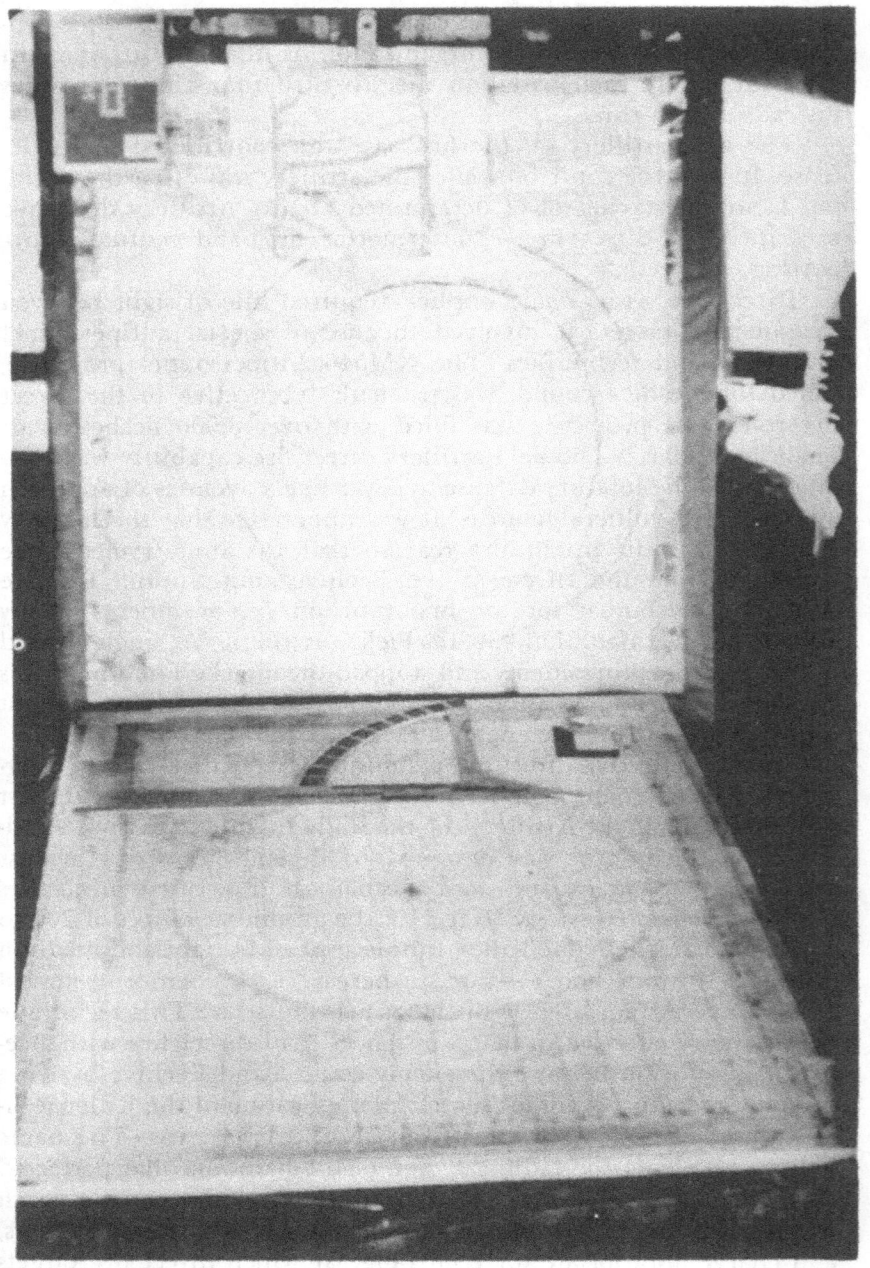

6,400-Mil Chart. *Map on back shows area coverage.*

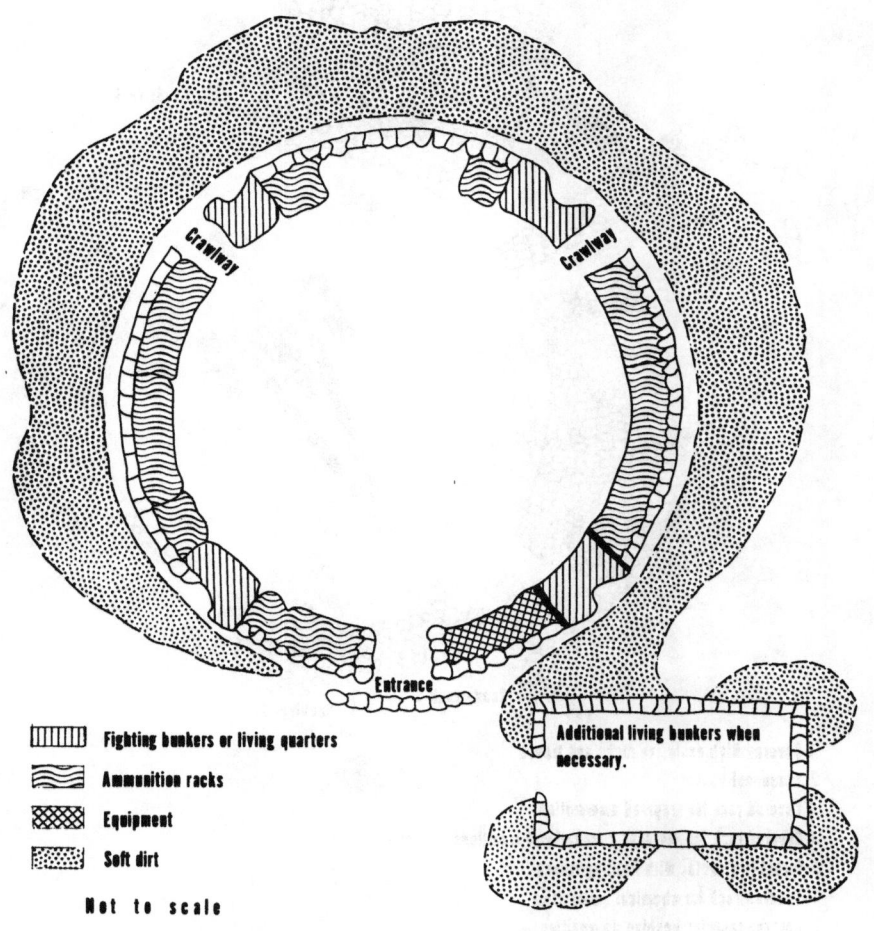

Diagram 1. M101 105-mm. artillery field position.

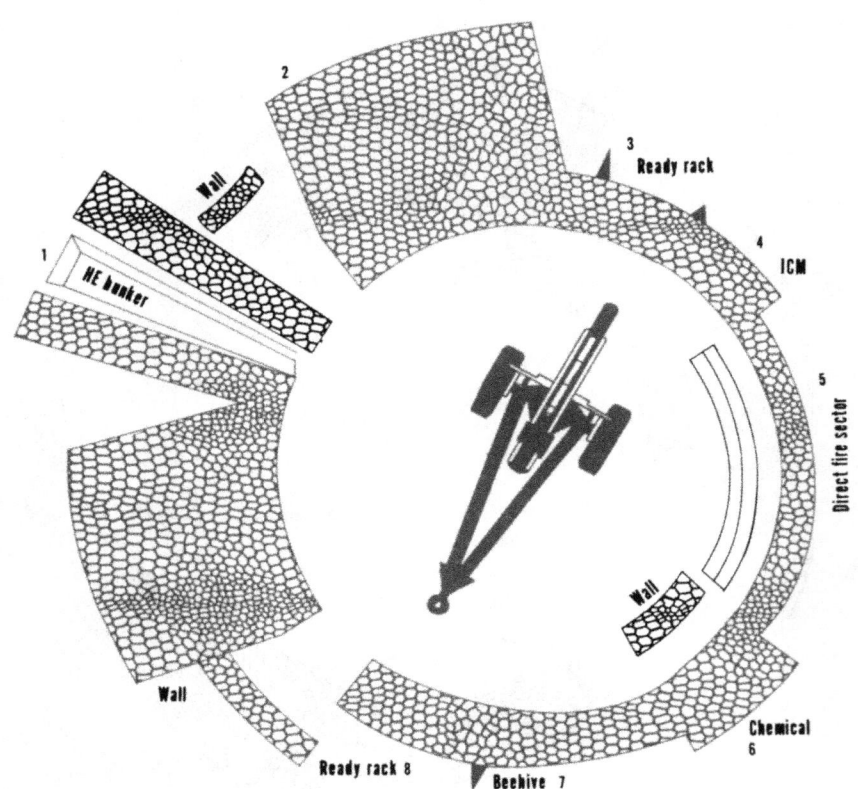

1 Covered High explosive racks and trench
2 Personnel bunker
3 Covered rack for prepared ammunition
4 Covered rack for improved conventional munitions
5 Direct fire sector with fighting trench
6 Covered rack for chemical ammunition
7 Covered rack for Beehive ammunition
8 Second covered ammunition ready rack

Diagram 2. M102 105-mm. emplacement.

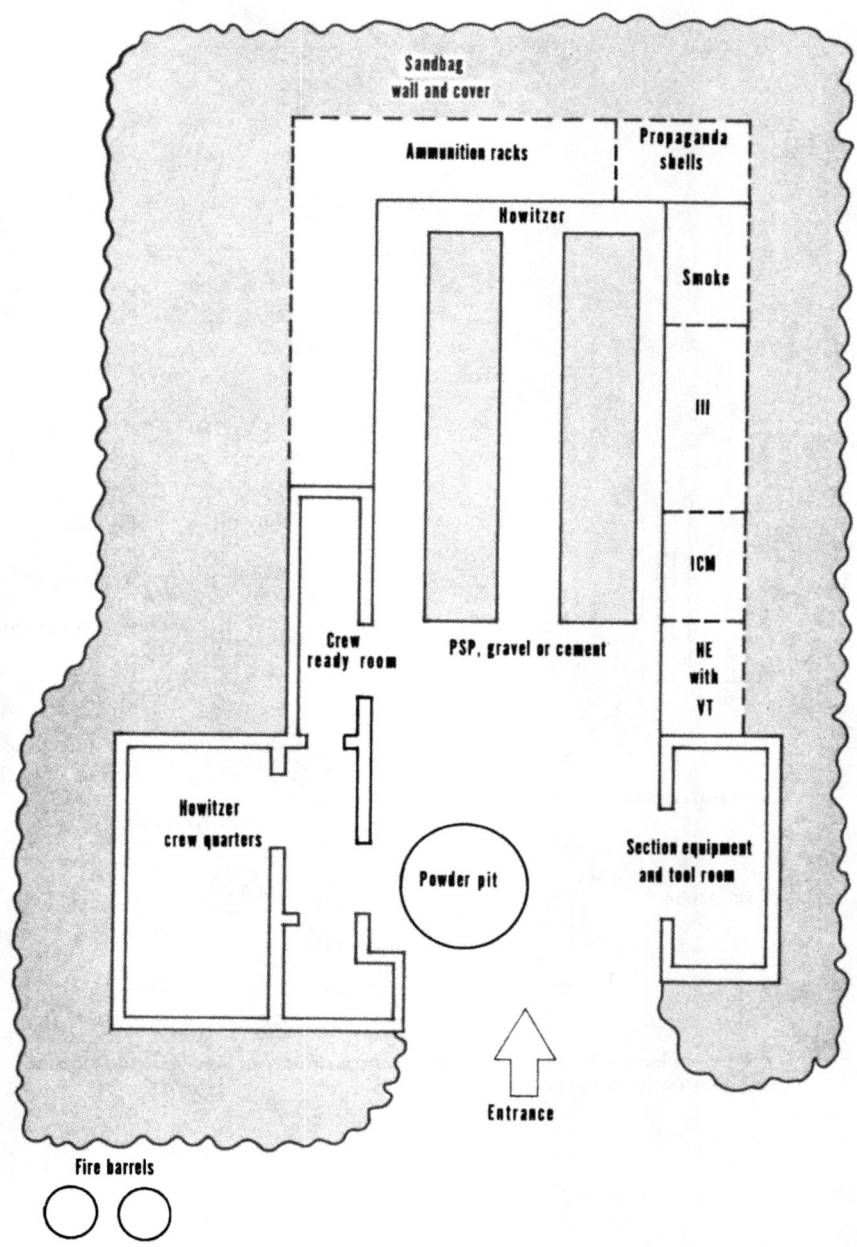

Diagram 3. Semipermanent 105-mm. self-propelled howitzer emplacement.

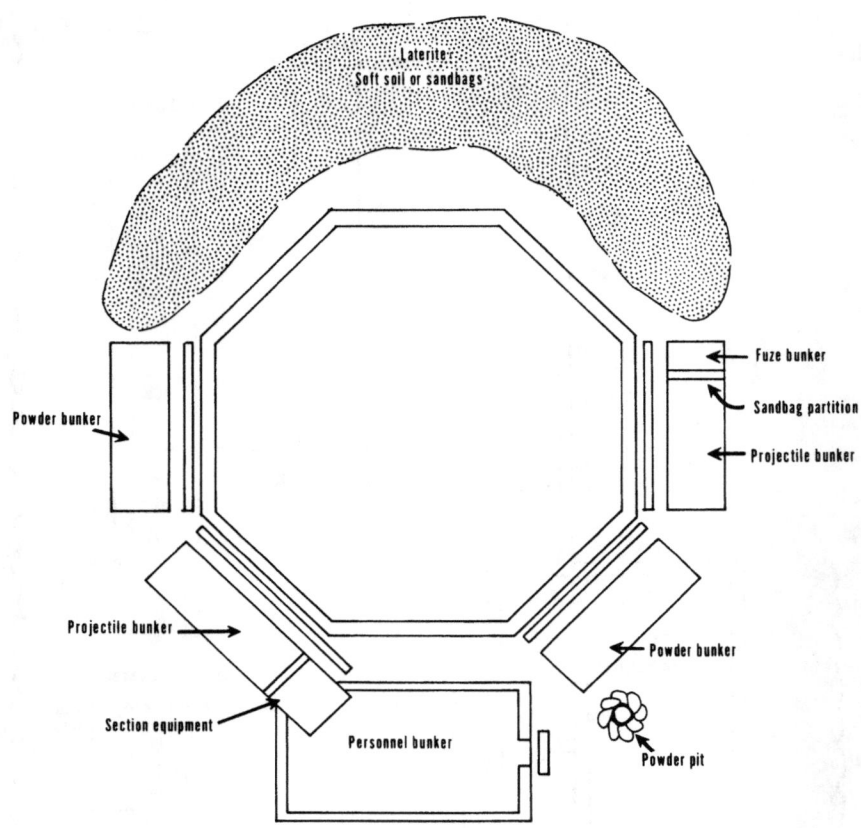

Diagram 4. Towed 155-mm. howitzer emplacement.

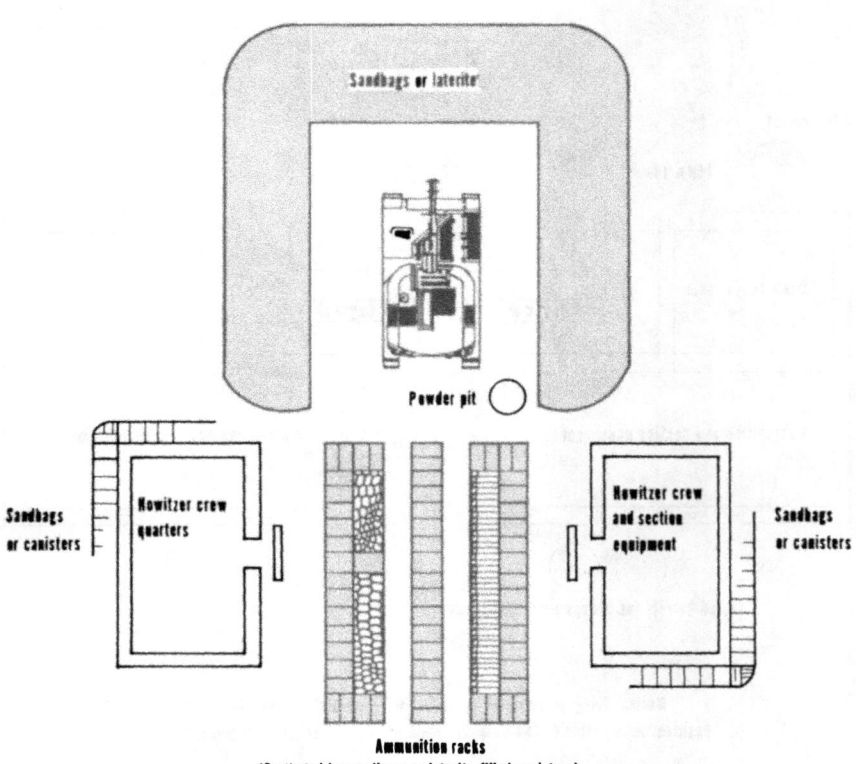

Diagram 5. Self-propelled 155-mm. howitzer emplacement.

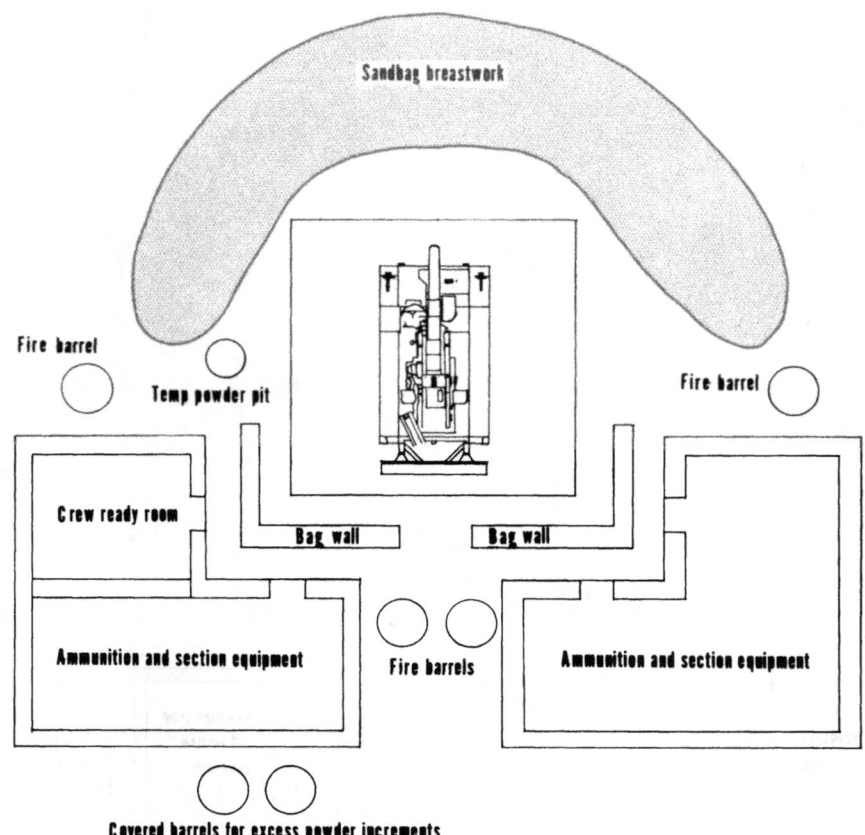

Normal living quarters for personnel were separated from the firing position when possible. The howitzer pads were constructed by engineers.

Diagram 6. Heavy (8-inch or 175-mm.) artillery emplacement.

executed in the event the fire base underwent an enemy rocket or mortar attack, either as part of a ground attack or as a "standoff" attack using rocket or mortar fire alone. A field artillery forward observer or liaison officer chose likely positions for enemy weapons from a map and from information provided by aerial reconnaissance. Firing data to the positions were computed and a fire plan was prepared. The fire plan was retained in the battery fire direction center, where it could be executed immediately when requested. This procedure might at first glance appear to depend

ARTILLERY HILL AT PLEIKU. *An artillery base camp containing a field artillery group, three field artillery battalion headquarters, and nine firing units.*

to a great extent on luck, but it proved to be quite effective. An experienced artilleryman knowing the optimum range of enemy weapons, the likely routes into the area, and the criteria for good weapons positions could be very accurate in predicting future locations of enemy weapons.

Mutually supporting fires, the third type of artillery defensive fire, were indirect fires provided by one fire base in support of another. Whenever a new base was established, field artillery forward observers and liaison officers contacted responsible personnel on other bases within range and made plans to support one another if attacked. Planning included choosing and prefiring targets close to the defensive perimeter of each fire base. The firing data were retained in the fire direction centers and used when requested. Immediately available close-in fires were thus assured. Subsequent corrections could be made if necessary.

Time and again the indirect fires from mutually supporting artillery proved to be a principal factor in successfully countering an enemy attack on a fire base. Having mutually supporting bases was considered so important that whenever a battery was required to occupy a position beyond the range of any friendly artillery, every effort was made to readjust other artillery positions to bring them within range. If that was not possible, batteries often split into three-gun platoons and occupied two separate but mutually supporting positions.

The various designs of individual weapon emplacements constructed by batteries on fire bases reflected a great deal of initiative and individuality. The design normally was standardized within a battalion and, in some cases, throughout a division or group. Whatever the design, it provided for all-round protection of weapons and crews from direct fire, readily available overhead cover for the crews, and protection of ammunition. Common materials used were sandbags, ammunition boxes, powder canisters, pierced-steel planking, heavy timbers, and corrugated steel roofing. Steel culverts covered with sandbags were used to provide hastily constructed, yet effective, personnel cover. Standard cyclone fencing placed 20–25 feet in front of positions protected howitzers, which, with their high silhouettes, were particularly vulnerable to enemy rocket attack.

The loose soil of coastal areas and the saturated soil of the lowlands during the monsoons made it difficult to prevent the shifting of light and medium howitzers during firing. Logs were used to brace the M101A1 105-mm. howitzers. Firing platforms on the M102 105-mm. howitzers frequently were staked through pierced-steel planking or ridged-aluminum planking. The M114A1 155-mm. howitzer was particularly prone to shifting. A common field expedient to help stabilize this weapon was 55-gallon drums filled with soil and buried vertically and flush with the surface. Logs were often dug in horizontally in a circle around the weapon to brace its trails during firing. One method that proved effective in reducing displacement was devised by the 1st Battalion, 84th Artillery. Old tank tracks with the ends linked together were buried vertically flush with the surface and in a circle. The howitzer was positioned in the center, with its trails against the tracks.

The 6,400-mil environment required that gun sections be thoroughly versed in techniques to allow weapons to be shifted rapidly to a new direction of fire. Two sets of reference points, which normally consisted of two sets of aiming posts or one set of aiming posts and an infinity collimator, provided a visible angular reference in any direction. Azimuth markers or stakes around the gun positions provided easy reference and facilitated the frequent shifting of trails from mission to mission. In the case of the 155-mm. towed howitzer, shifting trails was a time-consuming, laborious

AN/MPQ-4 COUNTERMORTAR RADAR, *positioned on a large tower for better area coverage.*

TPS–25 Ground Surveillance Radar

task. Through the initial efforts of Lieutenant Nathaniel Foster of the 8th Battalion, 6th Artillery, 1st Infantry Division, a pedestal that eliminated the need for lowering the howitzer off its jack before shifting trails was developed. Modification of Foster's initial platform led to the float jack, which made the weapon more responsive and flexible.

Central to the firing battery was the fire direction center. This was a small, well-bunkered position. It had the personnel and equipment necessary to receive fire requests from forward observers with the supported force and to convert these requests to data that were usable at the guns. Fire direction centers, too, had to follow new techniques in order to respond to calls for fire from all directions. Firing charts had to allow for a 6,400-mil range of fire, and much experimentation was done in this area to devise the best system. Generally, an oversized firing chart mounted on a large table proved to be the most effective solution.

The fire base proved its worth in Vietnam: it could be quickly constructed virtually anywhere; it could withstand the most formidable assaults that an unsophisticated enemy could bring against it; and it permitted the field artillery to provide fire support of the same high quality as that provided in past wars.

Base Camp Defense

The base camp was an installation occupied by a headquarters larger than a battalion. Whereas the fire base performed a combat mission, the base camp was larger and contained controlling headquarters for combat activities as well as essential combat service support activities. A perimeter of bunkers encircled the base camp, and beyond the bunkers were intricate barriers of barbed wire reinforced with flares and mines. Headquarters and combat service support personnel, augmented where required by infantry, manned the perimeter. Ground forces conducted continuous patrolling around the base camp, usually out as far as the range of enemy rockets.

The field artillery also contributed to the defense of a base camp. Cannons fired harassing and interdiction fires on likely enemy routes and positions, answered calls for observed fire from patrols, fired illumination rounds, and provided direct fires against enemy ground attacks. The number of cannons required for the defense of base camps varied; a brigade or artillery group base camp might require only a platoon of artillery, whereas a division base camp might need several batteries.

In addition to cannons, field artillery targeting devices such as radars and searchlights, when available, were integrated into the defense. The AN/MPQ-4 countermortar radar, organic to direct support artillery battalions, and the AN/TPS-25 ground surveillance radar, organic to division artillery, were used in conjunction with shorter range infantry antipersonnel radars for locating targets. Once targets were located, they were engaged by cannons or other suitable supporting fires. Searchlights provided either visible or infrared illumination. They were oriented for direction on the same angular reference as the artillery weapons. If the enemy was spotted, an azimuth and an estimated distance could be relayed directly to the battery fire direction center.

The responsibility for defense of a base camp was often assumed by the senior artilleryman occupying the installation. Phu Loi base camp, for example, was occupied by the 23d Artillery Group headquarters plus other combat support and combat service support activities. No infantry unit was permanently assigned, and on two occasions the group commander was designated as Phu Loi defense commander. Senior ground commanders at times also delegated responsibility for the defense of their base camps to their senior artillery commanders, as in the 4th Division, first at Camp Enari and later at Camp Radcliff. As installation defense commander the division artillery commander controlled that area around the base

30-INCH XENON SEARCHLIGHT. *Battery I, 29th Field Artillery, at Fire Support Base Horseshoe, February 1970.*

camp within a fourteen-kilometer radius. He co-ordinated patrol and reconnaissance activities in the area, co-ordinated the perimeter defense effort, and established the installation defense co-ordination center, in which all efforts concerning reconnaissance, ground defense, reaction to enemy attack, target acquisition, and fire support were centralized. Sizable portions of base camp defense responsibilities were also delegated to the artillery commanders of the 1st Cavalry Division and the 1st Infantry Division. The former was given operational control of a cavalry battalion in Area of Operations CHIEF, encompassing the division base camp at Phuoc Vinh. The latter directed maneuver operations around the Big Red One artillery base camp at Phu Loi.

Riverine Artillery

The terrain of the Mekong Delta was a serious hindrance to fighting forces in Vietnam. The delta is comprised of rivers and canals coupled with swamps and rice paddies. Roads and dry ground are scarce, and hamlets and villages have long since been built on what little dry ground there is. If artillery shared dry ground with a hamlet, the firing unsettled the people whose support the allies were trying so hard to win. Even when field artillery was positioned on dry ground, it was difficult to employ because the high water table made the ground soft. Without a firm firing base, cannons bogged down, were difficult to traverse, and required constant checks for accuracy. All this lessened their responsiveness and effectiveness.

A fighting force in the delta could not rely on ground vehicles for transportation or supply. Vehicles could seldom move the infantry close to the enemy, they were vulnerable to ambush, and the scarcity of dry ground overly cramped and restricted supply operations and the activities of control headquarters and supporting field artillery. Helicopters were used successfully to transport troops and artillery to the area of operations. The airborne platform was developed to solve problems of the inadequacy and scarcity of dry ground. The platform, a 22-foot square, was similar to a low table with large footpads on four adjustable legs to distribute its weight. The platform could be lifted by Chinook and placed rapidly in boggy or inundated areas. A second Chinook brought in a 105-mm. howitzer M102 and ammunition and placed it on the platform. (The howitzer and platform could be lifted together by a CH–54 Crane.) The platform provided space for the howitzer, the crew, and a limited amount of ammunition and permitted traverse of the howitzer in all directions. If one or more of the legs was mired when

CH–47 Emplacing Airmobile Firing Platform

the platform was to be moved, the footpad was disconnected and left in place to be recovered separately. A principal disadvantage of the airmobile platform was that the gun crew was overexposed to enemy fire. It was impossible to construct bunkers or overhead cover since the nearest ground was under water, though sandbags positioned around the edge of the platform provided some protection. Another disadvantage was that ammunition resupply and storage was difficult because of limited space on the platform.

Even more significant than the use of helicopters in the delta was the formation of a riverine task force, which relied on watercraft to provide transportation, fire power, and supply. The task force consisted of the 2d Brigade of the 9th Infantry Division and the U.S. Navy River Assault Flotilla 1.

Field Artillery support for the new riverine task force was initially provided from fixed locations, but the support was less than adequate. Field artillery needed to move and position itself to best support the ground action. This need was satisfied by the 1st Battalion, 7th Artillery, in December 1966 when the battalion first employed the LCM–6 medium-size landing craft as a firing platform for howitzers. The LCM could be moved to a desirable position and secured to the riverbank. Internal modification was required so that the craft could accommodate the M101A1 howitzer,

RIVERINE FIELD ARTILLERY BATTALION COMMAND POST, *with fire direction center on left, helicopter pad in center, and living quarters on right.*

but even then it was not wide enough to permit the howitzer trails to be spread fully. As a result, the on-carriage traverse was limited. Other shortcomings were that the craft did not afford as stable a firing platform as was desired and that excessive time was required to fire.

More successful were floating barges. The concept originated from a conference in the field between Captain John A. Beiler, commander of Battery B, 3d Battalion, 34th Artillery, and Major Daniel P. Charlton, the battalion operations officer. Their ideas prompted a series of experiments to determine the most suitable method of artillery employment with the riverine force.

The first experiment used a floating AMMI ponton barge borrowed from the Navy and an M101A1 105-mm. howitzer. Although the AMMI barge served its purpose, it was difficult to move and had a draft too deep for the delta area. The barge finally used was constructed of P–1 standard Navy pontons (each 7 by 5 feet) fastened together into a single barge that was 90 feet long by 28 feet 4 inches wide. Armor plate was installed around its sides for protection of the gun crews. Ammunition storage areas were built on either end and living quarters in the center. This arrangement

RIVERINE BATTERY POSITION. *Six M102 howitzers preparing for an operation (fire direction center located in center right barge).*

RIVERINE PLATOON MOORED TO CANAL BANK. *Living quarters are located in center, ammunition storage on each end.*

provided two areas, one on each side of the living quarters, that could be used to position 105-mm. howitzers. Initially the M101A1 howitzer was used but, as the newer M102 weapon became available in Vietnam, it replaced the older howitzer. A mount for the M102 was made by welding the baseplate of the howitzer to a plate welded to the barge deck. This mount permitted the howitzer to be traversed rapidly a full 6,400 mils.

Three barges and five LCM-8's constituted an average floating riverine battery. Three LCM's were used as push boats, one as the fire direction center and command post and one as the ammunition resupply vessel. Batteries could move along the rivers and canals throughout the delta region; they frequently moved with the assault force to a point just short of the objective area. All the weapons had a direct fire capability, a definite asset in the event of an ambush. Then the howitzers often responded with Beehive rounds, which usually broke up the ambush in short order.

When a location for the battery was selected, the barges were pushed into position along the riverbank. The preferable position was one where the riverbank was clear of heavy vegetation. This facilitated helicopter resupply, which could then be accomplished on the bank as close as possible to the weapons. Clear banks also

Riverine Gun Section in Traveling Configuration. *Note the five Beehive rounds at left of trails.*

provided better security for the battery. The barges normally were placed next to the riverbank opposite the primary target area so that the howitzers would fire away from the shoreline in support of the infantry. This served two purposes: weapons could be fired at the lowest angle possible to clear obstructions on the far bank, and the helipad was not in the likely direction of fire.

The barge was stabilized with grappling hooks, winches, and standoff supports on the bank side of the barge. Mooring lines were secured around the winches and reeled in or out to accommodate tide changes so that the barges would not be caught on either the bank or mudflats at low tide. Equipment to provide directional reference for the weapons—including aiming circle, collimator, and aiming posts—was emplaced on the banks. Accuracy of fires proved to be comparable to that of ground-mounted howitzers.

Without these new developments in riverine artillery, U.S. maneuver force activities in the delta area would have been seriously curtailed or often would have had to take place out of range of friendly field artillery. Instead, the field artillery was able to provide support when and where it was needed.

CHAPTER IV

The Buildup (1965–1967)

The Buildup Begins and Early Actions Around Saigon

At 0530 on 5 May 1965, the first of 150 sorties of C–130 aircraft loaded with men and equipment of the 173d Airborne Brigade and its support elements landed at Bien Hoa Air Base in Saigon. Battalion-size elements of the U.S. Fleet Marine Force, Pacific, had been operating around Da Nang in the northern portion of South Vietnam since March, but the arrival of the 173d, consisting of two airborne infantry battalions, marked the first commitment of a U.S. Army ground combat unit in Vietnam. The brigade, under the command of Brigadier General Ellis W. Williamson, formed a defensive perimeter around the air base. In direct support of the brigade was the 3d Battalion, 319th Artillery (Airborne), a two firing-battery 105-mm. battalion commanded by Lieutenant Colonel Lee E. Surut.

Counterinsurgency operations dictated new tactics and techniques, and, as they affected maneuver units, so they affected their supporting artillery. Although the brigade had undergone rigorous training in Okinawa before its departure for Vietnam, the "first unit in" could not be totally prepared. Nevertheless, the airborne troopers of the 173d performed admirably. No sooner had the brigade unloaded its gear than it began to conduct operations around Bien Hoa, primarily search and destroy operations and patrol actions. The men of the 319th had a "jump" of two months on fellow artillerymen, which enabled them to compile an impressive list of firsts. The first field artillery round fired by a U.S. Army unit in the Republic of Vietnam came from the base piece of Battery C, 3d Battalion, 319th Artillery, during a registration mission. With that round, the U.S. field artillery role in the Vietnam war began.

On 31 May 1965 the 3d Battalion, 319th Artillery, as part of Task Force SURUT, participated in the largest air assault conducted in Vietnam to that date. The task force, consisting of the 319th reinforced by a cavalry troop, an engineer platoon, and a composite platoon made up of volunteers from the support battalion, secured a landing zone and guided in CH–37 Mohave helicopters carrying

105-MM. BATTERY FIRING FROM HASTY POSITION

the howitzers. Up to this point in the war, the Mohaves had been doing yeoman duty as all-purpose aircraft. So smoothly and efficiently did this initial move go that three hours later these same howitzers mounted preparation fires on another landing zone for Task Force DEXTER, a reinforced infantry element of the 173d Brigade. This was the first such operation ever conducted in actual combat by a U.S. Army unit—one that had been in Vietnam less than thirty days.

The 173d soon had an opportunity to participate as the reserve force in an offensive operation. In June a Viet Cong regiment launched an attack on Dong Xoai, a district town ninety miles north of Saigon. With the press corps closely following the events, the 173d moved to a forward airfield in case relief forces were needed. Although South Vietnamese troops ultimately relieved Dong Xoai, the Redlegs of the 3d Battalion, 319th Artillery, became the first U.S. Army unit in Vietnam to engage in an offensive operation by providing fire support for the South Vietnamese troops relieving Dong Xoai.

After the Dong Xoai support operations, the 3d Battalion returned to Bien Hoa to ready for a history-making operation that commenced on Sunday, 27 June. Fifty kilometers north of Bien Hoa lies the southern edge of a huge tangle of double-canopy forest and thick undergrowth. Called War Zone D, it had long been a guerrilla haven, unpenetrated even by the French in their many years of fighting. In a massive, businesslike operation, five maneuver battalions penetrated deep into the area. The 3d Battalion (Airborne), 319th Artillery, provided co-ordinated fire support for the 1st and 2d Battalions (Airborne), 503d Infantry, of the 173d Airborne Brigade and the 3d and 4th Battalions of the South Vietnamese Army 2d Airborne Brigade. The Royal Australian Regiment joined the operation after the second day. The size of the assaulting force determined the significance of the operation for the artillery. It necessitated the close co-ordination of large volumes of artillery fires augmented by close air support and armed helicopters.

Before the operation began, the brigade commander directed that artillerymen "exercise the complete system." Exercise it they did. One hundred forty-four aircraft providing support for the operation assisted in the displacement of five infantry battalions, a field artillery battalion, a support battalion, and a composite battalion of cavalry, armor, and engineers. Throughout the entire operation, no serious incidents or major breakdowns in the system occurred. The artillery provided ten forward observers (including the battalion property book officer), three liaison officers (including the battalion communications officer), and two aerial observers in addition to those forward observers and liaison officers normally provided. Three communication nets were used and all fires were cleared through the brigade fire support co-ordination center. The 319th fired nearly 5,000 rounds of 105-mm. ammunition during the four-day period while maintaining contact and effecting co-ordination with the supporting Vietnamese and Australian artillery units.

Known only as OPORD 17–65, the designation of the original operation order, this venture into War Zone D yielded satisfying results. By conservative estimates, the enemy suffered 75 casualties and lost several trucks and nearly 250 tons of food and supplies. In an honest appraisal of the field artillery role shortly after the conclusion of the operation, Colonel Surut admitted having discovered some "bugs" in the fire support system:

> Fire support coordination initially slowed some missions, but by D+2 this bottleneck was overcome. Safety checks slowed the firing somewhat; however the checks are necessary for close support, particularly with three major maneuver elements abreast.

General Williamson, the brigade commander, in a letter to the commandant of the Field Artillery School, discussed the initial operations of the 3d Battalion, 319th Artillery:

> The artillery over here is doing a fabulous job. My Artillery Battalion Commander is having experiences that far exceed what most others have had. . . I would suggest that the Artillery make every effort to get the most promising young officers out here for some very worthwhile experiences.

The 173d Airborne Brigade again tested its fire support system in War Zone D on 6 July. Along with a battalion of the Royal Australian Regiment and units of the 43d Regiment of the Army of the Republic of Vietnam, the brigade conducted four multiple air assaults supported by helicopter sorties just north of the Dong Nai River. The operation resulted in 56 enemy killed, 28 captured, 100 tons of rice seized, and several tons of documents destroyed.

For the field artillerymen, this second venture into War Zone D provided an opportunity to correct the mistakes of the previous operation. Clearance and safety checks now were routine and the liaison and co-ordination efforts functioned smoothly. General Williamson, in complimenting the co-ordination efforts of all involved, said:

> . . . as I looked at it from above, it was a sight to see. We were withdrawing from the center Landing Zone while some friendly troops were still in the western Landing Zone. We had a helicopter strike going in a circle around the center Landing Zone. The machinegun and rocket firing helicopters kept making their circle smaller and smaller as we withdrew our landing zone security. Just to the west side we had another helicopter strike running north to south. We also had something else that was just a little hairy but it worked without any question. The artillery was firing high angle fire to screen the north side of the landing zone. The personnel lift helicopters were coming from the east, going under the artillery fire, sitting down on the LZ to pick up troops and leaving by way of the southwest. In addition to that, we had an airstrike going to the northeast. All of these activities were going on at the same time. We could not have done that a few weeks ago. The only reason we can do it now is that (we know) where our troops are and the fire support coordination center can coordinate fire and other activities.

The 3d Battalion, 319th Artillery, maintained continuous "feedback" to the U.S. Army Artillery and Missile School (later the Field Artillery School) at Fort Sill, Oklahoma. Correspondence included letters, memorandums, and copies of debriefings and after-action reports which contained numerous insights on the employment of artillery. At the school the correspondence was thoroughly studied and discussed with a view toward including any new and valuable information in classroom instruction. The fol-

AERIAL ROCKET ARTILLERY UH-1B WITH XM3 WEAPONS SYSTEM, *which carried forty-eight 2.75-inch folding fin aerial rockets.*

lowing are only a few of the important insights and tips received from the 3d Battalion:

1. Dense foliage in Vietnam made it particularly difficult to identify friendly troop dispositions and enemy targets to close air support aircraft. One system adopted to help correct this shortcoming was to employ white phosphorous projectiles as marking rounds.
2. Commanders must make every effort to preclude the check firing of one fire support system to accommodate another. General Williamson's description of actions in War Zone D was evidence that the 173d Airborne Brigade was getting good results with the continuous and concurrent employment of various fire support systems.
3. Responsive shelling report (SHELREP) personnel were necessary to establish an effective countermortar and counterbattery program. To this end, correspondence from the 173d Airborne Brigade recommended the use of artillery survey personnel in crater and shelling report teams.
4. Whenever possible clearances of large zones should be obtained in advance of an operation. This foresight in opera-

tional planning would result in more responsive on-call supporting fires.

New Arrivals

The 3d Battalion (Airborne), 319th Artillery, relinquished its position as the only U.S. Army artillery unit in Vietnam on 16 July 1965 with the arrival of the 2d Brigade, 1st Infantry Division (the "Big Red One"), and its supporting field artillery, the 1st Battalion, 7th Artillery. Less than two weeks later the 1st Brigade, 101st Airborne Division, arrived by ship at Cam Ranh Bay with the 2d Battalion (Airborne), 320th Artillery. In September the 1st Cavalry Division (Airmobile) arrived and brought with it the first U.S. Army division artillery to arrive in Vietnam.

The organization of the 1st Cavalry Division Artillery was typical of other division artilleries that followed. The division artillery consisted of three light 105-mm. howitzer battalions with three batteries of six guns each and an aerial rocket artillery battalion with thirty-nine aircraft. Most division artilleries contained three 105-mm. battalions but also included a fourth battalion of three 155-mm. howitzer batteries and one 8-inch howitzer battery. Whether aerial rocket artillery or heavy cannon artillery, the fourth battalion augmented and extended the range of the three 105-mm. battalions, each of which was in direct support of a brigade of the division.

Before the end of 1965, the remainder of the 1st Division Artillery arrived to provide support for the Big Red One in III Corps. Its organization was typical of most of the division artilleries that would arrive later, its fire power coming from three 105-mm. battalions and a composite 155-mm. and 8-inch battalion. The initial field artillery buildup also included the first few separate battalions that provided the general support and reinforcing fires needed to complement the divisional artillery.

As the number of U.S. troops committed to Vietnam grew, organizational changes to facilitate command and control were required. U.S. Army Support Command, Vietnam, was redesignated U.S. Army, Vietnam (USARV). Task Force ALPHA was activated on 1 August 1965 and based at Nha Trang with control over all U.S. units in the II and III Corps areas. III Marine Amphibious Force (III MAF) functioned as controlling headquarters for U.S. units in the I Corps area. In early 1966 Task Force ALPHA was redesignated I Field Force, Vietnam (IFFV), with responsibility for II Corps area. II Field Force, Vietnam (IIFFV), was activated. II Field Force was then assigned responsibility for III Corps area.

Coinciding with the activation of the II Field Force headquarters was the creation of controlling artillery headquarters. On 30 November 1965, XXX Corps Artillery arrived at Nha Trang and assumed control of U.S. and allied artillery units under Task Force ALPHA. On 15 March 1966, XXX Corps Artillery was redesignated I Field Force Artillery. To the south, II Field Force Artillery, organized in January, arrived in Vietnam in March 1966. The force artilleries functioned as controlling headquarters for all nondivisional artillery. Commanded by a brigadier general, the field force artillery was similar to a corps artillery, long a part of the U.S. Army organization. The force artillery was made up of all separate artillery battalions, batteries, and detachments in addition to the artillery groups under its control. The artillery group made its debut in the war with the arrival of the 23d Artillery Group in November of 1965. The group functioned as the controlling headquarters for its assigned battalions and normally had a mission of general support of the field force and reinforcing the fires of specific artillery units within the field force area of responsibility. Although many smaller organizational changes occurred in the course of the war, these first few significant steps laid the basic framework for the artillery command structure that by 1969 would support the operations of over a half million U.S. troops.

The Pleiku (Ia Drang) Campaign

In the early days of the buildup, units could not be permitted time for detailed planning and rehearsing. The North Vietnamese Army (NVA) had increased its forces significantly and had to be engaged at once. The situation was particularly critical in II Corps Tactical Zone, where at least three regiments of North Vietnamese regulars and one Viet Cong main force battalion were threatening to cut the country in half. Part of their mission was to meet and humiliate the newly arrived 1st Cavalry Division.

The 1st Cavalry Division did not arrive in Vietnam until September 1965, some of its units in early October. Yet on 22 October 1965 the commanding general of the division received the following order:

> Commencing first light 23 Oct 65, 1st Air Cav. Deploys one BN TF (Minimum 1 Inf Bn and 1 Arty Btry) to Pleiku with mission to be prepared to assist in defense of Key US/GVN installations. Vic Pleiku or reinforce II Corps Operations to relieve Plei Me CIDG Camp.

The Pleiku campaign, sometimes called the battle of the Ia Drang Valley, started with only a small force but eventually involved the entire division; Before the battle was over, the division

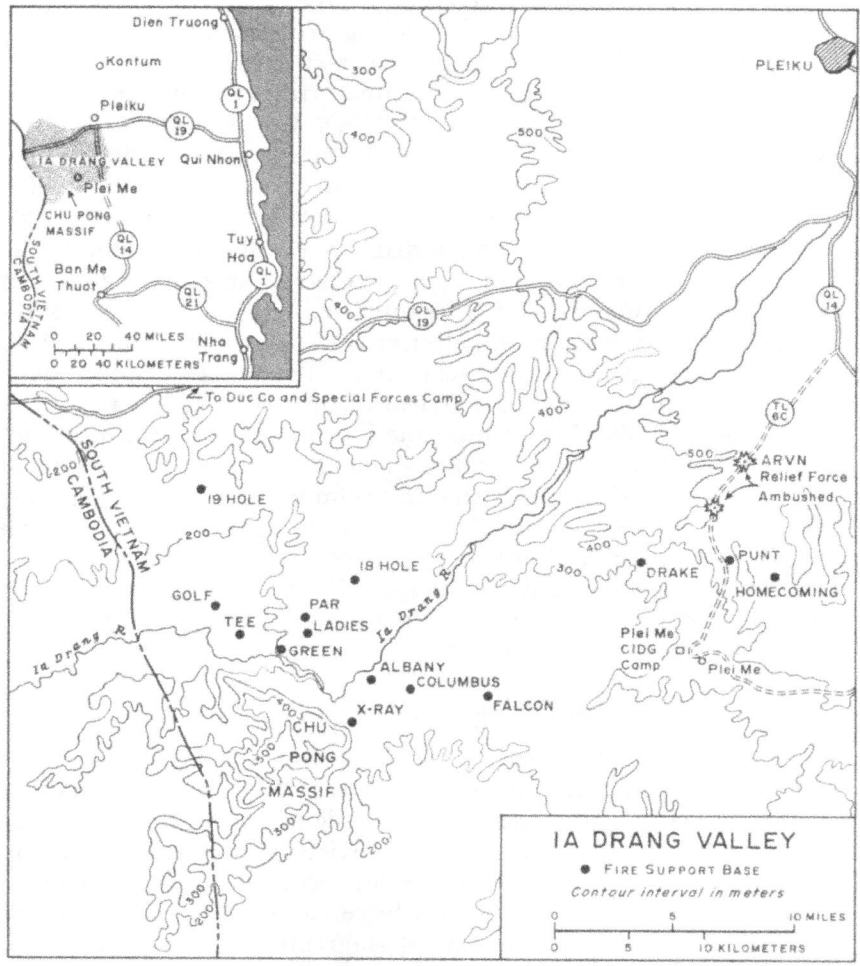

MAP 4

accomplished several significant feats. (*Map 4*) Among these was the first air deployment and supply of tube artillery in an area of extremely rugged terrain and no roads. The operation proved that infantry units could always have tube artillery, as well as aerial rocket artillery, in support of their ground operations regardless of the terrain. The Pleiku campaign saw the first night employment of aerial rocket artillery in extremely close support of ground troops and in conjunction with tube artillery and tactical air. Also, for the first time large American units met and defeated battalion-

and regiment-size North Vietnamese Army units under control of divisional headquarters. This was also the first real combat test of the airmobility concept.

The campaign opened on the morning of 23 October. Task Force INGRAM, composed mainly of the 2d Battalion, 12th Cavalry, and Battery B, 2d Battalion, 17th Artillery, moved by air from An Khe to Camp Holloway at Pleiku to reinforce the area. The commanding general of the 1st Air Cavalry Division received permission to move his entire 1st Brigade to Camp Holloway to assist in the security mission.

While the 1st Brigade was repositioning its forces, a South Vietnamese task force was moving from Pleiku to the relief of the Plei Me civilian irregular defense group camp, which had been attacked by a North Vietnamese regiment. Unfortunately, the relief column was engaged and halted by two or three enemy companies. The South Vietnamese commander absolutely refused to move unless he was provided U.S. artillery support. In an effort to get the relief column moving, the artillery battalion commander placed an artillery liaison team with the task force and provided the support of two artillery batteries. Still, the attempt to get the column moving was initially unsuccessful because the Vietnamese commander then refused to move until he had been resupplied from Pleiku. It was several days before the relief column started to move, and then only after the U.S. artillery forward observer mounted the lead vehicle of the convoy and literally walked artillery fires down the road in advance of the moving column. With this support, the column received only sporadic small-arms fire and this was silenced by attack helicopters and Air Force tactical air strikes. The South Vietnamese column finally arrived at the Plei Me camp at dusk on 25 October.

The reluctance of the Vietnamese commander to move on 23 October was probably a blessing in disguise, because it allowed the cavalry to reposition two batteries of the 2d Battalion, 19th Artillery, better to support the future battle. This proved a significant advantage later. The delay also gave the brigade time to learn more about the enemy disposition in the area.

On the morning of 26 October, the Vietnamese task force conducted a sweep around the Plei Me camp. Five minutes after noon the task force encountered mortar, small-arms, and recoilless rifle fire. The force immediately took casualties and faltered. The two batteries of the 2d Battalion, 19th Artillery, responded at once with supporting fires, which enabled the task force to regroup, withstand the attack, and take the offensive. The North Vietnamese forces suffered 148 killed and 5 captured in this action. The two artillery units were credited with drawing first blood for the 1st Cavalry Division. Had they not been in position, what became the first friendly victory could well have been a defeat.

The division started hunting for the enemy force with all available means. It planned to support any engagement by rapid air movement of artillery batteries and by tactical air strikes. The airmobility concept had envisioned the movement and supply of maneuver and support forces by helicopter, and the 1st Cavalry Division had been organized accordingly with light equipment and aircraft. From 27 October until the morning of 1 November, the enemy proved to be elusive. He attempted to retreat toward sanctuary areas and avoided contact whenever possible. A few skirmishes occurred, but they were mainly between small forces.

On the morning of 1 November, an air cavalry troop discovered a small enemy force guarding a regimental aid station. Before the action terminated, an enemy battalion was engaged by the air cavalry troop. The air cavalry habitually operated beyond artillery range; its mission was to find the enemy and fix him in position, when possible, until the division ground forces and supporting artillery could be brought to the scene. In this case all friendly artillery was out of range, but even so the enemy lost the effectiveness of most of one battalion before the battle was over. The enemy withdrew pursued by division scout and aerial rocket artillery aircraft as well as Air Force tactical air strikes.

On 2 and 3 November, light action continued and ambush positions were established throughout the area. One of the ambushes caught an enemy platoon-size force by surprise and totally destroyed it. The ambush patrol then pulled back into the patrol base area and established a tight defensive perimeter. At midnight of the 3d, the patrol base was attacked by an enemy battalion-size force. It was evident that reinforcements were needed at once. The patrol base, which had been established by Troop B, 1st Squadron, 9th Cavalry, had a landing zone within the perimeter sufficient to accommodate five helicopters. Into this landing zone came Company A, 1st Battalion, 8th Cavalry, in platoon-size lifts, making this the first time that a perimeter under fire had been relieved by a heliborne force. Although cannon artillery was not within range of the patrol base initially, aerial rocket artillery was available and for the first time fired at night in very close support—as near as 50 meters to friendly positions. Aerial rocket artillery continued to support the defense of the patrol base until the morning of 4 November, when tube artillery was moved to a supporting position. The enemy broke contact shortly after artillery rounds began to fall on their positions. Although a large number of the enemy dead was carried away by the retreating forces, the body count was 112, with an estimated 92 others killed in action. Intelligence discovered that this enemy force was a North Vietnamese Army unit that had just arrived in the country. The cavalry division had insured that they received a warm welcome.

The artillery also proved instrumental in defeating an enemy force engaged by elements of Company B, 2d Battalion, 12th Cavalry. While on a sweep operation, Company B came upon an enemy element guarding a cache of weapons and ammunition. The artillery fire caused the enemy to disengage and abandon the cache. He lost 120,000 rounds of small-arms ammunition; 126 rounds of mortar ammunition, recoilless rifle ammunition, and hand grenades; and 26 weapons, including mortars and recoilless rifles.

Again, on 6 November, aerial rocket artillery fire was decisive in battle. Company B, 2d Battalion, 8th Cavalry, became engaged with a battalion of the 33d North Vietnamese Army Regiment. The enemy battalion had attempted to encircle Company B, but the company's fire power plus artillery and air strikes held off the enemy threat. Company C was able to reinforce Company B before dark. After dark, when the most intense part of the firefight was over, the enemy withdrew his main force and left snipers behind to harass the perimeter of the two companies. He was soundly defeated. His last cohesive fighting unit east of the Ia Drang River had sustained an estimated 460 killed and wounded. Many of these casualties must be attributed to the fires of both tube and aerial rocket artillery.

The enemy wanted no further engagements until he could regroup his forces after the mauling the 1st Brigade of the 1st Cavalry Division had given him. Sufficient intelligence had been gathered to determine that the division was fighting three separate North Vietnamese regiments—the 66th, which had just arrived in the country; the 32d, which had ambushed the South Vietnamese task force on its way to Plei Me; and the 33d, which had attacked Plei Me. These regiments formed a full North Vietnamese Army division, which was being used offensively for the first time in South Vietnam.

Of the three North Vietnamese Army regiments, the 33d had been particularly hard hit. When the unit attacked Plei Me, its strength was 2,190 men. In actions against the 1st Brigade, the regiment had lost 890 men killed, more than 100 missing, and still more suffering incapacitating wounds. Materiel losses had also been heavy. The regiment lost 13 of its 18 antiaircraft guns as well as

11 mortar tubes and most of its recoilless rifles. In addition, there had been crippling losses of ammunition, food, and medical supplies.

The North Vietnamese division headquarters next planned an attack for the morning of 16 November against the original target —the Plei Me civilian irregular defense group camp. With this objective in mind, the three enemy regiments regrouped and headed eastward toward Plei Me.

During the lull in battle, the 3d ("Gary Owen") Brigade relieved the now battle-tested 1st Brigade of the 1st Cavalry Division on the battlefield. The 1st Brigade returned to Camp Radcliff at An Khe for a well-deserved rest. No significant action occurred until 12 November, when the enemy, seemingly just to let the 3d Brigade know that he was still around, staged a violent battalion-size attack against the 3d Brigade base at Landing Zone STADIUM. Aerial rocket artillery aircraft positioned at STADIUM responded immediately. All seven aircraft were airborne within five minutes after the attack started, and their combined fires stopped the mortar barrage.

As the 3d Brigade began search and destroy missions to the east of Plei Me, it also set the stage for a sudden thrust to the west by pre-positioning artillery at Landing Zone FALCON, twelve kilometers to the west of Plei Me. This artillery move took place on 13 November. The field was now prepared for what was to be the major battle of the campaign, Landing Zone X-RAY.

The 3d Brigade waited until the North Vietnamese assault elements were moving toward Plei Me. Then, at noon on 14 November, the 1st Battalion, 7th Cavalry, landed at the foot of the Chu Pong Massif, at X-RAY. The enemy was totally surprised. Instead of launching a divisional attack on Plei Me and possibly gaining the tactical initiative, the North Vietnamese Army division was now required to defend its own base area in the Chu Pong Mountains and the Ia Drang Valley, long a sanctuary for Viet Cong and North Vietnamese forces. Such so-called secret bases provided the insurgents with a secure area in which to store supplies, conduct training, carry out administrative functions, manufacture and repair arms and equipment, and provide an operating base for combat units. Not since the French occupation had Vietnamese government units penetrated the Chu Pong Massif; it was from this sanctuary and supply base in the Ia Drang Valley that the Field Front Headquarters and the 32d and 33d Regiments had moved to Plei Me on 19 October.

Reacting swiftly to the cavalry landings, the enemy Field Front ordered the 66th Regiment to attack the landing zone. Strong elements of the regiment were established on the ridge line overlooking the landing zone to provide a base of fire for the attack. The 9th and 7th Battalions of the 66th and a composite battalion of the 33d (the combined forces of what remained of the 2d and 3d Battalions) provided the initial assault forces.

When the troops of the 1st Battalion, 7th Cavalry, landed at X-RAY, they expected to engage enemy forces, but they did not expect to face an entire North Vietnamese Army regiment before the day was over. The enemy attacked with great ferocity against all elements of the 7th Cavalry. At least two cavalry platoons were immediately cut off and completely surrounded. The only thing that saved the platoons was the combined fire of the aerial rocket artillery unit and the two batteries of artillery at Landing Zone FALCON. The tube artillery support was frequently called to within less than 100 meters of the friendly positions. An additional company from a sister battalion of the 7th Calvary was helilifted into X-RAY and filled a vacant and vulnerable position on the perimeter.

Throughout the night, the North Vietnamese Army forces attempted to crack the perimeter of one of the isolated platoons but intensive artillery protective fires that ringed the position broke up every attack. The main perimeter was also subjected to repeated probes, and these too were repulsed. Batteries A and C, 1st Battalion, 21st Artillery, located at FALCON, fired over 4,000 rounds of high-explosive ammunition during the night in close support of X-RAY. The probing attacks continued into early morning. At first light, a North Vietnamese Army force of over two companies once again attempted to penetrate the perimeter. Despite intensive air strikes and cannon and aerial rocket artillery fires, the enemy closed to hand-to-hand combat range, attacking from all directions. Artillery fire was brought to within 50 meters of the hard-pressed perimeter. This devastating curtain of steel finally broke the back of the attack. By mid-morning the fight had been reduced to the point that reinforcements could again be helilifted into X-RAY and the wounded air evacuated.

To provide additional artillery support, Landing Zone COLUMBUS was established $4\frac{1}{2}$ kilometers to the northeast of X-RAY. This landing zone was midway between X-RAY and FALCON, where Batteries A and C of the 1st Battalion, 21st Artillery, were located. Battery B of the 1st Battalion, 21st Artillery, and Battery C of the 2d Battalion, 17th Artillery, were now moved into COLUMBUS.

The enemy broke contact and filtered back into the mountains after suffering tremendous losses. He was pursued with heavy fire power: cannon artillery continually pounded the area; Air Force tactical air provided continuous support with a fighter bomber on a target run on an average of once every fifteen minutes; but the most devastating support was provided by B–52 bombers which struck without warning six kilometers west of X-RAY. Though the bombers had been employed initially in Vietnam some six months earlier, this was their first use in direct support of U.S. troops on a tactical operation. For the next five days, the big bombers systematically bombed large areas of the Chu Pong Massif.

Early on the morning of the 16th, the enemy attempted again to overrun X-RAY and again there was a bloodbath. The defenses were just too tough to penetrate. The enemy lost 834 soldiers by actual body count and an estimated 1,200 more.

On 17 November, X-RAY was evacuated in preparation for a B–52 strike (referred to as an Arc Light) that was to be virtually on top of the landing zone. The 2d Battalion, 7th Cavalry, was moving overland from X-RAY toward a clearing to the northeast, which was to be used as a landing zone designated ALBANY. About 300 meters short of the objective, the battalion became involved in an intense battle with the 8th Battalion, 66th Regiment, of the North Vietnamese Army.

As all too often happens in a meeting engagement, the exact locations of friendly and enemy positions were uncertain. Although artillery aerial observers were overhead and two batteries of 105-mm. and one battery of 155-mm. howitzers were well within range, none could fire initially. It was solely an infantryman's battle for several hours. By midafternoon heavy supporting fires began falling among North Vietnamese Army elements. The first strikes were by aerial rocket artillery, followed by a tactical air napalm run on an enemy company that was forming for an attack. The attack never started.

Reinforcements were quickly brought into ALBANY, and the perimeter was consolidated before dark. Actually, two separate perimeters were established—one by the 2d Battalion, 7th Cavalry, and one by two companies of the 1st Battalion, 5th Cavalry, which had moved toward ALBANY as reinforcements. The hard-hit 2d Battalion, 7th Cavalry, was able to expand the perimeter and recover friendly casualties from the battle area. This freedom of movement was afforded by the continuous artillery fire from COLUMBUS and FALCON and the illumination provided by Air Force flare ships.

The punishment taken by both friendly and enemy units was severe during the short battle at ALBANY. Over 270 troopers were casualties. The enemy lost 403 soldiers by body count and an estimated 100 others killed. No estimate of wounded was made.

The next morning, the battle area around ALBANY was relatively quiet. The enemy had moved on toward his new objective—the artillery units at COLUMBUS. At 1735 on 18 November, the last enemy offensive of the Pleiku campaign began. The remnants of two enemy regiments attacked COLUMBUS with heavy mortars and automatic weapons. Because the artillery based at FALCON was being moved to another location, tactical air strikes and aerial rocket artillery were used along with direct fire from the artillery weapons within COLUMBUS to repulse the enemy attack. After three hours the enemy attack lost momentum and subsided into sporadic small-arms fire and then quiet. The battle of the Ia Drang Valley was, for all practical purposes, over.

The 2d Brigade now entered the battle area and relieved the 3d Brigade. The new brigade continued to search for the enemy. Contacts were made with scattered North Vietnamese Army elements of squad or platoon size, and then only after they had been flushed out and chased by heliborne cavalry or foot patrols.

During the Pleiku campaign, the enemy lost over 1,500 confirmed killed and an estimated 2,000 more. His losses were so extensive that an entire North Vietnamese Army division was made ineffective. His casualties were produced by all types of weapons, ranging from the B–52 bomber to the individual rifle. But a very large proportion of those casualties must be attributed to the artillery of the cavalry division. The enemy was driven back time and again, primarily by the intensity of artillery fire power. The division fired 40,464 artillery rounds and rockets during the campaign. Of the total casualties, 562 enemy killed and an additional 1,863 estimated killed and wounded were officially credited to the artillery.

Although the Pleiku campaign was the first time an entire U.S. division was committed in battle in Vietnam, the division had been committed piecemeal, one brigade at a time. Piecemeal commitment in this case had certain benefits. As one brigade was committed, the relieved brigade along with its supporting forces, including the direct support artillery battalion, was withdrawn to a rest area and allowed to refit and to consider what had taken place in the battle.

The artillerymen had learned much from this campaign. First, the concept of displacing and supplying artillery by air was proved valid, particularly in support of an airmobile force. During the campaign, artillery units of the cavalry division artillery had made a total of 79 tactical moves—67 of them by air. Continuous air movement by maneuver and support forces unsettled the enemy. Properly executed airmobile operations could keep constant pressure on him, wearing him down and destroying his will to resist. Second, aerial rocket artillery was shown to be extremely responsive and effective in augmenting cannon fires. Ground forces learned that aerial rocket artillery was reliable and extremely accurate, characteristics that were particularly important in close support missions. By controlling helicopter fires through artillery fire support channels, as was done with aerial rocket artillery, cannon and helicopter fires could be closely co-ordinated by a single individual, thus insuring that both were complementary. Third, artillerymen learned of the necessity of having artillery positions that were mutually supporting. Though Landing Zone COLUMBUS had stood off an enemy attack without mutually supporting artillery, its defenders had required air support, which in poor weather might not have been available. Fourth, because of the rugged terrain and dense foliage, target acquisition was a definite problem. Forward observers were still the best means of target acquisition because they were always with maneuver companies. To augment the forward observers, aerial observers were added whenever possible and were particularly effective in support of overland ground movements. Fifth, it was shown that the 105-mm. howitzer was a particularly good weapon for reconnaissance by fire. As the unit moved, the artillery forward observer would adjust artillery rounds in advance of the unit. This provided two benefits: the artillery could disrupt any activity or ambush site the enemy might have, and the location of the last round fired was a good indicator of the unit's location. This second advantage would allow for rapid delivery of artillery in the event the enemy ambushed the ground force.

The Buildup and Major Combat Operations During 1966

During 1966 three divisions—the 4th, 9th, and 25th—came to Vietnam. Two separate brigades—the 196th and 199th Light Infantry Brigades—and the 11th Armored Cavalry Regiment also arrived. The organization of supporting artillery varied somewhat. The divisional artillery of the three infantry divisions consisted of three 105-mm. howitzer battalions and one composite battalion of 8-inch and 155-mm. weapons. The separate, or nondivisional, brigades were organized for independent operations. For that reason, they each had an organic 105-mm. howitzer battalion. The armored

FIELD FORCE ARTILLERY. *Eight-inch howitzer ready to fire (note gunner's quadrant held by man on left).*

cavalry regiment, roughly equivalent to a brigade, had no artillery battalion. Instead, each of its three subordinate squadrons had an organic 155-mm. self-propelled howitzer battery, which together equalled an artillery battalion. The absence of an artillery battalion headquarters, however, precluded the co-ordination of all fires.

As 1966 began, artillery in the Republic of Vietnam consisted of one 105-mm. battalion in direct support of each maneuver brigade, plus two additional 105-mm. battalions, one 155-mm. battalion, one 155-mm. and 8-inch battalion, one aerial rocket artillery battalion, four 8-inch and 175-mm. battalions, and two artillery group headquarters. Before the end of 1966, the amount of artillery in Vietnam was to increase over 100 percent. There would be four group headquarters, six 8-inch and 175-mm. battalions, six 155-mm. or 155-mm. and 8-inch battalions, twenty-four 105-mm. battalions, and the one aerial rocket artillery battalion. There would also be two artillery 40-mm. "Duster" battalions that had been reactivated from Reserve and National Guard assets.

175-MM. GUN. *Battery C, 1st Battalion, 83d Field Artillery, at Fire Support Base Bastogne.*

The very number of the operations during 1966 was particularly important for those concerned with artillery employment. Operation MASHER/WHITE WING, conducted by the 1st Air Cavalry Division in early 1966, was the first large-scale operation to cross corps boundaries, and it involved a tie-in with U.S. Marine Corps forces as well as allies of the Army of the Republic of Vietnam and the Republic of Korea. The effect of the operation on the enemy was devastating; it was the largest of the nineteen major operations conducted during 1966 and resulted in 2,389 enemy casualties.

The operation took place mainly in Binh Dinh Province, largely controlled by the enemy and considered a very "hot" area. Binh Dinh is bounded by the South China Sea on the east, by foothills on its northern boundary with Quang Nga Province, and by large hill masses on the west and south. In the eastern part of the province, the terrain is mostly flat coastal plains; to the west, the terrain becomes rugged but is interspersed with flat plateaus. Reliable in-

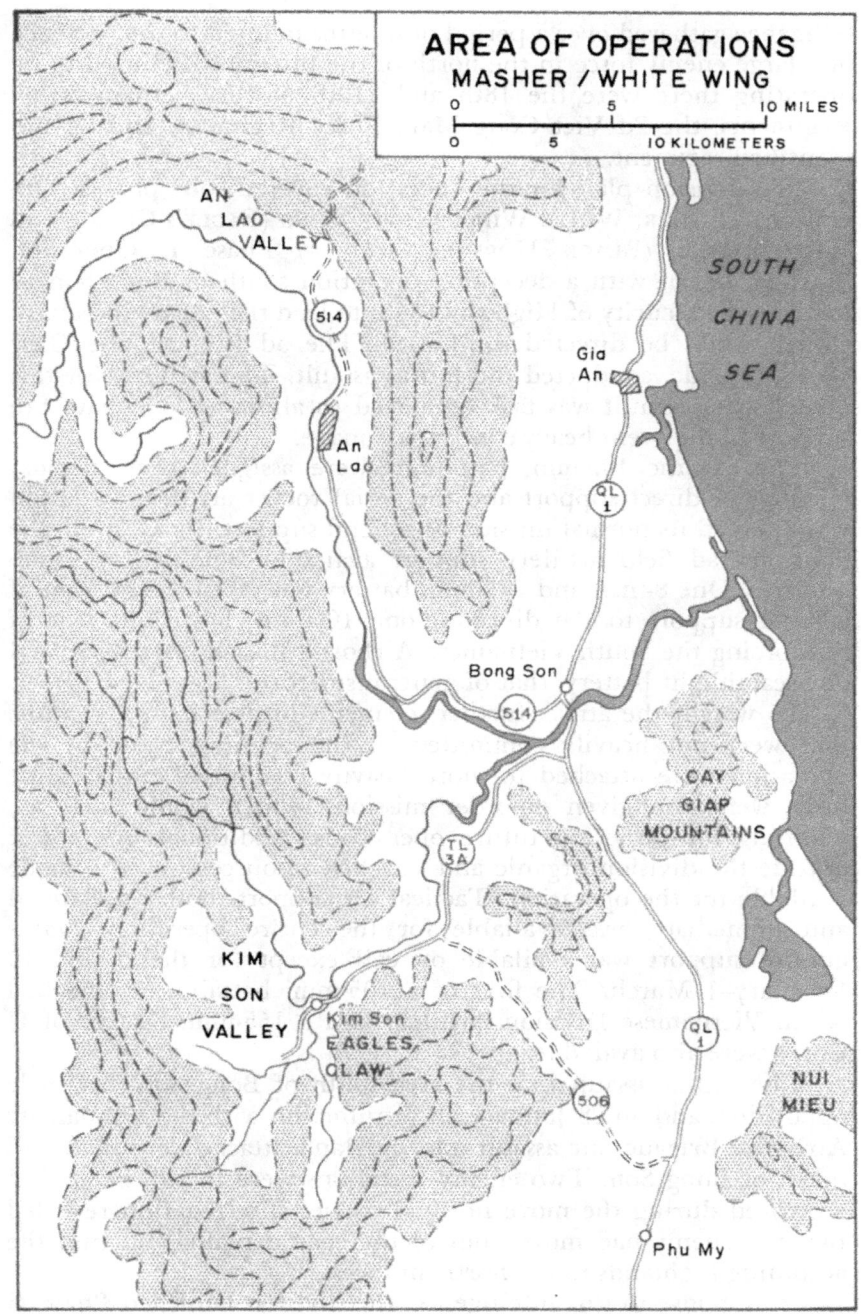

MAP 5

telligence gathered over a period of months pointed to the presence of a large enemy force in the north of the province. Believed to be operating there were the 18th and 210th North Vietnam Army Regiments, the 2d Viet Cong Main Force Regiment, and an unidentified regiment.

The division plan for the operation covered four phases: Operations MASHER, WHITE WING, WHITE WING (EAGLE's CLAW), and WHITE WING (BLACK HORSE). (*Map 5*) Phase I, Operation MASHER, began with a deception operation south of Bong Son to increase the security of Highway 1 and to lead the enemy to believe efforts would be directed southward. The 3d Brigade, the Gary Owen Brigade, conducted the initial assault. The artillery for this diversionary assault was task organized to allow for adequate fire support in the event heavy contact was made.

The organic 105-mm. battalions were assigned their normal missions of direct support and the aerial rocket artillery battalion was assigned its normal mission of general support. In addition, the division had field artillery support available from higher headquarters. One 8-inch and 175-mm. battery was given the mission of general support to the division; one 105-mm. battalion, that of reinforcing the South Vietnamese Airborne Brigade Artillery; and one searchlight battery, that of general support.

To weight the attack further, elements of direct support units that were not heavily committed in the opening phase of the operation were attached to more heavily committed units. Some units were also given on-order missions, which would facilitate planning for projected future operations. Additional fire power outside the division organic and attached resources was also made available for the operation. Tactical air support, both preplanned and immediate, was available for the entire operation. Naval gunfire support was available on call except for the period 10 February–1 March. The fires of a 105-mm. battalion of the 22d South Vietnamese Division Artillery and a 155-mm. battery of II Corps were also available.

The initial assault into the area south of Bong Son met little opposition, and on 28 January, in conjunction with the Vietnamese Airborne Brigade, air assault and overland attacks were launched north of Bong Son. Two enemy battalions were found, fixed, and destroyed during the move north. Prisoner interrogation revealed that the enemy had moved out of the coastal plains and into the adjoining highlands to the north and west.

In response to this intelligence, the division launched Phase II of the operation, WHITE WING. Originally scheduled for 4 February, the initial assaults were delayed for 48 hours because of bad weather. On 6 February, with a battalion of Marines holding blocking positions to the north, the 2d Brigade, 1st Air Cavalry Division, launched a co-ordinated five-battalion attack from both sides of the An Lao Valley and swept south toward the 22d Division.

As the 2d Brigade moved south, the 3d Brigade launched Phase III, a series of attacks into the area southwest of Bong Son. Highlighted by valleys, this area was appropriately nicknamed the "Eagle's Claw." A number of light to moderate contacts were made as enemy units within the valleys were caught between converging forces. Meanwhile, the 2d Brigade received some valuable intelligence information. Among the prisoners captured by the division was a battalion commander of the 22d North Vietnamese Army Regiment. He revealed that his unit held defensive positions in an area south of Bong Son. The brigade responded to this intelligence with an assault into the area and, in three days of continuous fighting, destroyed the 22d Regiment. While the 2d Brigade was engaged, the 1st Brigade relieved the 3d Brigade in the Kim Son Valley and in a matter of days rendered the 18th North Vietnamese Army Regiment ineffective, capturing all of the enemy antiaircraft weapons and recoilless rifles.

The final phase of the operation, WHITE WING (BLACK HORSE), was a sweep into the Cay Giap Mountains southeast of Bong Son. The sweep, conducted with the South Vietnamese 22d Division, met only sporadic enemy resistance. By 6 March, 1st Cavalry skytroopers had made a complete sweep of Bong Son and the area could no longer be considered an enemy stronghold. The division had maintained contact with a determined enemy for 41 consecutive days and had again proved the effectiveness of airmobile operations.

For the supporting field artillery involved in Operation MASHER/WHITE WING, the success of the operation is of particular significance. The artillery showed that it could follow the fast pace of the airmobile troopers. Displacements were made quickly and efficiently without loss of the fire support capability.

At the outset of Operation MASHER on 25 January, the division artillery forward command post displaced to Bong Son Special Forces Camp, where it was collocated with the division tactical operations center and the Vietnamese division command post. The move greatly facilitated clearance procedures and created a quick fire channel, which permitted immediate U.S. response to Vietnamese calls for fire and Vietnamese response to U.S. calls for fire.

Although every attempt was made throughout the operation to position artillery so that displacements were held to a minimum, the speed with which ground troops moved and the size of the area

CH–54 Emplacing 155-mm. Howitzer

M102 Firing High-Angle. *1st Battalion, 21st Field Artillery, received the first M102 howitzers in Vietnam in March 1966.*

of operations nonetheless dictated an unusually high number of artillery displacements. Shown below are battery displacements for the 41-day period:

Operation	Displacements by	
	Air*	Road
Masher	2	30
White Wing	28	27
White Wing (Eagle's Claw) (11–28 February)	27	35
White Wing (Black Horse) (1–6 March)	0	17
Total	57	109

*Average of 12 CH–47 sorties per battery displacement

When a field artillery unit is moving, it cannot support the maneuver forces; the displacement that becomes necessary requires a considerable amount of planning and co-ordination to avoid depriving the ground troops of the support they need. Nevertheless, 1st Cavalry artillerymen at all levels of the command met this challenge. Although most of the personnel assigned to the division were not strangers to airmobility, many of the supporting units were; yet they, too, completed air moves without major difficulty.

In early February during Operation WHITE WING, a CH–54 Crane moved a 14,000-pound 155-mm. towed howitzer for the first time in combat. The weapon belonged to Battery A, 1st Battalion, 30th Artillery. This feat showed that medium towed artillery could go virtually anywhere the lighter (105-mm.) artillery could go; thus greater flexibility of the artillery and its supported forces was achieved. Much of the credit for the move must go to the men of the 1st Cavalry Division Support Command, who fabricated and tested the special slings required to lift the 155-mm. howitzer.

The large number of displacements by air put a tremendous strain on the air resources of the division. When the artillery was displaced by helicopters, ammunition was transported separately. During MASHER/WHITE WING, artillerymen attempted to determine a means of economizing on "blade time" in the displacement of artillery. The product of this experimentation was a double-sling system that allowed the CH–47 to lift the 105-mm. howitzer as well as a load of ammunition. The ammunition was suspended underneath the howitzer by means of a long (18- to 20-foot) sling. With crew riding inside the CH–47, this new method proved invaluable in subsequent operations, since it permitted the displacement of a complete firing section in one aircraft sortie. The initial attempt to test this concept during combat was not made until Operation JIM BOWIE, which took place a few days later, though its development is attributed to the experiences of MASHER/WHITE WING.

The development of procedures to displace artillery during MASHER/WHITE WING is of secondary importance to the actual shooting done by the field artillery. Operation MASHER/WHITE WING testifies to the ability of the field artillery to maintain a devastating volume of fire and still move and communicate with the supported forces. During the operation, 141,712 artillery rounds of all types were fired during 16,102 missions. A breakdown of expenditures by size and mission is shown below:

Phase	Preparations	Time on Target Missions	Enemy Contact Missions	Total
MASHER	5	26	28	59
WHITE WING	6	1	20	27
(EAGLE'S CLAW)	50	124	66	240
(BLACK HORSE)	36	6	15	57
Totals	97	157	129	383

ARTILLERY MISSIONS AND AMMUNITION EXPENDITURES
DURING OPERATION MASHER/WHITE WING

Phase	105-mm.		155-mm.		8-inch		175-mm.		2.75-inch		Total	
	Msn	Exp	Msn	Exp	Msn	Exp	Msn	Exp	Msn	Exp	Msn	Exp
I—Masher	1,167	25,738	457	6,182	316	711	20	78	711	10,686	2,671	44,095
II—White Wing	654	16,800	306	1,797	133	657	200	522	139	3,512	1,432	22,288
III—White Wing (Eagle's Claw)	8,557	38,824	1,064	3,777	829	3,525	340	717	352	18,033	11,142	64,876
IV—White Wing (Black Horse)	501	6,700	224	1,233	112	491	0	0	20	1,729	857	10,153
Total	10,879	88,062	2,051	12,889	1,380	5,354	560	1,317	1,222	33,960	16,102	141,712

In addition to the artillery expended, the U.S. Navy supported the operation with 3,212 5-inch rounds, and the U.S. Air Force flew 515 tactical air sorties during which over 1,000 tons of ordnance were dropped.

Both tube and aerial artillery received a fair share of credit for enemy killed. Of particular value in this respect was information gleaned from prisoner interrogations. For example, a prisoner from the 8th Battalion, 18th North Vietnamese Army Regiment, revealed that on 3 February 1966, at the end of Operation MASHER, his unit had discovered and buried 200–400 bodies killed by artillery. All told, Operation MASHER/WHITE WING yielded 2,389 enemy casualties, of which 358 confirmed dead were credited to the field artillery.

On the whole, Operation MASHER/WHITE WING was a tremendous success in defeating the enemy and freeing the civilian populace of the Bong Son area from enemy control. The complete fire support system functioned effectively throughout this operation. Target acquisition resources, artillery survey, artillery aviation, firing batteries, and support elements all acted as a team. The co-operative effort and enthusiastic response of the South Vietnamese artillery contributed significantly to the over-all fire support co-ordination effort. On the U.S. side, the 2d Battalion (Airborne), 19th Artillery (Airmobile), and the 1st Battalion (Airmobile), 77th Artillery, exchanged liaison personnel during the operation to permit the direct support battalion of one brigade more easily to provide support for maneuver units of another brigade. Artillery communications functioned smoothly throughout the operation, and, last but not least, despite the vast area covered by the operation, artillery survey personnel from both division artillery and the support battalions traversed in excess of 190,000 meters and established 18 survey control points during the operation. If there had been doubts as to how an entire division artillery would fare in its first large-scale operation, MASHER/WHITE WING erased them.

Another significant 1966 field artillery action occurred during Operation BIRMINGHAM. This operation is noteworthy because it involved a major movement of supporting field artillery that required detailed planning and co-ordination.

The operation was initiated when Military Assistance Command directed a search and destroy operation into northwest Tay Ninh Province. Controlled by the U.S. 1st Infantry Division, Operation BIRMINGHAM was directed at locating and destroying Viet Cong forces and base camps in the area. The 1st Division was operating in the Phu Loi area, 50 kilometers southeast of Tay Ninh, when the division commander received word to displace to Tay Ninh Province within a week. The 1st Division Artillery had to plan and co-ordinate the displacement of elements from seven field artillery battalions. The result was the smooth displacement of 72 pieces of field artillery into Tay Ninh Province using all available means of transportation. The 1st Division Artillery Headquarters, functioning as the convoy control element, moved by road, with the 1st Battalion, 7th Artillery, and the 8th Battalion, 6th Artillery, in the formation. Security for the convoy was provided by the 1st Squadron, 4th Cavalry ("Quarter Horse"). One battery of the 2d Battalion, 33d Artillery, moved by C-130 aircraft from Lai Khe to Tay Ninh city. Air Force C-123 aircraft were used to displace a second battery of the 2d Battalion, 33d Artillery, from Binh Gia, southeast of Saigon, to Tay Ninh. An attached battery of the 2d Battalion, 13th Artillery, was airlifted by CH-47 helicopter from Phu Loi. The 3d Battalion, 319th Artillery, under operational control of the 1st Division and in support of the South Vietnamese Airborne Brigade, moved separately by road; and a battery of 175-mm. guns, in general support of Operation BIRMINGHAM, moved by road to Soui Da. To insure continuous and sufficient fire support for the road moves, the 1st Division Artillery Headquarters utilized its headquarters battery executive officer to co-ordinate fire support along the route of march.

Brigadier General (then Colonel) Marlin W. Camp, 1st Division Artillery commander, was justifiably proud of the manner in which the move was conducted. The success of the move is especially significant because friendly units had not ventured deep into northwest Tay Ninh Province in the past.

For field force artillery to provide maximum area coverage, certain of its firing units were required to occupy extremely remote positions. In such cases, movement to the positions and position preparation required detailed planning. Those weapons that provided the best area coverage by virtue of their long ranges were self-propelled weapons—8-inch howitzers and 175-mm. guns—too heavy to move by helicopter. For the most part, the "heavies" were restricted to movement by road.

Some of the roads over which self-propelled weapons moved were in remote areas which had long been in enemy hands. These roads could be expected to be heavily mined with their bridges destroyed. Extensive engineer support was required to open those roads and the engineers, like the artillery that followed, were subject to ambush at any time. Infantry and armor support was required to help open the roads, provide protection, and keep the roads open at least until the artillery movement was completed and support withdrawn.

In a war characterized by the frequent movement of field artillery, the displacement of Battery B, 7th Battalion, 8th Field Artillery, in September 1967 is particularly impressive. The movement of Battery B was unusual because it was accomplished by Air Force tactical airlift. The battery, under the cammand of Captain Edward G. Walker, was moved from Bien Hoa air base to a landing strip at Song Be in heavily contested Phuc Long Province. To make the move, the weight of the weapons had to be reduced to the lift capacity of the aircraft. This was done by removing the weapons' spades and tubes and transporting them by C–130 aircraft. The carriages could then be lifted by C–124's. B Battery was positioned at the end of the Song Be airstrip from where its weapons could easily reach to the Cambodian border. The men of B Battery worked on their new position for a month and then turned it over to B Battery, 6th Battalion, 27th Field Artillery. Both batteries swapped their weapons to avoid the problem of having again to move weapons to and from a remote area. The artillery position at Song Be was occupied until June 1971. The weapons could not be withdrawn by air in the same manner in which they had been moved to Song Be, since the landing strip was able to accommodate aircraft landing at peak capacity loads but was insufficient to allow them to take off with these same loads. The weapons were, therefore, withdrawn over a road that had been opened and improved during the four years that the Song Be position was occupied.

As noted earlier, the first combat firing of the Beehive round occurred in November 1966. But it was the battle at Landing Zone BIRD in December that really woke up field artillerymen and infantrymen to the effectiveness of this new round.

BIRD was a fire base located in the Kim Son Valley some 50 kilometers north of Qui Nhon. (*Map 6*) No strangers to the valley, the 1st Cavalry Division had operated throughout the area since Operation MASHER/WHITE WING early in 1966. The landing zone had only one half-strength infantry company (Company C, 2d Battalion, 12th Cavalry) for security in addition to twelve howitzers (six 105-mm. and six 155-mm.). The surrounding terrain afforded good cover for an enemy force that might decide to attack the base. On the night of 26 December 1966, two companies of the 22d North Vietnamese Army Regiment decided to test the light defenses and silently moved to within feet of the outer perimeter of BIRD.

Shortly after midnight the enemy launched a co-ordinated mortar and ground attack against the position. The attack penetrated

THE BUILDUP

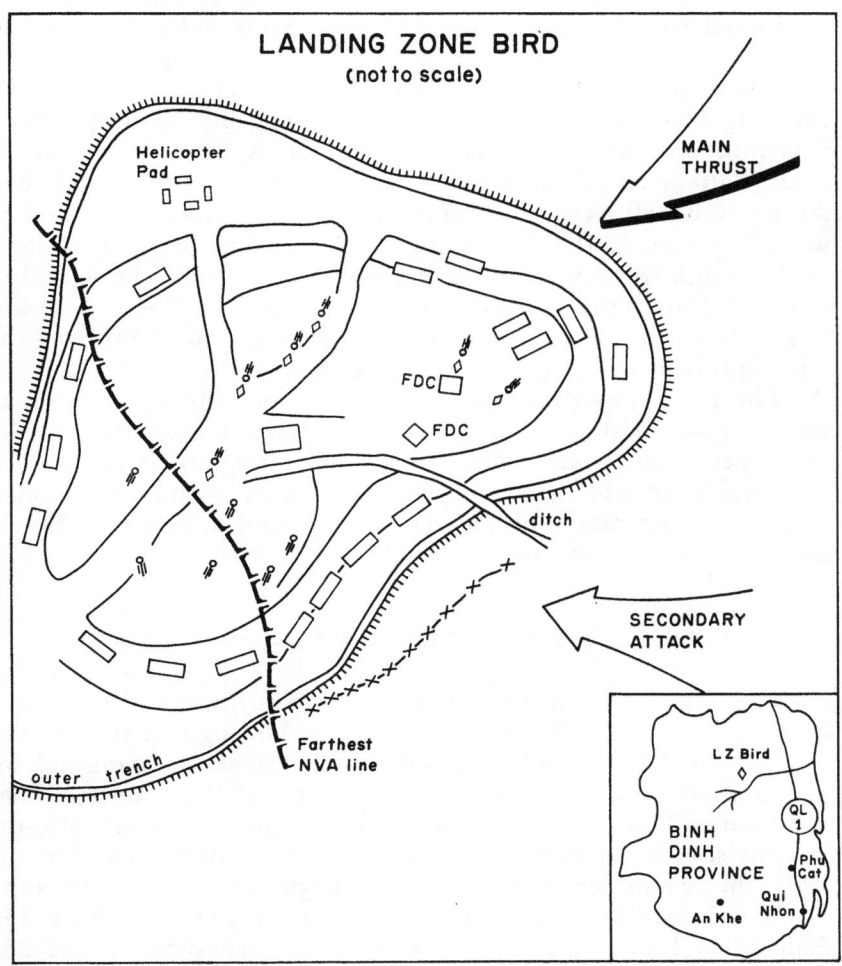

MAP 6

the base from both the northeast and southeast. Driven slowly back, the defenders found themselves cornered in the south end of the base in the vicinity of gun number 2 of the 105-mm. battery position. Almost in desperation, Captain Leonard L. Schlenker, the battery commander, ordered the firing of Beehive and First Lieutenant John T. Piper, the battery executive officer, loaded the round, yelled a warning, and fired the round to the northeast in the direction of the enemy main attack. One hundred enemy soldiers were at the northeast corner of the fire base, in and around the number 1 gun position of the 155-mm. battery. Piper fired one additional round and the attack was halted as suddenly as it had begun.

The United States lost 30 men killed in action at BIRD while claiming 266 known enemy dead. For doggedly beating back a determined and numerically superior enemy, the three units at BIRD (Battery B, 2d Battalion, 19th Artillery; Battery C, 6th Battalion, 16th Artillery; and Company C, 2d Battalion, 12th Cavalry) were all presented the Presidential Unit Citation. Sergeant Delbert O. Jennings, weapons platoon sergeant, was awarded the Medal of Honor for his bravery, and Lieutenant Piper and Staff Sergeant Carrol V. Crain, Battery B chief of firing battery, both received the Distinguished Service Cross for their action.

The most important benefit derived from the action at BIRD was recognition that the Beehive round was a tremendously valuable asset to the over-all fire base defense program. It had gained the confidence and respect of both artillerymen and infantrymen and would continue to play a vital role in position defense throughout the remainder of the war.

The Buildup and Major Combat Operations During 1967

The year 1967 saw a continued growth in the number of field artillery units in the Republic of Vietnam. During that year, eleven nondivisional field artillery battalions arrived in Vietnam and began supporting operations in various parts of the country. They were joined by three additional division artilleries. In January, the 9th Division Artillery set up its headquarters in Bearcat, and in late 1967, the remainder of the Screaming Eagles of the 101st Airborne Division joined their 1st Brigade. In a ceremony held at Chu Lai in September 1967, Task Force OREGON was redesignated the 23d (Americal) Division and thus was also born the Americal Division Artillery. The task force had been in existence since mid-1967 and was composed of three separate infantry brigades.

In contrast to the previous year, 1967 was highlighted by large-scale, multidivisional operations. The year was only a week old when Operation CEDAR FALLS began. Controlled by II Field Force, CEDAR FALLS involved the 1st and 25th Divisions, the 173d Airborne Brigade, the 11th Armored Cavalry Regiment, and separate battalions of the Army of the Republic of Vietnam. The operation was directed against the enemy Military Region IV headquarters and strongholds in the Iron Triangle region of III Corps. The success of the operation (389 enemy killed, 471 defectors) attested to the ability of the Free World forces to work together, fight side by side, and produce a well co-ordinated, multidivision offensive.

While CEDAR FALLS was in full swing in the Iron Triangle, II Field Force planners were putting the final wraps on plans for subsequent operations. The largest offensive planned to date, Operation JUNCTION CITY had been on the drawing boards for months. It was aimed at Viet Cong and North Vietnamese Army strongholds in War Zone C, in northern Tay Ninh Province, which had long been a major Viet Cong stronghold and the location of the headquarters for the Central Office of South Vietnam (COSVN). COSVN, the controlling headquarters for all Viet Cong activities in South Vietnam, had always been an elusive target and continued to be throughout the war.

Committed to JUNCTION CITY were two U.S. divisions (1st and 25th), five brigades (173d Airborne; 196th Light Infantry; 199th Light Infantry; 3d Brigade, 4th Division; and 1st Brigade, 9th Division), and the 11th Armored Cavalry Regiment. II Field Force, Vietnam, under the command of Lieutenant General Jonathan O. Seaman, was the controlling headquarters for the operation. II Field Force Artillery, commanded by Brigadier General Willis D. Crittenberger, Jr., provided six field artillery battalions and four batteries of Dusters and quad.-50 machine guns from the 5th Battalion (AWSP), 2d Artillery. II Field Force assets were divided equally between the 1st and 25th Divisions, the two major subordinate elements. An additional eleven artillery battalions were committed to the operation in various support roles. A list of the participating field artillery units is shown below:

II Field Force Artillery Units
    7–9 Arty (105 T) attached 1st Div
    2–13 Arty (105 T), attached 1st Div
    2–11 Arty (155 T)
    6–27 Arty (8/175)
    2–32 Arty (8/175)
    2–35 Arty (155 SP)
    5–2 Arty (AWSP)
25th Infantry Division Artillery
    1–8 Arty (105 T)
    7–11 Arty (105 T)
    2–77 (Arty 105 T)
    3–13 Arty (105 T)
    3–82 Arty (105 T) OPCON, DS 196th Bde
    Btry A, B, C, 11th ACR, OPCON, Supporting 11th ACR
1st Infantry Division Artillery
    1–5 Arty (105 T)

1–7 Arty (105 T)
2–33 Arty (105 T)
8–6 Arty (155/8)
3–319 Arty (Abn) (105 T), OPCON, DS 173d Abn Bde

JUNCTION CITY was initially a two-phase operation; Phase I (22 February–17 March 1967) called for a co-ordinated assault into western War Zone C and search and destroy operations against the Central Office and enemy forces and installations in the area. Phase II (18 March–15 April 1967) called for a shift of emphasis to eastern War Zone C and continuation of search and destroy operations throughout the remainder of the war zone. The success of these first two phases resulted in a third (16 April–14 May), which called for a continuation of search and destroy operations to the southern edge of the war zone and the provision of security for the city of Tay Ninh and the town of Soui Da. (*Map 7*) For Phase III, II Field Force passed control of the operation to the 25th Infantry Division.

The objectives of Operation JUNCTION CITY were accomplished to varying degrees. The Viet Cong lost 2,728 soldiers. A number of his base camps and supply caches were destroyed, forcing him to move. Although the operation did not destroy the enemy's capability to wage war, JUNCTION CITY can be said to have put him significantly off balance and to have eliminated War Zone C as a haven for enemy units. During the operation, U.S. forces constructed in War Zone C three C–130 airfields and two civilian irregular defense group camps, giving Free World forces readily accessible points from which to launch future operations in the area should the need arise.

JUNCTION CITY required most of the U.S. ground forces available in the III Corps area, and a commensurate amount of field artillery supported the operation. The massive co-ordination effort dictated by the employment of the equivalent of seventeen field artillery battalions was effected with surprising ease. The completeness with which the operation was planned is, in large part, the explanation for its success. To facilitate command and control of the operation, II Field Force for the first time displaced a tactical headquarters to the field. Collocated with the tactical command post was the II Field Force Artillery command post. In addition, II Field Force Artillery tapped the resources of its 54th Artillery Group to provide a controlling headquarters for the separate howitzer batteries of the 11th Armored Cavalry Regiment. The technique proved to be a success in aiding the co-ordination between firing units. For the remainder of the field artillery battalions, existing liaison sections proved sufficient in strength to provide liaison between units. Unit boundaries were used as fire coordination lines throughout the operations, and the II Field Force fire support plan authorized direct co-ordination between divisions and supporting artillery groups. Field artillery fire planning was accomplished by division and separate brigades.

The most significant combat action during Operation JUNCTION CITY took place around Fire Support Base GOLD, seventeen miles northwest of Tay Ninh. The fire base was occupied jointly by the 2d Battalion, 22d Infantry, of the 3d Brigade, 4th Division, and the headquarters and all firing batteries of the 2d Battalion, 77th Field Artillery. At 0640 on 21 March infantry patrols sweeping the area around GOLD made contact with elements of a Viet Cong force apparently preparing to attack the base. The contact prematurely triggered the enemy attack which began with heavy fire from recoilless rifles, rocket-propelled grenades, and 60-mm. and 82-mm. mortars. At 0715 the Viet Cong launched a co-ordinated ground assault from the east, southeast, and north with elements of five battalions under the control of the 272d Viet Cong Regiment. So violent was the assault that the enemy carried portions of the perimeter, but actions by the field artillery turned the tide. All batteries of the 2d Battalion, 77th Field Artillery, commanded by Lieutenant Colonel John W. Vessey, engaged the enemy with over 1,000 rounds in direct fire including 30 rounds of Beehive, the largest number of these rounds fired in a single engagement to date. At the same time three batteries within range added their fire. The batteries included Battery C, 1st Battalion, 8th Artillery (105-mm., towed), to the south which delivered more than 1,000 rounds; Battery B, 3d Battalion, 13th Artillery (155-mm., self-propelled), which delivered almost 400 rounds; and a composite 8-inch and 175-mm. battery from II Field Force Artillery to the south which provided additional support. Further fire support was provided by Air Force tactical air. During the attack two maneuver battalions of the 3d Brigade, 4th Infantry Division, were rushed to the scene, catching the enemy forces as they were attempting to withdraw and inflicting further casualties. The action in and around GOLD resulted in 635 Viet Cong killed (confirmed by body count) and 7 captured together with 65 crew served weapons and 94 individual weapons. U.S. losses were 31 killed and 109 wounded. The action was given the name Battle of Soui Tre after the fact.

Field artillery units involved in Operation JUNCTION CITY gained invaluable experience in employment, tactics, and techniques in a large-scale, multidivision offensive operation. To help preserve the element of surprise, field artillery units usually fired preparations of short duration; the fires of large numbers of units

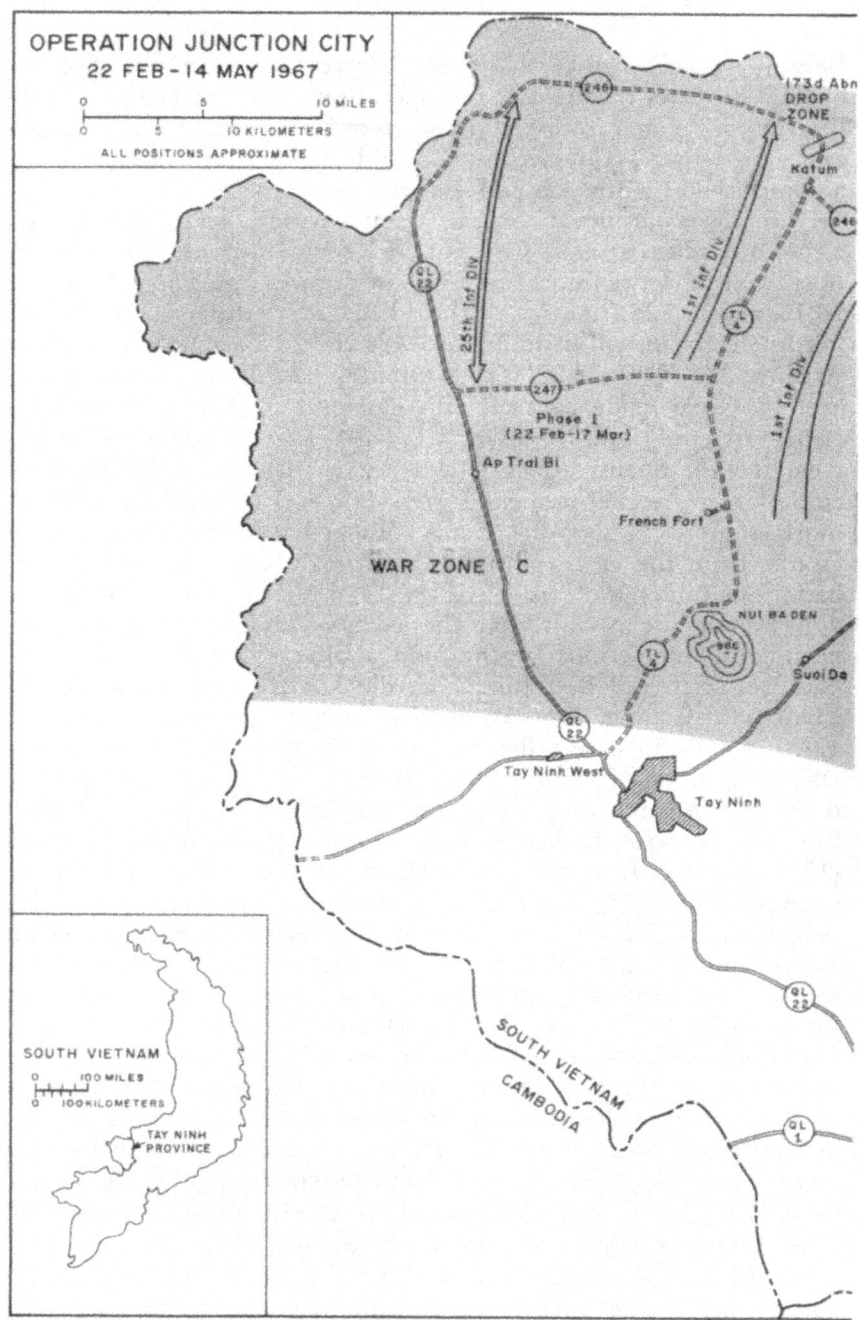

MAP 7

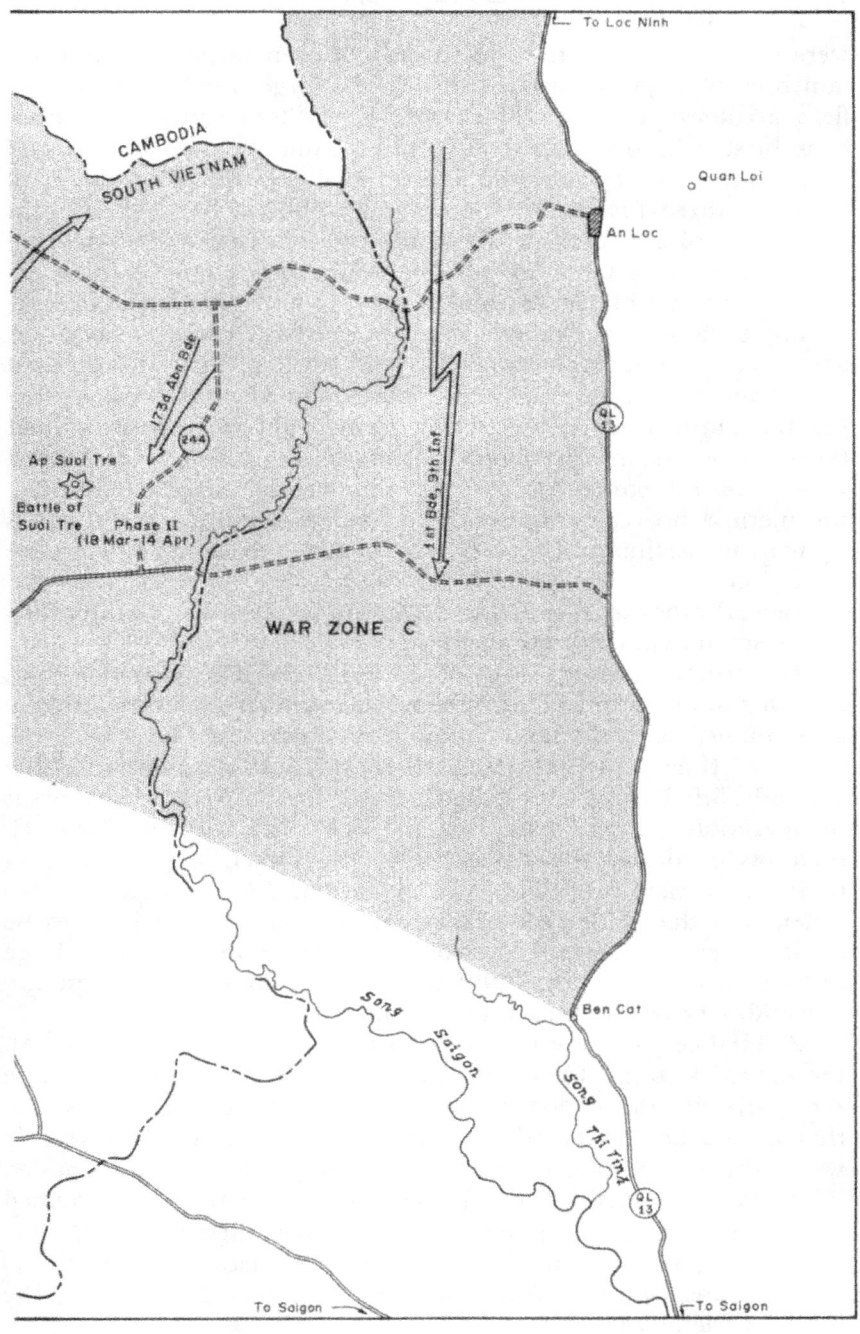

were massed to insure the effectiveness of preparations yet to maintain brevity. A problem was the lack of a large number of suitable field artillery positions. Thus, several artillery units were often consolidated at one location. Landing Zone BLACKHORSE at one point in the operation housed 52 field artillery tubes—five 105-mm. batteries, three 155-mm. batteries, and an 8-inch battery. The disadvantages of crowding artillery into one location and presenting a lucrative target were far outweighed by being able to mass accurately the fires of a large number of weapons from a few locations.

Since the element of surprise was essential, extensive position area surveys were impractical; the field artillery instead employed a relatively new technique called photogrammetric survey. Basically, the technique utilized air reconnaissance photos, the prominent terrain features in the photos serving as registration points and survey control points for position area survey. Although limited, the method proved far superior to that of obtaining co-ordinates by map inspection and served as a valuable expedient during the operation.

Several other artillery-related techniques used successfully during JUNCTION CITY deserve mention:

1. Artillery warning control centers (AWCC's) played a vital role in the operation. The tremendous number of aircraft in the area coupled with the large amount of constant artillery firing necessitated timely and accurate artillery advisories for aircraft. The 1st and 25th Divisions operated centers for their respective areas of operation during Phase I of the operation. During Phase II, such responsibility was delegated to the direct support artillery battalion in each brigade area of operation. The advantage of this system was that data were always current and did not have to be consolidated at a central location. One center in an area as large as that encompassed by JUNCTION CITY would necessitate an unacceptably heavy volume of radio traffic.

2. High-angle fire was proved to be more effective in penetrating the thick jungle foliage than low-angle fire, principally because the projectile descended steeply, paralleling the tree trunks, so that the chance of its hitting a tree and detonating prematurely was reduced. High-angle fire in the jungle also assured added safety for supported ground troops. If high-angle fires detonated prematurely, they did so almost directly over their target. On the other hand, if low-angle fires detonated prematurely they did so some distance laterally from the target, possibly directly over the heads of friendly troops.

3. During the operation, the effectiveness of the AN/MPQ-4A radar was proven. Careful planning prior to the operation resulted

in the placement of radars to provide mutual and overlapping coverage of the various units and fire support bases. Each radar had a primary direction of coverage as well as alternate directions. If a fire base came under attack, usually a radar at another fire base would pick up the enemy rounds before the radar on the fire base under attack would. This flexibility greatly enhanced the ability of U.S. forces to deliver rapid counterbattery fire.

4. On D-day, 22 February 1967, the artillerymen of Battery A, 3d Battalion, 319th Artillery, under operational control of the 2d Battalion, 503d Infantry, 173d Airborne, participated in the only U.S. parachute assault conducted in the war. Led by the battery commander, Captain Charles C. Anderson, the entire battery parachuted into the area around Katum. The howitzers were dropped into the landing zone by C–130's. From a position established in the vicinity of the landing zone, Battery A provided direct artillery support for search and destroy operations conducted by maneuver elements in the vicinity of Katum.

In spite of the magnitude of the operation and the amount of artillery involved in JUNCTION CITY, there were surprisingly few problem areas of major significance. The most significant was in fire support. During the operation, field artillery fires were frequently lifted to accommodate tactical air support, which is a bad practice. If supporting fires are properly co-ordinated, the need to check fire field artillery should rarely occur. When it does occur maneuver forces are slighted because only when all available supporting fires, regardless of type, are able to function simultaneously will they provide the best possible support.

On the whole, JUNCTION CITY was a successful operation. In the years of combat that followed, U.S. and allied forces maintained the capability of re-entering War Zone C at will. All artillerymen participating in the operation could take great pride in having contributed so effectively to the accomplishment of the mission.

Perhaps it is only fitting that 1967, the "year of the big battles," should end as it had begun. Operation JUNCTION CITY began the year; the battle for Dak To ended it. Although much of the heavy fighting in 1967 took place in the south (for example, CEDAR FALLS, JUNCTION CITY, and the battle at Loc Ninh), Dak To was to the north in the Central Highlands of Kontum Province. The battle for Dak To was part of MACARTHUR, an operation that extended into early 1969.

Reacting to intelligence reports that indicated a large buildup of enemy troops in Kontum Province, the 4th Infantry Division deployed its 1st Brigade to the Dak To airfield in late October

1967. On 2 November, a North Vietnamese Army reconnaissance sergeant defected and revealed that four infantry regiments and an artillery regiment were preparing to launch a large-scale attack against the Dak To–Tanh Canh area. This would have been the largest enemy offensive in the Central Highlands area to that time.

The 1st Brigade initially made heavy contact with the enemy to the south and southwest of Dak To throughout the first week in November. Augmented by the 173d Airborne Brigade, the 1st Brigade maintained heavy contact throughout the Ben Het–Dak To area. Additional assistance came from the 42d South Vietnamese Army Regiment, operating to the east of Dak To, and from the 1st Brigade, 1st Air Cavalry Division, which blocked enemy withdrawal routes to the south of Ben Het–Dak To. As the fighting intensified, the enemy was forced to commit his reserves to cover his withdrawal toward the southwest. The bitter fighting that followed ranks with the fiercest of the war. The turning point of the action was the fight for Hill 875, which was finally taken by elements of both the 4th Division and the 173d Airborne Brigade but not before the hill "received the heaviest concentration of Tac Air and all calibers of artillery bombardment of any single terrain feature in the II Corps area."

After the operation, Major General William R. Peers, commander of the 4th Division, acknowledged the role played by the artillery in the battle: "The large number of enemy in the area and the fact that many of the contacts were against elaborately constructed enemy fortifications required that Tac Air and artillery be used at the maximum rates possible. The responsiveness of both air and artillery and the cooperation between them contributed greatly to the victory and was a real tribute to integrated direct support under difficult circumstances."

The artillery committed in the battle of Dak To consisted of 15 batteries of all calibers, with a total of 77 artillery pieces available for support. These figures do not include the battery of aerial rocket artillery that became available when the 1st Brigade of the 1st Cavalry Division joined the operation on 11 November. Battery A (ARA), 2d Battalion, 20th Artillery, assumed a general support-reinforcing role. The U.S. aerial rocket artillery, coupled with the enemy's use of rockets, led to the unfamiliar sight of rockets being employed against rockets.

Artillery expenditures for the 37-day period exceeded 150,000 rounds of all calibers. Artillery units completed 48 tactical displacements to meet the constantly changing demands of the battle. To eliminate fire support co-ordination problems, the 4th Infantry Division Artillery sent a tactical command post to Dak To on 9

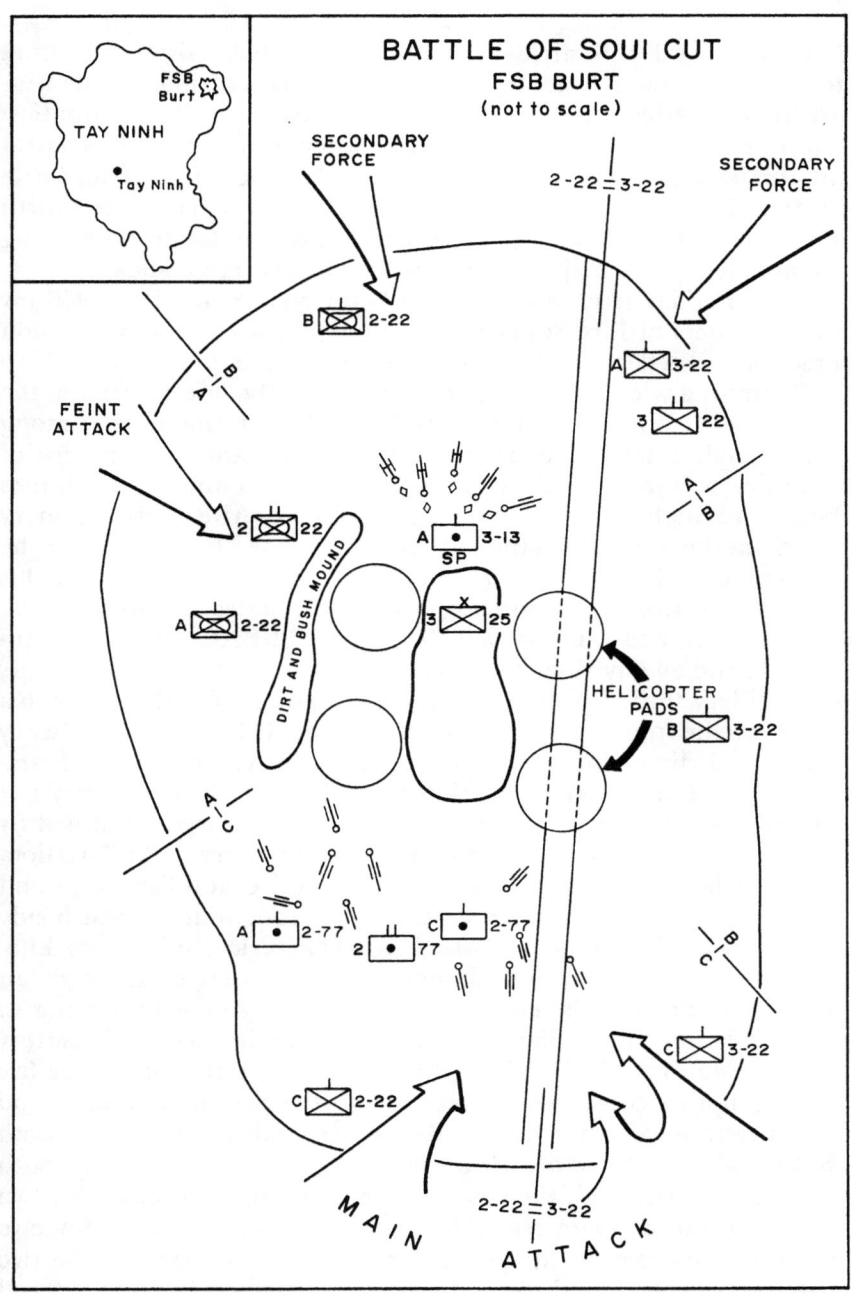

MAP 8

November and U.S. artillery batteries provided liaison personnel to the fire direction centers of the three supporting Vietnamese artillery batteries. The effectiveness of the fire support co-ordination effort is evidenced by the successful integration of 2,096 tactical air sorties and 45 B–52 strikes during the operation. The battle of Dak To cost the enemy 1,644 lives and rendered three North Vietnamese Army infantry regiments ineffective, totally disrupting enemy plans for a major victory in the Central Highlands.

The holiday truce ended abruptly on New Year's Day 1968 for the defenders of Fire Support Base BURT, a 25th Infantry Division base located ten kilometers south of the Cambodian border. (*Map 8*) Beginning with sporadic mortar attacks in the late afternoon, the enemy sent four Viet Cong battalions against the base. Among the defenders were two batteries of 105-mm. and one battery of 155-mm. howitzers. The enemy ground attack commenced minutes before midnight, the official end of the truce. After a diversionary attack on the west side of the perimeter, defended by elements of the 2d Battalion, 22d Infantry (Mechanized), the enemy launched his main attack from the southeast, a sector defended by Company C, 3d Battalion, 22d Infantry, and Battery C, 2d Battalion, 77th Artillery. As the enemy slowly worked his way toward the bunker line, the artillery shifted from countermortar to direct fire in answer to a call from the infantry command post. Battery C began firing a heavy volume of direct fire with both high explosive and Beehive ammunition. The enemy attack slowed in the face of the artillery but picked up to the south of the fire support base, a sector manned by Company C, 2d Battalion, 22d Infantry, and Battery A, 2d Battalion, 77th Artillery. Battery A commenced direct fire, and flare ships and armed helicopters were used extensively throughout the south side of the base. Fire Support Base BEAUREGARD, located twelve kilometers to the west, provided supporting fire west of BURT in an attempt to prevent the enemy from reinforcing or withdrawing in that direction. The 155-mm. (self-propelled) howitzers of Battery C, 3d Battalion, 13th Artillery, located on the north side of the fire base, supplied continuous direct fire to the north, northeast, and northwest. In addition to the direct fire, indirect fire from both BURT and BEAUREGARD was shifted out to the road running south from BURT. Although they were not discovered until daylight, two enemy battalions were assembled on that road as a reserve force to exploit weaknesses in the perimeter, If weaknesses existed, the two battalions never found them. By 0300, tactical air had arrived and was pounding the area to the south. The fires of the artillery gunships and tactical air broke up the Viet Cong attack: by 0600 contact was broken and 400 enemy lay dead in and around the base.

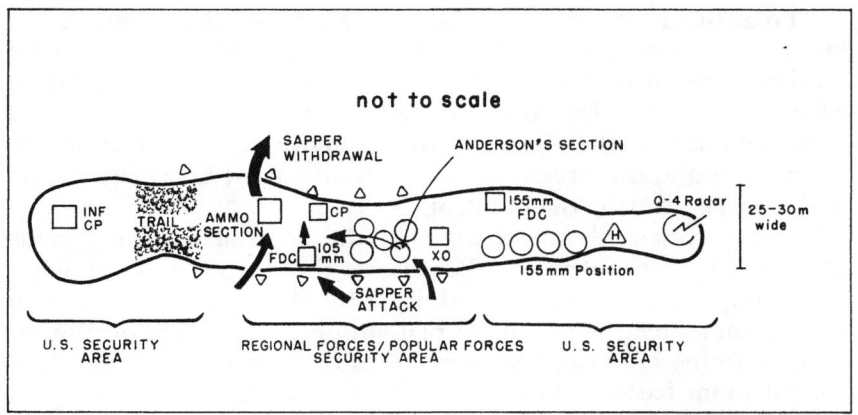

Diagram 7. Battery A, 2d Battalion (Airborne), 320th Artillery, fire base.

The artillerymen of the 25th Division played a vital role in the success of the operation. In addition to maintaining a constant stream of both direct and indirect fire, artillery personnel cut out hasty landing zones for resupply aircraft and broke out and distributed over 1,500 rounds of artillery and mortar ammunition and 200,000 rounds of small-arms ammunition, all during the hours of darkness and in the heat of battle. In addition, they established an improvised air station in the fire direction center of Battery C, 2d Battalion, 77th Artillery, and assisted in the treatment and evacuation of the wounded.

Despite the heroic actions of the 25th Division personnel, the battle cost 23 lives and 153 wounded. The successful integration of infantry, artillery, and air power had saved Fire Support Base BURT. The battle of Soui Cut is a typical example of many such actions that occurred during the war in Vietnam. It is representative of well co-ordinated position defense and fire support.

A second example of a determined defense by field artillerymen occupying a fire base occurred during the early morning hours of 14 October 1967. Battery A, 2d Battalion (Airborne), 320th Artillery (105-mm.), and Battery C, 3d Battalion, 16th Artillery (155-mm.), were occupying an unnamed fire base on a ridge line in support of elements of the 1st Battalion (Airborne), 327th Infantry, of the 1st Brigade, 101st Airborne Division, during Operation WHEELER. The fire base, which had been occupied for almost a month, was located halfway between Tam Ky and Thien Phuoc in the I Corps region.

To assist in the defense of the base, a force of 75 civilian irregular defense group (CIDG) personnel manned the perimeter bunkers. For further security, Battery A nightly posted guards at each howitzer, the fire direction center, and the ammunition section. Because of the difficulty in distinguishing them from the enemy at night, the irregulars had been instructed to remain within their bunkers during the hours of darkness.

The perimeter bunkers were on the edge of a steep dropoff along the narrow ridge line. Because of the steepness of the slope, it was impossible to observe activity directly below the bunkers. It was up these steep slopes that a platoon of sappers crept during the early morning hours and pre-positioned themselves for an attack on the 105-mm. battery. Their objective was to capture the weapons and turn them on the 155-mm. battery and infantry battalion headquarters, which were located on either side of the 105-mm. battery position.

At 0320, in extreme darkness, mortars, rockets, and recoilless rifles unleashed a devastating barrage on the area in conjunction with the sapper attack. Every position within the battery area was known to the enemy before the attack. The radios in the fire direction center were destroyed immediately. A sapper tossed a grenade into the center and then reached in and placed a satchel charge directly on top of the two VRC–46 radios. The enemy so effectively infiltrated the battery area that the artillerymen had no chance to repulse the initial attack; instead, the fighting began within the parapets. That the crewmen of the weapons were able to return fire with their howitzers testified to their discipline and courage. Although the enemy seemed to be everywhere in the battery area, the battery commander, executive officer, and first sergeant, though wounded, moved from weapon to weapon, helping the more seriously wounded and assisting in the delivery of fire.

Each weapon parapet had its own private war going by this time. All the men of number 1 section had been wounded by the initial mortar attack; nevertheless, the section chief, Staff Sergeant Webster Anderson, and his men moved into the parapet and directed fire upon the enemy. Grenades fell all around them, but neither Anderson nor his men faltered. Two mortar rounds landed at Anderson's feet and severely mangled his lower legs. Although in great pain, he managed to move around in the protective parapet and continued to inspire his men. When a grenade landed next to one of his wounded cannoneers, Anderson grabbed the grenade and threw it from the parapet. In the process, his hand was blown off. The executive officer came upon number 1 weapon at this time and, seeing Sergeant Anderson's condition, moved him to medical aid.

Battery A, 2d Battalion, 320th Field Artillery, in Position on Operation Wheeler. *An example of a small, crowded ridgeline position.*

For his actions, Sergeant Anderson later received the Medal of Honor.

By now the battery commander had retrieved the sole remaining radio and had directed defensive fires upon the enemy weapon positions. These fires, in conjunction with direct fires from the 105-mm. howitzers, silenced the enemy. The Viet Cong were finally driven from the battery perimeter after more than two hours of close combat. The infantry battalion headquarters and the 155-mm. battery had not received a single enemy round during the battle. Because of the unknown nature and size of the enemy force, these two units were forced to man their own defenses and were initially unable to assist Battery A. Because of extremely bad weather, the only aircraft flying that night were medical evacuation helicopters, and even they had to be directed into the fire base by the battalion Q–4 radar, which was collocated with the 155-mm. battery. A total of three medevac aircraft evacuated the wounded and dead from the battery area under the worst possible flying conditions.

Morning found Battery A with 6 killed and 29 wounded out of

an initial strength of 49. Twenty-two of the wounded required evacuation. The civilian irregulars lost 6 killed and 5 wounded. Fifty-six craters from 82-mm. mortar rounds were counted in the battery position. At least five mortar rounds had landed in each section parapet. Rocket and recoilless rifle flashes had been observed and fired upon by the 105-mm. and 155-mm. batteries. Although the 105-mm. battery was hurt badly during the attack, the objective of the enemy force was not realized. The field artillerymen stood by their weapons in the face of overwhelming odds and repulsed the enemy from the battery area without losing a single howitzer.

Still another example of determined defense of a fire support base occurred on 18 November 1967 at the opposite end of the country from Operation WHEELER, at Fire Support Base CUDGEL. It was one of three bases established in support of 9th Infantry Division units participating in Operation KEN GIANG in western Dinh Thong Province.

The operation began at dawn on 15 November from a staging area at Dong Tam, the 9th Division command post. In order to locate an area of dry ground large enough to accommodate four guns of his 105-mm. howitzer battery, the commander of Battery C, 2d Battalion, 4th Artillery, Captain Dennis J. Schaible, accompanied the first flight of infantry. For security reasons, reconnaissance of the area had been limited to one brief flyover three days before the operation. Forty-five minutes after the insertion, the battery commander had located an area suitable for the four howitzers. This area was later named Fire Support Base CUDGEL. Fifteen minutes after the crews had lowered the first howitzer to the mushy ground, Battery C commenced preparation fires in support of positions previously selected for the other two fire bases. Later in the morning after the insertion of two infantry battalions into the area of operations, three howitzers of Battery D, 2d Battalion, 4th Artillery, joined Battery C at CUDGEL. Battery D was the first battery employed in Vietnam with the airmobile firing platform, and this was its first operation. The four guns of Battery C were positioned near the northern perimeter and the three guns of Battery D flanked the southern portion of the perimeter. With the addition of elements (battalion headquarters, Company C, and the reconnaissance platoon) from the 5th Battalion, 60th Infantry, which would join the two artillery batteries at CUDGEL on the 17th, the cast of players was set for the battle of Fire Support Base CUDGEL.

The base was bordered on the west by a canal approximately 33 feet wide and 10 feet deep. On the north was a canal with similar dimensions and running east to west. To the south were scrub woods and thick undergrowth, and to the east were open rice paddies. The reconnaissance platoon was deployed on the western portion of the perimeter across the north-south canal, since the canal offered a good line of protection against enemy advance and was a good terrain feature on which to fix the two flanks of the company defensive position. The right flank of the reconnaissance platoon, on the west side of the canal, was linked with the left flank of the 2d Platoon, Company C, which was on the east side of the canal. The 2d Platoon stretched to the east and linked up with the 4th Platoon, which extended south. The right flank of the 4th Platoon linked with the 3d Platoon, which deployed south and west to tie in with the 1st Platoon on the south. The right flank of the 1st Platoon, on the east side of the north-south canal, joined with the left flank of the reconnaissance platoon, along the west side of the canal. In addition to the perimeter established by the infantry company and reconnaissance platoon, Battery C had prepared automatic weapons positions on the east side of the north-south canal as a backup defensive position. A hot line between the battery fire direction center and the infantry battalion command post provided vital communications for the integrated defense.

Intelligence had disclosed a heavy concentration of Viet Cong forces in the area. Battery C cannoneers prepared sandbagged positions as a precaution before dark on their first night at the fire support base. They improved their positions at every opportunity during the occupation of CUDGEL. Preparations were extremely difficult because the water level was less than one foot below the ground. All the foxholes filled with water and most of the protection had to be constructed above the soggy surface of the base.

Soon after the occupation of the perimeter by the reconnaissance platoon, one member of the platoon saw what he thought to be someone wearing a helmet and crouching next to a stand of palm trees directly west of the position. The soldier was unarmed at the time; when he returned with his weapon to investigate, he could find nothing and did not report the incident.

At 2130 the men of one of the listening posts set out by the reconnaissance platoon intercepted a Viet Cong scout and killed him with a burst from an M60 machine gun. Around 0150 the south side of the fire support base perimeter came under heavy fire. The 1st Platoon of Company C was in danger of being overrun. Within minutes, an intense mortar barrage fell on the positions occupied by the reconnaissance platoon and Battery C. This seemed to be a signal for enemy forces on the southwest of the perimeter to attack the reconnaissance platoon positions. It was later estimated that one company assaulted the reconnaissance platoon on the south and west to provide a base of fire with mortars and

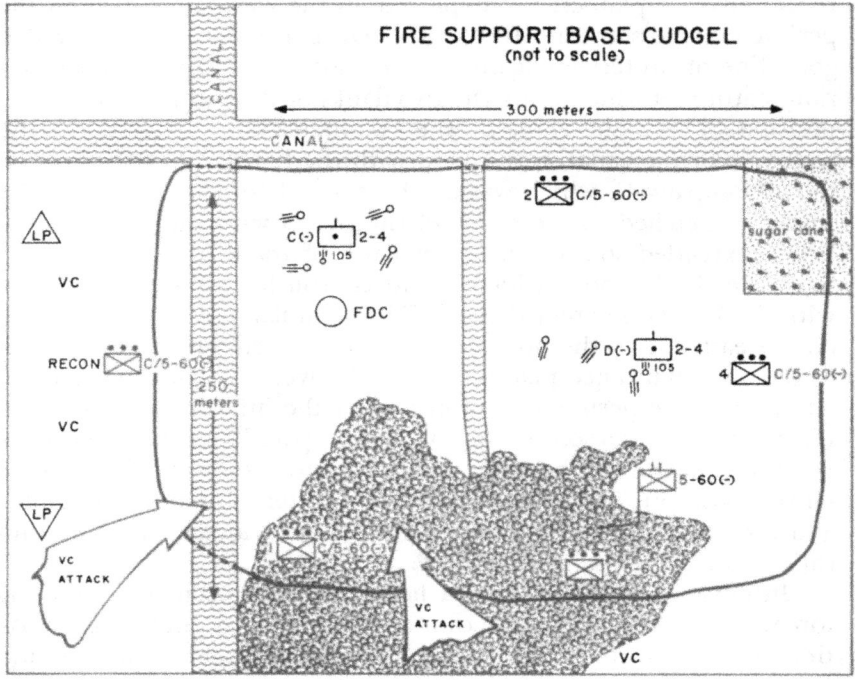

MAP 9

recoilless rifles while two companies maneuvered against Company C on the south.

When the mortar barrage began in the Battery C area, most of the men cried "incoming" and dived for protection. The battery commander and the fire direction officer (FDO) were in the fire direction center. Within seconds after the first mortar rounds burst in the battery area, the officer was on the radio requesting that supporting artillery prepare to fire the defensive concentrations to the south and west of the battery position. At the same time the battery commander was on the hot line to the infantry battalion command post and informed the infantry battalion commander that the fire direction center was in contact with the mutually supporting artillery and requested permission from the battalion commander to call for defensive concentrations. Though permission was quickly granted, it was ten to fifteen minutes before the first artillery support from a sister battery was received. The enemy had also mortared Fire Support Base MACE, a few kilometers away, just before the ground and mortar attack on CUDGEL. (*Map 9*)

The battery supporting CUDGEL was also supporting MACE and was already engaged in a fire mission when the call from the Battery C fire direction center was received.

In the battle that raged for the next 1½ hours, the Viet Cong forces made a desperate attempt to penetrate the southwest portion of the perimeter by overrunning the reconnaissance platoon left flank and Company C right flank. They came perilously close to achieving their goal.

The reconnaissance platoon and the 1st and 3d Platoons of Company C were the most heavily engaged infantry forces during the battle. The fighting in their sector was so fierce and at such close range that each position seemed to be isolated by intense enemy fire in a struggle for individual survival. The battle had been going on for approximately 30 minutes when the reconnaissance platoon leader gave the order to pull back across the canal to the positions occupied by Battery C. As the platoon evacuated its position, the enemy rushed forward and set up recoilless rifle and automatic weapons positions aimed point blank into the Battery C position across the canal.

As soon as the reconnaissance platoon began to withdraw across the canal, Battery C was subjected to intensive automatic rifle, rifle grenade, and recoilless rifle fire. The battery commander requested and received permission from the infantry battalion commander to engage the advancing Viet Cong units with direct artillery fire. Permission to fire Beehive rounds was withheld, however, until the reconnaissance platoon had crossed the canal. Three of the four howitzers had been firing an illumination mission when the attack began and were pointed away from the direction of the enemy advance. Within a few minutes, the crews had turned the pieces around and taken the onrushing enemy under fire. The battery commander and the chiefs of sections adjusted the high-explosive direct fire while the fire direction officer was on the radio adjusting the indirect supporting fire.

The Viet Cong countered with recoilless rifle and heavy machine gun fire. The first round from the recoilless rifle missed the guns and its flash provided a target for howitzer number 2. The cannoneers of number 2 fired at the recoilless rifle, but their first round was low. It struck the canal just below the target, exploded on contact with the bank, and sent mud and fragments back into the battery position. As the crew was about to fire a second round, a recoilless rifle scored a direct hit on the front carriage of the howitzer. The blast wounded the entire section. The tires and sling-load cushioning on the howitzer burst into flame. One of the cannoneers, Private First Class Sammy L. Davis, struggled to his feet and returned to the now furiously burning howitzer. Disregarding a hail of small-arms fire directed against the position, he aimed and fired the howitzer. The damaged weapon recoiled violently and slammed Davis to the ground. Undaunted, he returned to the piece, but a mortar round exploded within 20 meters of his position and compounded his wounds. Private Davis loaded the howitzer, aimed it, and fired; this time he destroyed the recoilless rifle. Again the recoil of the howitzer knocked him to the ground, sent the howitzer skidding into a hole, and rendered it inoperable.

By this time, most of the reconnaissance platoon had reached the friendly side of the canal. The artillerymen of Battery C dragged many of the infantrymen from the canal. Three men from one of the platoon listening posts were not so fortunate; the Viet Cong attack had cut them off. As the battle progressed, a round from another battery landed immediately in front of them. They decided that they must abandon their position or be annihilated by their own artillery. As they started back, another artillery round landed behind them and wounded two of the three men. They continued to low crawl back toward the canal. As they reached the bank of the canal, they saw the recoilless rifle that Davis had knocked out. Not knowing that the round that had knocked out the recoilless rifle had also put the howitzer out of action, they yelled across to the artillery to cease firing. Hearing their cries for help, Davis and another member of number 2 gun section, Private First Class William H. Murray, went to help the wounded men. Despite his painful wounds and his inability to swim, Davis picked up an air mattress and he and Murray struck out across the deep canal to rescue three men. Upon reaching the men, all of whom had by this time sustained wounds, Davis took up a position on the canal bank and fired on the Viet Cong, who were swarming the western bank, while Murray ferried the most seriously wounded infantryman across the canal. After emptying five magazines into the charging enemy, Davis and Murray floated the remaining two wounded infantrymen across the canal. Though still suffering from neglected wounds, Davis refused medical attention, joined another howitzer crew, and assisted in firing until the attack was broken later in the morning. For his action, Private Davis received the Medal of Honor, which was presented to him by President Johnson at the White House exactly one year from the date of the battle.

While Davis was fighting his private battle with the recoilless rifle, the other howitzer sections were also heavily engaged. By 0245 the 3d Platoon, manning the southern perimeter, had fallen back to the battery position. The platoon leader had been seriously wounded and the platoon sergeant killed. With a second side of the perimeter now open, gun number 4 once again shifted trails to level direct fire south into the vacant perimeter area. Throughout the raging battle, the battery commander continually requested permission to fire Beehive in hopes of breaking up the attack. Finally permission came, and Battery C fired a total of 21 Beehive rounds. Just after the first of these was fired, number 3 gun received a direct hit from a recoilless rifle. Although the recoil mechanism was leaking oil, the crew continued to fire the Beehive rounds until the piece would no longer return to battery. As the last of the Beehive rounds was fired, and almost as quickly as the firing had begun, that attack withered. By this time helicopter gunships and a C–47 Spooky had arrived on station to add their fire power against the retreating enemy forces.

When the battle was over, 22 of the 44 artillerymen of Battery C had been wounded. Two of the 4 howitzers had been destroyed and over 600 direct fire rounds, including the 21 Beehive rounds, had been fired at the enemy. The infantry suffered 6 killed and 76 wounded. The official number of enemy killed in the operation was placed at 83, but estimates of the actual enemy losses were more than twice that number. The efforts of Private Davis and the other field artillerymen in Battery C turned what could have been a Viet Cong victory into a clear defeat.

Overview: 1965 to Pre-Tet 1968

As 1967 drew to an end, the enemy was busy formulating plans for an offensive to be launched throughout Vietnam in celebration of *Tet* 1968. The eve of *Tet* is a good vantage point from which to look back on the U.S. field artillery's first 2½ years of combat in Vietnam.

Beginning on 5 May 1965, with the commitment of the 3d Battalion (Airborne), 319th Artillery, the U.S. Army involvement had increased until 54 artillery battalions were in various supporting roles throughout Vietnam. In nearly 1,000 days of combat, artillery progress and accomplishments contributed significantly to the success of the U.S. tactical mission. Artillerymen adapted to the unique situation posed in Vietnam. The length of time between the Korean War and the start of combat operations in Vietnam had deprived the Army of a high level of combat experienced personnel. Combat experience was the exception rather than the rule at company and battalion levels in all branches. Further, the nature of the Vietnam war negated much of the conventional war experience possessed by those who had previously been in combat. To overcome this inexperience and unfamiliarity with counterguerrilla operations, the field artilleryman needed to be more creative, innovative, and flexible than ever before. Artillerymen fulfilled this need with the utmost professionalism.

From the first few informal reports from the field in 1965 through the volumes of operational reports and lessons learned that became formalized by 1967, the message was clear: the basic doctrine, tactics, and techniques that had been followed for years by artillerymen were still valid, but some modifications of the manner in which they were applied were necessary. These modifications initially resulted in problems, which were listed and discussed to determine expeditiously the best and most feasible solutions. Experiences were shared with artillerymen worldwide to insure against repetition of the same mistakes and to better provide adequate fire support.

Probably no artilleryman of any grade or position proved more flexible in the face of adversity than the forward observer. Every maneuver company was assigned a field artillery forward observer who traveled with the company and called for and adjusted supporting fires. The "eyes and ears of the artillery," as he is often called, the forward observer in Vietnam faced many disadvantages in the early months of the war. A lieutenant by table of organization and equipment, the observer was often a young noncommissioned officer or enlisted soldier, in his first combat tour, and trained in the principles of conventional war. In Vietnam he encountered thick forest and jungle and, more often than not, lack of visibility of the target area. This often necessitated the adjustment of artillery by sound, something he was not trained to do. The nature of operations in Vietnam often resulted in infantry platoons and squads operating semi-independently, away from the company command post. Control of the platoons and squads kept company commanders so busy that the forward observer's responsibilities often included maintaining accurate and current locations of the company and subordinate elements. This was a significant problem, compounded by the fact that vegetation often obscured prominent terrain features and visible reference points. The 1st Cavalry Division reported in 1965 that their forward observers, hampered by dense jungle, had improvised a rope and sling device with which to climb trees in order to observe artillery fire. Common methods of resolving map reading problems were the "pace and count" method of land navigation and the firing of a spotting round of smoke or white phosphorus, which was detonated in the air above a location that had been predetermined by the fire direction center and passed to the forward observer. In a series of taped interviews with company commanders who had served in Vietnam, the general consensus was

AERIAL FIELD ARTILLERY COBRA IN FLIGHT

that map reading and responsibilities for maintaining unit locations were best left in the hands of the artillery forward observer.

Another problem area for the observer was the employment of aerial rocket artillery, which was relatively new. The forward observer had received little if any training in aerial rocket artillery adjustment. He had to gain confidence in the system, but once that was accomplished, aerial rocket artillery inevitably became his "trump card."

Artillery commanders in Vietnam were quick to recognize the need for well-trained, able observers. In 1965, a large proportion of "combat notes" and reports from the field emphasized the importance of the forward observer section to the successful accomplishment of the fire support mission. Initial reports from the 173d Airborne Brigade stressed the need for cross-training of personnel in these sections. The reconnaissance sergeant and the radiotelephone operator often had to assume fire-support responsibilities

AERIAL FIELD ARTILLERY COBRA AND LIGHT OBSERVATION HELICOPTER *form hunter-killer team.*

and some were not qualified to do so. In addition, it was believed that forward observers were not being properly utilized as a source of intelligence. It was concluded that more emphasis should be given to correcting these shortcomings during training in the continental United States.

Firing batteries throughout Vietnam experienced several common problems. Tables of organization and equipment prescribed personnel levels and authorizations that made 24-hour operation a severe strain on personnel. Modification of tables was necessary to permit round-the-clock operations, particularly in the fire direction center. Large areas of operation and great distances between battalions and their batteries put the emphasis on the battery center as the primary source of firing data. Often the battalion fire direction control mission became more a matter of control than direction. Too, mountainous terrain often hampered communications and thus the battery center had to check its own firing data. The frequent splitting of batteries meant that a battery had constantly to maintain the personnel and equipment to establish and maintain several fire direction centers. Another challenge for the field artilleryman was his new-found mobility resulting from the extensive use of the helicopter. Few individual replacements had much if any training in airmobility, yet all towed artillery units had to be ready to move on a moment's notice. The versatility of the artilleryman offset his lack of experience. Units that had never displaced by air learned, and learned quickly. Occasionally peacetime habits, both good and bad, cropped up in Vietnam. One such habit, a negative one but easily correctable, was cited by the 23d Artillery Group. Delays in firing often occurred in firing sections with new section chiefs. The explanation was that these chiefs, with considerable peacetime experience, were in the habit of waiting for the safety officer to check firing data. A further problem was that firing batteries equipped with the M107-mm. gun were hampered by the weapon's extremely short tube life. After firing 300 full charge rounds, it was necessary to replace the tube, a six-hour procedure. The artillery lived with this problem until a new tube with four times the tube life was developed. Stateside production of the tubes caught up with Vietnam demands in early 1968. In addition, the field time required to change tubes was reduced to two hours, principally the result of the efforts of an enterprising artilleryman who fabricated an adapter which prevented the nitrogen in the weapon's equilibrators from escaping. Previously, equilibrators were permitted to empty during tube change and additional time was required to replenish the lost nitrogen.

Initially, many combat experiences, creative ideas, and new tactics and techniques were peculiar to particular units or areas of Vietnam and were passed informally by word of mouth. To prevent disjointed concepts and ideas and to standardize procedures, information pertinent to artillery procedures was given wide dissemination. The best source was lessons learned reports, and information from them was distributed throughout Vietnam as well as up through channels, ultimately to be used in training by units and service schools in the United States.

To standardize procedures in Vietnam and to reinforce written standing operating procedures, training schools were established at division artillery, artillery group, and field force artillery levels to train newly assigned personnel in artillery procedures and techniques peculiar to Vietnam or to the particular area or unit to which they would be assigned. The emphasis was primarily on forward observer and fire direction center procedures and techniques. These schools ranged in duration from three days to a week and were staffed and equipped from units already in Vietnam. Typical of this training was a six-day course in fire direction conducted by I Field Force Artillery for all its newly assigned fire direction officers. The 41st Artillery Group conducted a five-day orientation course for newly assigned forward observers. Similar schools were conducted by II Field Force Artillery and its subordinate units.

To improve co-ordination and liaison between U.S. forces and other Free World Military Assistance Forces units, many U.S. units conducted artillery orientation schools for allied personnel. The 9th Infantry Division conducted such a school in 1967 in preparation for a joint U.S. and Thai operation. To facilitate artillery co-ordination in the II Corps area, the 41st Artillery Group conducted fire support training for South Vietnamese Army personnel. When the language barrier was overcome, the result of such training was a marked improvement in the speed and quality of artillery support.

The ultimate in training experiences was on-the-job training (OJT) in a unit engaged in actual combat operations. As time progressed and personnel were "infused" between units to prevent large rotational humps, individual training became possible. To insure adherence to basic artillery doctrine and safety procedures and to allow for standardization of artillery techniques, artillery staffs at group and division levels established various means of testing the proficiency of subordinate units. The most common technique was the formation of a team which visited a subordinate unit to render assistance and evaluate the artillery procedures used. The 23d Artillery Group conducted unannounced proficiency tests (UPT) of the basic artillery fundamentals and principles in their subordinate units. Requirements consisted of firing a registration mission, a time-on-target mission, and two adjust fire missions. The objective of such tests was to evaluate and assist, not to harass, and the practice proved quite successful.

As lessons learned reached the continental United States, every effort was made to ease the training burden of combat units in Vietnam and to incorporate Vietnam-related procedures and lessons learned into instruction and training.

At the Field Artillery School (then the United States Army Artillery and Missile School) at Fort Sill, Oklahoma, the emphasis was on instruction and training geared to meet the artillery requirements in Vietnam. The Field Artillery School dispatched liaison teams to Vietnam "to determine the actions required to improve the products of the [Artillery] Training Center and the Artillery School at Fort Sill for officers, enlisted men and deployable units." These visits included one in September of 1967 by Major General Charles P. Brown, Fort Sill commander and Artillery School commandant. Extensive interviews at all levels of artillery command were conducted during these visits and a list of matters requiring the attention of the Artillery School was made. Essentially, the ba-

Major General, Then Colonel, David E. Ott, 25th Division Artillery Commander (Right), Demonstrates FADAC to Major General Tillson, 25th Infantry Division Commander, *July 1967.*

sic message gleaned from these trips was that although the over-all state of training of artillery personnel assigned to Vietnam was excellent, increased Vietnam-oriented training was required. Specifically, it was determined that increased emphasis was necessary in 6,400-mil fire direction center procedures; counterguerrilla reconnaissance, selection, and occupation of position training; and fire support co-ordination responsibilities at all levels, particularly those of the artillery liaison officer.

By mid-1967, the Artillery School had begun to make significant progress in implementing changes in instructional programs to satisfy Vietnam requirements. A field artillery officer's Vietnam orientation course (FAOVOC) was instituted in July 1967. Four to five weeks long, the course concentrated solely on tactics and techniques used in Vietnam. In fiscal year 1968, 239 officers completed the course; in fiscal year 1969, over 1,000. The course was offered in addition to the officer basic schooling and was designed better to prepare officers for Vietnam service. The officer basic course was increased from 9 to 12 weeks, and the Artillery Officer Candidate School enrollment increased from 3,000 in fiscal year 1966 to 9,600 in fiscal year 1967. Increased emphasis on Vietnam training for noncommissioned and enlisted students resulted in short (2–3 week) section chief courses and a noncommissioned officer candidate course designed to emphasize skill development in artillery procedures. Fire direction center training stressed 6,400-mil fire direction procedures, including chart preparation and wind cards. On the basis of information received in Vietnam during liaison visits, additional training on the field artillery digital computer (FADAC) was implemented. The Tactics and Combined Arms Department constructed two Vietnam-type artillery fire bases for instruction in battery defense, and field exercises included a counterguerrilla phase in the scenario as students participating in training for reconnaissance, selection, and occupation of position began occupying star-shaped and circular battery positions in addition to conventional linear positions. Throughout the Field Artillery School, every attempt was made to prepare the field artilleryman for combat duty in Vietnam.

The field artillery made genuine progress after its arrival in Vietnam in 1965. The quality of fire support was ever increasing as the artillery played a vital role in operations ranging from JUNCTION CITY, the largest combined operation to date, to small-unit actions such as those in the remote outposts of Landing Zone BIRD and Soui Cat. In over two and a half years of combat, the artillerymen had trained hard, fought hard, and shared experiences with personnel of other branches. As the 1968 *Tet* holiday season neared and the enemy made final plans for attack, seasoned artillerymen manned positions in 54 field artillery battalions scattered throughout Vietnam.

CHAPTER V

The Hot War (1968–October 1969)

The Viet Cong and the North Vietnamese Army in late 1967 launched several costly attacks. On 29 October the Viet Cong attacked the South Vietnamese district capital of Loc Ninh, ran up the flag of the National Liberation Front, and tried to hold the city. United States and South Vietnamese forces responded with massive air and artillery bombardment, but the enemy continued to press the attack despite heavy losses. Similarly, in early November four North Vietnamese Army regiments fought U.S. and South Vietnamese troops near Dak To. The U.S. command deployed the equivalent of a full division from the heavily populated coastal lowlands to the battle area. Again, as at Loc Ninh, the enemy sustained heavy casualties. A captured enemy document listed four objectives for the 1967 campaigns. These included encouraging units to improve, in combat, the technique of concentrated attacks to annihilate relatively large enemy units and effecting close co-ordination with various battle areas throughout South Vietnam to achieve timely unity. The activity of late 1967 was a prelude to *Tet* 1968. A high-level prisoner later revealed that the assault on Loc Ninh had been ordered to test mass formations and previously inexperienced troops in preparation for the 1968 offensive.

Tet, the festival of the Asian lunar new year, usually was the occasion for a formal cease-fire. In 1968, however, the North Vietnamese Army and the Viet Cong, using reserve forces and the larger supporting weapons, launched a series of massive co-ordinated attacks in what became known as the *Tet* offensive. As revealed by captured enemy sources, the strategy for the offensive was based on the belief that the war would culminate in 1968 and that large-scale continuous attacks, in conjunction with a general uprising of the people, would precipitate the withdrawal from Vietnam of U.S. forces and the collapse of the South Vietnamese government, which would then be forced to accept a coalition government dominated by the National Liberation Front.

Tet 1968

Political and military targets of the *Tet* offensive included provincial and district capitals, the government in Saigon and its agencies such as the Regional Development Cadres and the National Police, and the Republic of Vietnam Armed Forces. The enemy believed that if widespread attacks were successful, the inability of the government to protect the people would become obvious and the credibility of that government would be undermined. Installations and facilities that were essential to the conduct of the war and that were difficult to defend became tactical targets. (*Map 10*) In preparation for the *Tet* offensive, the enemy went to unprecedented lengths to assemble supplies and weapons and to infiltrate the cities. In Saigon, funeral processions concealed the movement of arms and ammunition. In Hue and Saigon, enemy troops in civilian dress escaped detection. In provincial centers such as Quang Tri, Da Nang, Nha Trang, Quin Nhon, Kontum city, Ban Me Thuot, My Tho, Can Tho, and Ben Tri, the enemy infiltrated in strength.

The offensive began at 0015 on 30 January at Nha Trang. The same night eleven other cities in I and II Corps zones, as well as several military installations and airfields, came under attack. Enemy documents later revealed that these attacks were premature; the forces operating in these areas had not received the order for a one-day postponement of the offensive. The main attack took place on the following night, 30–31 January, when enemy forces hit eighteen cities throughout the country. The allies cleared most of the cities within hours. However, in a few cities, particularly Saigon and Hue, the fighting continued for days.

The attack on Hue commenced at 0340 on 31 January. (*Map 11*) Elements of the 800th, 802d, and 806th Battalions, 6th North Vietnamese Army Regiment, and the 804th Battalion, 4th North Vietnamese Army Regiment, initiated a rocket, mortar, and ground assault on the city. Forces of the 4th Regiment soon occupied all of southern Hue except the Military Assistance Command compound. Meanwhile, to the north, two battalions of the 6th Regiment moved into the citadel, an old French fortress near the center of the city. By morning the flag of the National Liberation Front had been mounted on the flag pole of the citadel and the enemy controlled all of the fortress but the South Vietnamese Army 1st Division headquarters.

The allies acted immediately to relieve the pressure on the Military Assistance Command and South Vietnamese Army compounds. While U.S. and Vietnamese marines along with the 1st Division bore down on the enemy forces to the south and within the city itself, the 3d Brigade, 1st Cavalry Division, sealed off Hue to the north and west. Each of the maneuver forces fought exceptionally well, but the actions of the 3d Brigade, 1st Cavalry Division,

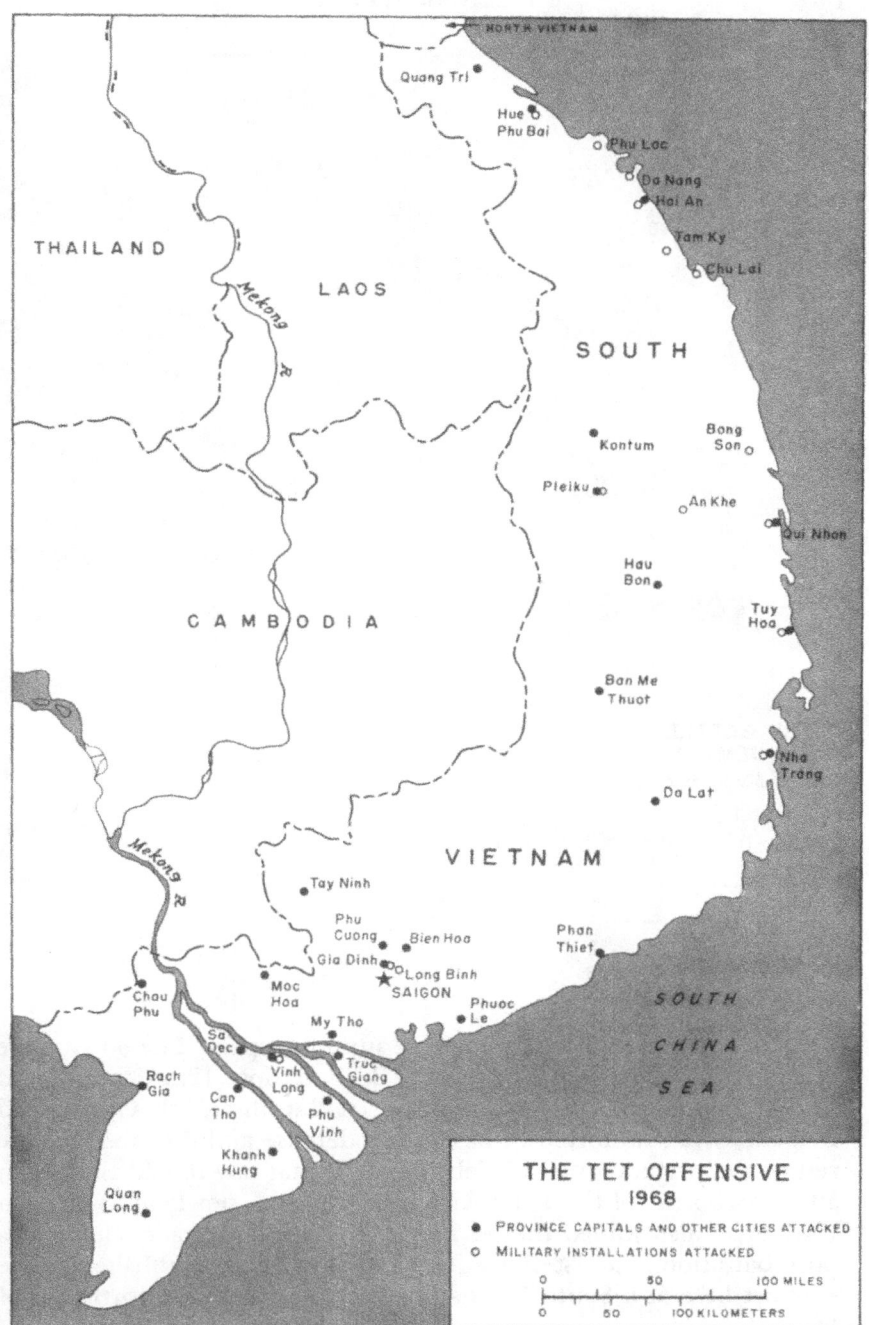

MAP 10

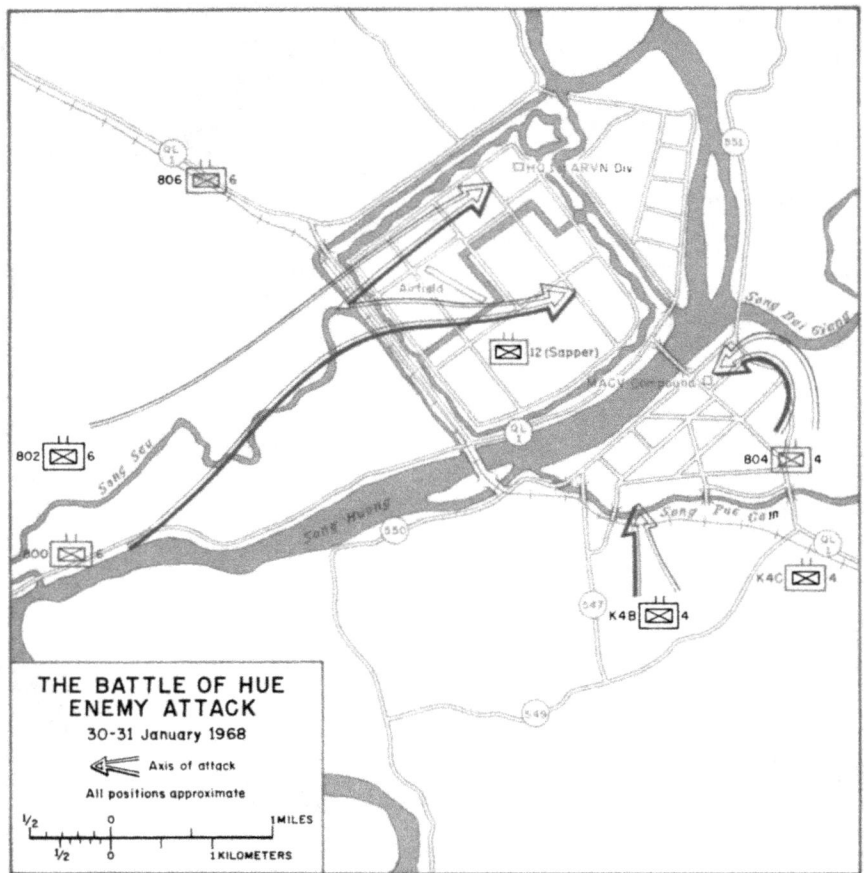

MAP 11

were the most significant from a fire support aspect. The 3d Brigade blocking force was comprised of the 2d Battalion, 12th Cavalry, and the 5th Battalion, 7th Cavalry. The 1st Battalion, 7th Cavalry, 3d Brigade, was committed to base camp defense and did not join the rest of the brigade until 19 February. On that day the 2d Battalion, 501st Airborne, of the 101st Airborne Division, newly arrived from III Corps, also joined the 3d Brigade. The 3d Brigade direct support battalion, the 1st Battalion, 21st Artillery, established a fire support base at a South Vietnamese Army compound northwest of Hue.

On 3 February the 2d Battalion, 12th Cavalry, detected a large North Vietnamese force positioned near Que Chu, west of Hue.

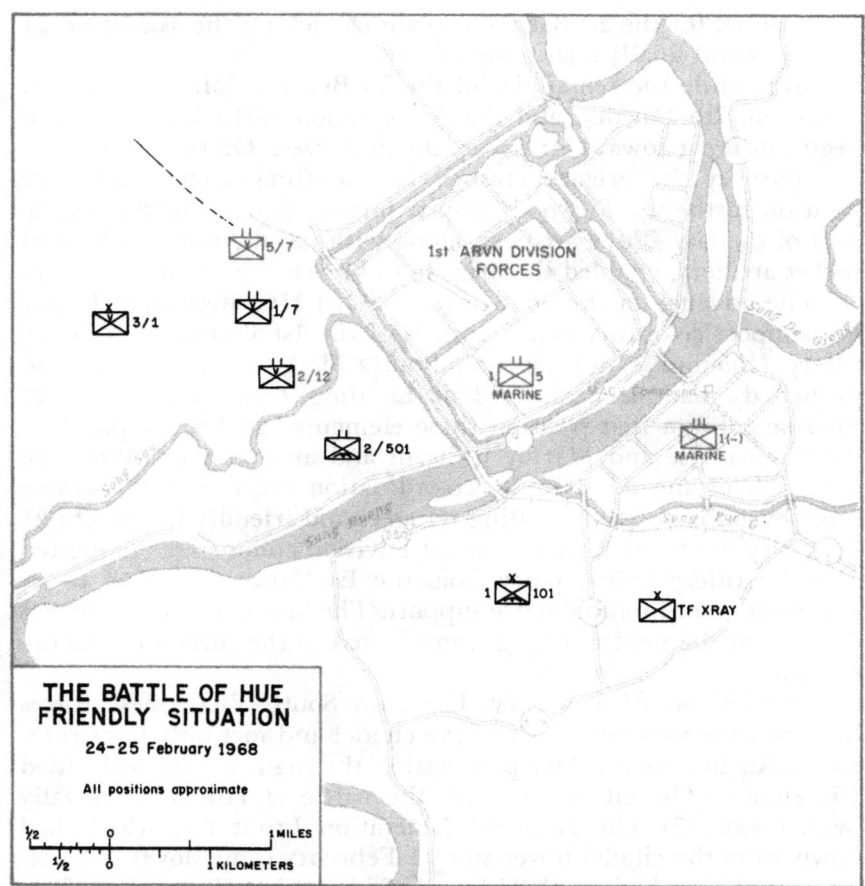

MAP 12

The battalion, supported by indirect artillery fire, aerial rocket artillery, and helicopter gunships, attacked the well-fortified enemy position. By 5 February the 2d Battalion controlled the high ground in the Que Chu area overlooking the surrounding plains and, with precise artillery fire, was able virtually to stop all enemy movement.

Beginning on 9 February, while the 5th Battalion, 7th Cavalry, maintained the blocking position, the 2d Battalion, 12th Cavalry, entered the village of Bon Tri to the south of Que Chu and encountered a well-dug-in regimental-size enemy complex. For three days U.S. artillery, air strikes, and naval gunfire pummeled the positions. On 12 February the 2d Battalion had to break contact without any substantial change in the situation. The 5th Battalion took over the assault, but it too was unable to dislodge the enemy.

It remained for the 2d Battalion again to pick up the assault on 21 February and finally secure the village.

Meanwhile the remainder of the 3d Brigade, joined by the 1st Battalion, 7th Cavalry, and the 2d Battalion, 501st Airborne, had begun its move toward Hue from the northwest. On the morning of 21 February the brigade crashed into a strong enemy defensive position in the Ti Ti woods, approximately five kilometers northwest of the city. Tube artillery, along with naval gunfire and aerial rocket artillery, enabled the brigade to breach the enemy positions.

The advance of the 3d Brigade toward Hue necessitated close fire support co-ordination. Elements of the 1st Battalion, 30th Artillery (155-mm.), and 1st Battalion, 83d Artillery (8-inch, self-propelled), had been situated at Landing Zone NOLE since 20 February. From that position these elements had been supporting the Vietnamese and Marine units in and around Hue. With the approach of the 3d Brigade, co-ordination requirements became more exacting to avoid shelling refugees and friendly forces. On 21 February the South Vietnamese 1st Division commander requested a field artillery liaison party from the 1st Cavalry Division to assist in the co-ordination of fire support. The liaison party, which was dispatched the next morning, contributed to the success of the operation.

At 0730 on 24 February, U.S. and South Vietnamese forces breached the southwest wall of the citadel and met only light resistance. An intense artillery preparation the night before had killed 161 enemy. The citadel secured, the battle of Hue was officially over. *(Map 12)* The National Liberation Front flag which had flown from the citadel tower since 1 February came down. The recapture of Hue had involved four U.S. Army battalions, three U.S. Marine Corps battalions, and eleven South Vietnamese battalions. Ten Viet Cong and North Vietnamese Army battalions had been committed in an attempt to hold the city.

Colonel Richard M. Winfield, Jr., 1st Cavalry Division Artillery commander, in summarizing the actions and problems of the artillery, emphasized the conventional quality of the operation and concluded with a description of clearance activities and the consequences:

> In the battle for Hue, the brigade was operating four battalions in the most conventional type of conflict that this division had ever been faced with. The brigade had their normal supporting artillery—three direct support batteries, a medium battery, and, during the latter periods of the attack, an 8-inch battery. Those units, from the 3d to the 26th of February, fired 52,000 rounds. In addition, 7,670 rounds of 5-inch to 8-inch naval ammunition, and 600 tons of Air Force-delivered munitions were expended in the area. In the last stages of the operation, the di-

vision commander and I went into Hue and worked with the commanding officer of the 1st ARVN forces. We took whoever was needed for fire control and clearance so that we wouldn't have any major accidents against US Army, ARVN, or Marine unit or civilian, who were all converging on Hue. This required tight and rigid fire control, which was exercised by both the GS battalion commanders, by myself, and by the senior officer whom I had placed in Hue to control those fires. We had 11 fire support agencies in Hue. Now, this of course, had an effect on our infantry units, which are used to operating when they want to shoot—they call for fire and the fire is there. When we have all these clearance requirements and you have to have minimum safe distances all around you, the fire becomes slow because of the clearance and becomes restricted both in the caliber of weapons and in the number of rounds you can fire. I would say that the fire support was adequate. It was tough to get, but it was certainly adequate.

U.S. plans in the III Corps Tactical Zone for early 1968 envisioned only fourteen allied battalions remaining within a 29-mile radius of Saigon. Since early December 1967, defense of the capital itself had been the responsibility of the South Vietnamese command. The 5th Ranger Group, with a U.S. 105-mm. howitzer battalion (2d Battalion, 13th Artillery) in direct support, was responsible for providing the necessary security. U.S. forces thus released from the defense of Saigon were incorporated into plans for assaults on enemy base camps in the Cambodian border region. Thirty-nine battalions were to operate against these camps.

As the U.S. plans were set in motion, however, General Weyand, commanding II Field Force, became concerned over the results. Enemy resistance along the Cambodian border was weak. This weakness, coupled with the large volume of enemy radio transmissions near Saigon, convinced him of the necessity for redeployment. He conveyed his conclusions to General Westmoreland. The result was a shifting of forces. By the time of the *Tet* attacks in the III Corps area, twenty-seven U.S. maneuver battalions were in the capital area and the remaining twenty-five outside.

The operational plan of the enemy in the III Corps Tactical Zone included:

1. Seizing the Bien Hoa–Long Binh complex. Key targets: Bien Hoa Air Base, II Field Force headquarters, III Corps headquarters, prisoner-of-war camp between Bien Hoa and Long Binh, Long Binh ammunition storage area.

2. Attacking targets in the Hoc Mon area northwest of Saigon while blocking allied reaction by interdicting Route 1 between Saigon and Cu Chi; maintaining readiness to exploit successes in the northern Saigon area.

3. Blocking any attempted reaction by the U.S. 25th Infantry Division from the Cu Chi–Dau Tieng region.

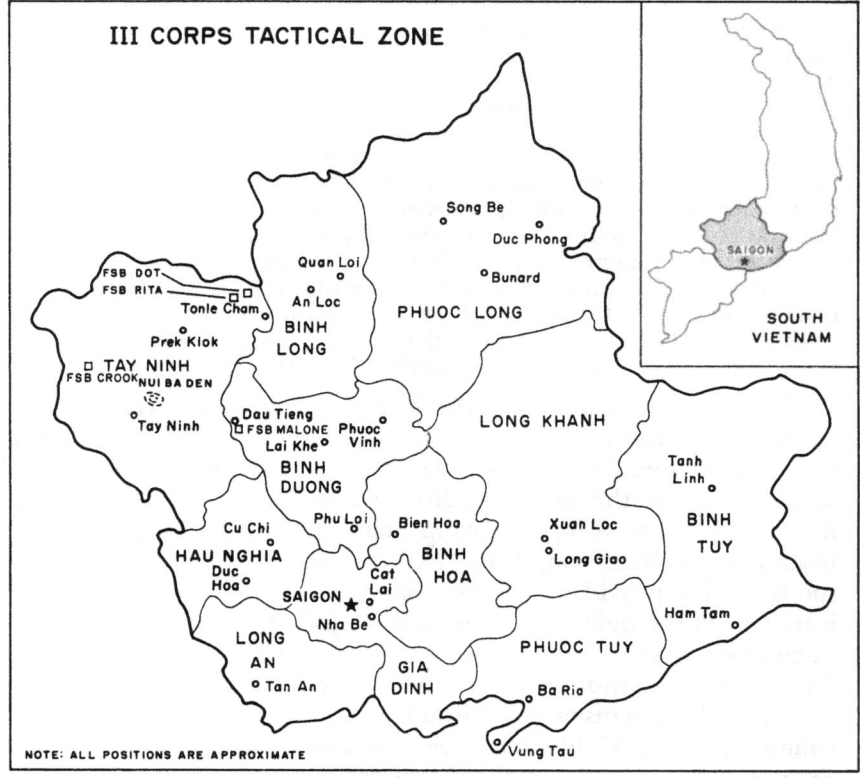

MAP 13

4. Attacking district and government installations in Thu Duc and destroying the Newport bridge over the Saigon River between Saigon and Long Binh.

5. Containing the 1st Infantry Division in the Lai Khe area and cutting off Highway 13 at An Loc.

6. Seizing Tan Son Nhut Air Base and possibly the adjacent vice-presidential palace; taking over the presidential palace along with the U.S. and Philippine embassies; holding or destroying installations of the government of Vietnam such as the National Police stations and power plants. Success here would cause the government and the United States to lose face and would propel a move to the conference table, where the National Liberation Front would negotiate from a position of strength.

7. Controlling Cu Chi, Duc Hoa (including the South Viet-

namese 25th Division headquarters), Ba Ria, Xuan Loc (18th Division headquarters), My Tho, Ben Tre, and Phu Loi–Phu Chang.

In the III Corps area the *Tet* offensive began at 0300 on 31 January in the Long Binh–Bien Hoa complex with a rocket and mortar attack on headquarters of the 199th Infantry Brigade and II Field Force. (*Map 13*) By 0321 Saigon and Tan Son Nhut were also receiving heavy fire. In order to control combat units in the Capital Military District (Gia Dinh Province), General Weyand ordered his deputy commander, Major General Keith Ware, and a small staff to Saigon to take operational control of all U.S. units. Task Force WARE, the operational headquarters, situated at Capital Military District headquarters, was operational by 1100 that same day and remained so until 18 February.

At the outset of the *Tet* offensive, only one U.S. infantry battalion and four 105-mm. howitzer batteries operated in Gia Dinh Province. Three of these batteries were in direct support of the South Vietnamese 5th Ranger Group. General Westmoreland, for political and psychological reasons, had refrained from maintaining U.S. maneuver units in Saigon and several other large cities. Once the *Tet* attacks began and American maneuver battalions arrived in the Capital Military District, division and field force artillery units relocated and supported the relief of the district.

Fire support for American units in the Capital Military District, particularly in Saigon, posed serious problems for the artillery. Numerous homes and shops and heavy concentrations of people within the city limited the area where artillery could be fired. When artillery could be employed, it was slow to respond because of difficulties in obtaining clearance to fire. Vietnamese military units in the city and the city government had not been placed under a single control headquarters. As a result, no centralized clearance activity was established. Artillery liaison officers were required to obtain clearance locally from the national police station in their area of operations. The situation was corrected in June 1968 when the Army of the Republic of Vietnam established a single military governor in the Capital Military District. Artillery support was further limited in Saigon because buildings and other structures restricted the view of forward observers. Gunships and tactical air proved more adept at providing support because the pilots had a better view of the target area. As a result specific enemy locations could be pinpointed and damage held to a minimum. For these reasons most of the major field artillery engagements in the Capital Military District during the *Tet* offensive and counteroffensive occurred in the outer edges of Saigon and in other areas of the zone.

Particularly impressive during *Tet* was the fire support provided to the 1st Infantry Division in III Corps Tactical Zone. The division killed over 1,000 enemy troops. The Big Red One estimated that artillery and air strikes accounted for 70 percent of these enemy losses. The volume of field artillery fire increased substantially during the *Tet* offensive. The 1st Infantry Division recorded the following:

Caliber	Daily Average Prior to *Tet*	Daily Average During *Tet*
105–mm.	2,376 rounds	5,616 rounds
155–mm.	925	1,459
8–inch	200	235
4.2–inch	1,100	1,570
Total	4,601	8,880

The most significant engagement during *Tet* for units of the 1st Infantry Division Artillery and the 23d Artillery Group began on 1 February. The division had shifted its artillery south along Highway 13 in order to meet increased enemy activity between Lai Khe and Saigon. On the morning of 1 February, elements of the division engaged units of the 273d Viet Cong Regiment at An My, approximately 4,000 meters north of Phu Loi. The artillery began by providing blocking fires. Then at 1330 the artillery placed destructive fires upon enemy forces entrenched in the village. Throughout the day 3,493 rounds hit the northern half of the village and caused approximately 20 secondary explosions. A survey of the area before dark confirmed 201 enemy killed and evidence supporting estimates of more than twice that number. Once darkness set in, the artillery again provided blocking fires. The next morning, the 1st Infantry Division found the remainder of the 273d Regiment still entrenched in An My. The action resumed at 1030 with the artillery continuing to provide blocking fires. When rounds were fired on the village, numerous secondary explosions again resulted. After several hours of bombardment, friendly elements swept and secured An My and found 123 Viet Cong killed. Prisoner reports later confirmed the import of the encounter. The 273d Regiment was moving south when it met the 1st Infantry Division at An My; the ensuing battle rendered the 273d ineffective before it could reach its assigned objective and contribute to the *Tet* offensive.

The performance of the field artillery in III Corps Tactical Zone during *Tet* caused General Weyand to observe that the field artillery was instrumental in blunting or defeating many of the assaults in the zone: "Timely response, especially in the moments of fluid uncertainty during the initial phase of the attacks, and in spite of clearance handicaps, contributed to the successes of the infantry and armored units."

Numerous smaller but significant field artillery actions occurred throughout Vietnam during *Tet*. For example, the 25th Infantry Division was plagued by enemy bunkers near the highway between Cu Chi and Saigon. Fires from the bunkers prevented free movement between the two locations. Numerous attempts to reduce the bunkers with artillery, air strikes, and infantry assaults were unsuccessful. An 8-inch howitzer delivering assault fire finally eliminated the bunkers. Also noteworthy were the actions of units of the 54th Artillery Group which prevented the collapse of the Xuan Loc base camp. On 2 February Xuan Loc came under heavy attack. The quick and devastating fire of Battery C, 1st Battalion, 83d Artillery, saved the post. Battery C fired thirty-five 8-inch rounds and killed 80 of the attackers. During the period 1–18 February similar missions supported the defense of Xuan Loc. The 2d Battalion, 40th Artillery, the direct support battalion of the 199th Light Infantry Brigade, was one of the first artillery units to respond to enemy attacks in III Corps. An observer detected the enemy launching rockets on II Field Force headquarters and shifted fire onto the launching sites. Several of the firing points were neutralized before the enemy had fired all his rounds. The enemy suffered more than 50 killed.

In IV Corps Tactical Zone the enemy offensive included attacks against My Tho and Vinh Long. On 31 January 1968, the Mobile Riverine Force was placed under operational control of the senior adviser in IV Corps. The riverine force initially was moved to the vicinity of My Tho, and two of its battalions conducted a three-day operation north of the My Tho River in response to a multibattalion Viet Cong attack on the provincial capital. Then, on 4 February, the riverine force moved to the provincial capital of Vinh Long and engaged three enemy battalions that were trying to seize the city. The 3d Battalion, 34th Artillery (105-mm., towed), was in direct support of the Mobile Riverine Brigade. One battery was equipped with airmobile firing platforms and two batteries were mounted on barges. The artillery battalion effectively delivered 8,158 rounds in support of the My Tho campaign. At one point a barge-mounted battery was required to make an airmobile deployment. The battery was provided a ¼-ton jeep and a ¾-ton trailer for a fire direction center. The barges were beached and the pickup was made directly from them. This type of movement opened possibilities for deeper penetration into the Mekong Delta.

Finally, in I Corps area on 12 February 1968, Battery C, 1st

Battalion, 40th Artillery (105-mm.), while in support of a South Vietnamese unit, became the first U.S. Army artillery unit to fire improved conventional munitions in combat. The target was 40–50 North Vietnamese troops in the open. The battery fired 54 rounds of the new ammunition, resulting in 14 enemy killed. The round was a controlled, fragmentation-type ammunition similar to the Air Force cluster bomb unit. FIRE CRACKER became the code word used when a forward observer wanted improved conventional munitions.

Khe Sanh

The 66-day battle of Khe Sanh, which began in January 1968, became a classic defensive operation for U.S. forces. It tested American concepts of defense and demonstrated that good fire support could effectively neutralize a superior force.

Khe Sanh sits atop a plateau in the shadow of the Dang Tri Mountains and overlooks a tributary of the Quang Tri River. Surrounding it on all sides are hills from which the North Vietnamese could shell the base. If controlled by the Marines, however, the hills would form a ring of protection for the base and afford good vantage points for detecting enemy movement. American involvement at Khe Sanh had begun in 1962, when Special Forces elements established a Civilian Irregular Defense Group camp at the site that was later known as the Khe Sanh combat base. Its purpose was to counter enemy infiltration through the area and provide a base for surveillance and intelligence-gathering operations in the western part of northern I Corps. Marine units occupied the base in late 1966 and the Special Forces moved southwest to the village of Lang Vai.

Between late 1966 and late 1967, activity around the base fluctuated from heavy contact to none at all. Then in December 1967 a surge of enemy activity began. Reconnaissance teams reported large groups of North Vietnamese moving into the area. The movement in itself was not irregular, but now the forces were staying, not passing through. The enemy was building up men and equipment in preparation for a siege. The enemy initiated major offensive action around Khe Sanh early in January 1968, when he shifted his emphasis from reconnaissance and harassment to actual probes of friendly positions.

On the night of 2 January an outpost at the western end of the base reported six unidentified figures walking around outside the wire. When challenged, they made no reply and were taken under fire. Five of the six were killed. Later investigation disclosed that the dead included a North Vietnamese regimental commander and

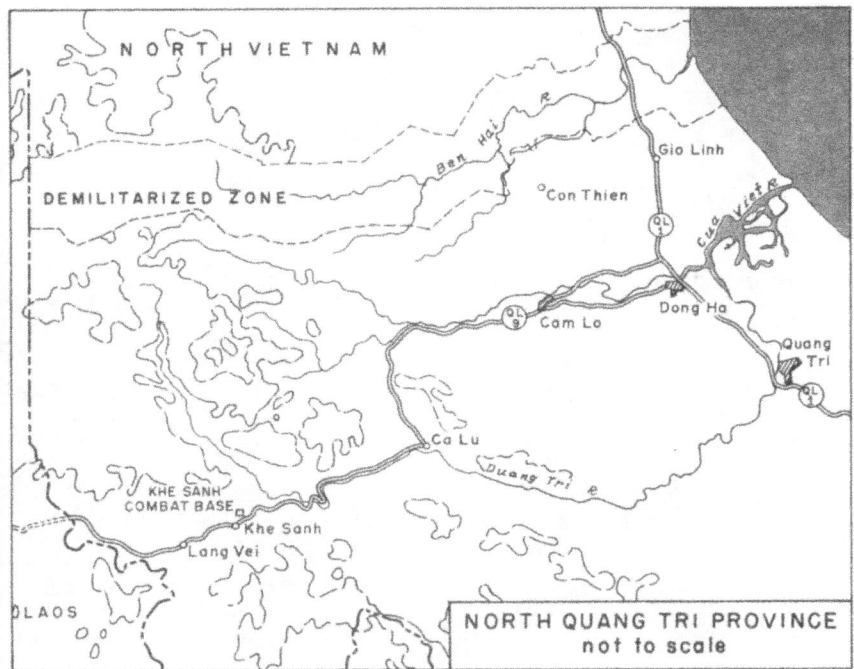

MAP 14

his operations and communications officers. The commitment of these key men to such a dangerous reconnaissance mission was a clear indication that something big was about to happen. *(Maps 14 and 15)*

In the predawn of 21 January, the enemy began his anticipated move against Khe Sanh. Just after midnight rockets and artillery shells began impacting on Hill 861 to the northwest of the city. A full-scale ground attack followed, only to be repulsed after several hours of fighting. At 0530 another intense barrage of 82-mm. shells and 122-mm. rockets hit Khe Sanh. Damage was substantial—a major ammunition dump and a fuel storage area were destroyed. When news of the attack reached the United States, many questioned the feasibility of defending Khe Sanh. The base was isolated and, with Route 9 interdicted, would have to be resupplied by air. Fearing that Khe Sanh would become an American Dien Bien Phu, critics favored a pullout.

The problem, therefore, was not merely how to defend the base but whether the base should be defended at all. General Westmoreland and General Cushman, commander of III Marine Am-

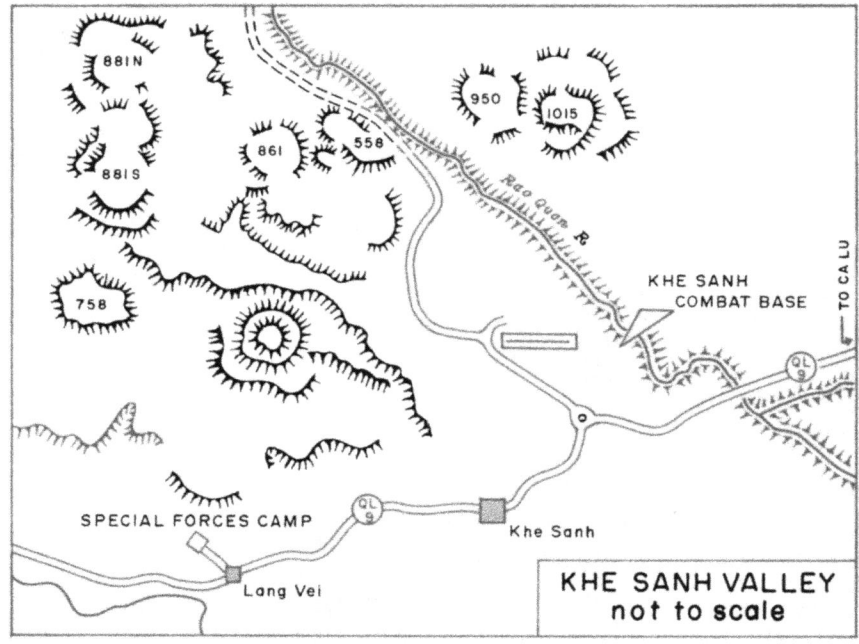

MAP 15

phibious Force, decided to defend Khe Sanh. The base and adjacent outposts commanded the plateau and the main avenue of approach into eastern Quang Tri Province. Although these installations did not stop infiltration, they blocked motorized supply from the west. Another advantage to holding the base was the possibility of engaging and destroying a heretofore elusive foe. At Khe Sanh, the enemy showed no desire to hit and run but rather chose to stand and fight. The marines could fix him in position around the base while air and artillery barrages closed in. Finally, two crack North Vietnamese divisions, which might otherwise have participated in attacks in other areas of South Vietnam, were tied down by one reinforced Marine regiment. The decision made, all that remained was to complete the buildup of men and materiel required to hold the base.

Air power and artillery played an important role at Khe Sanh and were given the highest priority. The Khe Sanh defenders had three batteries of 105-mm. howitzers, one battery of 4.2-inch mortars, and one battery of 155-mm. howitzers; all five batteries were Marine artillery. In addition, they were supported by four batteries of Army 175-mm. guns, one at the "Rockpile," north of the base, and three at Camp Carroll, to the east. These artillery pieces, 46 in all, were supplemented by 90-mm. tank guns, 106-mm. recoilless rifles, and tactical air support. The fire support co-ordination center, the 1st Battalion, 13th Marines (Artillery), located at Khe Sanh, controlled all supporting arms fire. Once the fighting began, the battalion commander, Lieutenant Colonel Lownds, said that the side which kept its artillery intact would win the battle. Only three American artillery pieces were destroyed during the entire siege.

Since the enemy maneuvered mainly under cover of darkness, the Marine and Army batteries were most active during these hours. Preplanned artillery fires included combined time-on-target fires from nine batteries, separate battalion time-on-target missions, battery multiple-volley individual missions, and battery harassment and interdiction missions. Fire support co-ordination progressed to the point that artillery was seldom check fired while tactical aircraft were operating in the area. Throughout the battle 158,981 rounds of various calibers of artillery were directed against enemy locations around the base.

During the siege, air-delivered fire support reached unprecedented levels. A daily average of 45 B-52 sorties and 300 tactical air sorties struck targets near the base. Eighteen hundred tons of ordnance a day laid waste wide swaths of jungle terrain and caused hundreds of secondary explosions. In seventy days of air operation, 96,000 tons of bombs, nearly twice what the Army Air Corps delivered in the Pacific during 1942 and 1943, pulverized the battle area.

In addition to volume, reaction time was a key factor. Relatively easy clearance procedures meant immediate response—unless friendly aircraft were in the target area—regardless of the weather. Artillery rounds were usually on the target area within forty seconds after the call for fire. This instant artillery impaired enemy movements within the tactical area of responsibility and helped to break up numerous attacks.

Protective fires were carefully planned in advance. The fires of the artillery batteries planned by the fire support co-ordination center prevented the enemy assault forces from reaching the perimeter wire. Because the North Vietnamese usually attacked with their battalions in column, the center also planned fires to isolate the assault elements from the reserves. When the enemy launched his attack, the center placed a three-sided artillery box around the lead enemy battalion. Three batteries of the 1st Battalion, 13th Marines, executed this mission. The fourth battery then closed the remaining side, which faced the friendly positions, with a barrage that

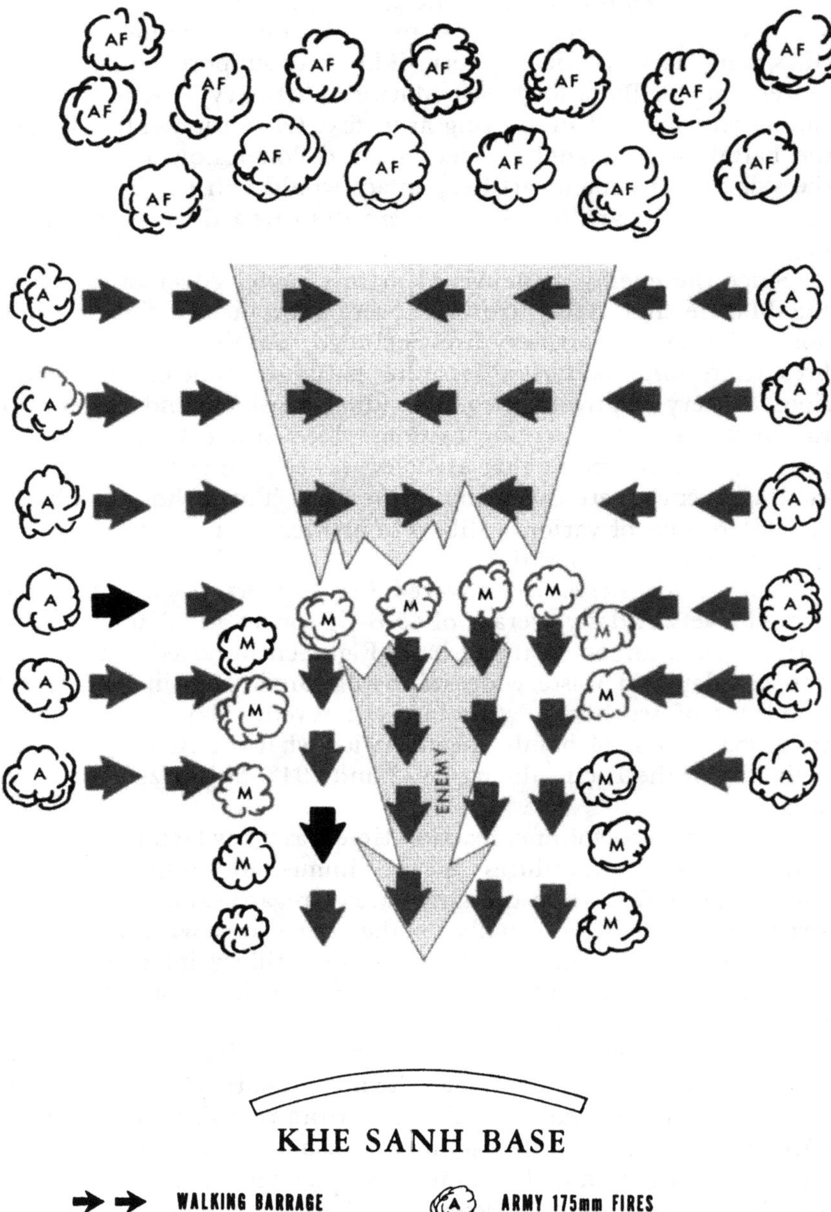

152 FIELD ARTILLERY

KHE SANH BASE

 WALKING BARRAGE
 ARMY 175mm FIRES
 MARINE 105mm FIRES
 AIR FORCE B-52 & TAC AIR STRIKES

Diagram 8. Artillery box.

rolled from one end of the box to the other much like a piston within a cylinder. The enemy force in the box could neither escape nor avoid the rolling barrage. Those North Vietnamese who spilled out of the open end of the box came under the final protective fires of the marines along the perimeter. At the same time, the fire support co-ordination center placed a secondary box around the North Vietnamese backup units. The four U.S. Army 175-mm. batteries were responsible for two sides, which were about 500 meters outside the primary box. On order, the gunners rolled their barrage in toward the sides of the primary box and back out again. The third side was sealed by continuous flights of aircraft under the control of radar. Whenever B-52's were available or could be diverted in time, arc light strikes saturated the approach routes to the battle area.

The manner in which the center co-ordinated its air and artillery support was another critical element in the defense of Khe Sanh. The mini arc light, devised by the assistant fire support co-ordinator, was used against area targets. The mini arc light was similar to a B-52 strike but could be organized and employed more rapidly. When intelligence reports indicated that enemy units were in a certain region, the fire support co-ordination center plotted a 500- by 1,000-meter block in the suspected area or across a likely route of march. Then the center called two Intruder tactical aircraft, each armed with twenty-eight 500-pound bombs, for a radar bomb run. Meanwhile the batteries at Khe Sanh, Camp Carroll, and the Rockpile were alerted for a fire mission. Thirty seconds before the bombs were dropped, the 175-mm. batteries, concentrating their fires on one-half of the block, salvoed the first of approximately 60 rounds. When the aircraft rippled their loads down the middle of the block, the Marine artillery batteries opened up on the second half with about 200 155-mm., 105-mm., and 4.2-inch rounds. The trajectory and flight times of all ordnance were computed so that the bombs and initial artillery rounds hit at the same instant. The saturation of the target area all but insured that any enemy soldier caught in the zone during the bombardment would be a casualty.

The micro arc light, developed and executed in the manner of the mini arc, used less ordnance and covered a 500- by 500-meter target block. The advantage of the micro arc light was that it could be in effect within ten minutes whereas the mini arc light required roughly 45 minutes. On an average night the fire support co-ordination center executed three to four mini arc lights and six to eight micro arc lights.

Artillery also functioned extensively in the direct fire role against targets of opportunity. The three Marine 105-mm. howitzers on Hill 881S demonstrated the effectiveness of this technique. An alert machine gunner on the hill spotted a twenty-man column of North Vietnamese slowly climbing Hill 758, due south of 881S. They were carrying what appeared to be several mortar tubes. The marines from a range of 1,200 meters managed to hit several of the enemy. Instead of scattering, the remaining soldiers clustered around their fallen comrades. The Marine gunners pushed aside their parapet, depressed the tube for a downhill shot, and slammed a dozen rounds into the midst of the tightly packed enemy group. All 20 were killed.

While supporting air and artillery whittled away the strength of the enemy, the defensive posture of the Khe Sanh combat base grew more formidable. A full-scale ground attack would be costly. However, the North Vietnamese forces remained determined and, during the last ten days in February, launched several attacks. The most significant attack occurred 29 February–1 March.

Early in the evening of 29 February, intelligence showed the enemy moving toward the eastern perimeter of the camp. The fire support co-ordination center called for saturation of the enemy route of march. Massed artillery, tactical air, and mini and micro arc lights were targeted in blocks to the east, southeast, and south. B–52 strikes added to the carnage in the area. The enemy attempted three ground assaults during the night at 2130, 2330, and 0315. All were stopped short of the perimeter by intense ground fire and air and artillery barrages. Later in the morning of 1 March, 78 enemy bodies were found, some still in their assault trenches, peppered with holes from the artillery airbursts. Although the exact number of enemy killed was never accurately determined, Montagnard tribesmen inhabiting the surrounding hill reported finding 200–500 bodies at a time stacked in rows along the trails and woods leading to the base. The North Vietnamese forces apparently had been caught while on the march and had been mangled by air raids and piston-like artillery concentrations.

Beginning in mid-March, U.S. intelligence personnel noted an exodus of major North Vietnamese units from the battle area. Most of one division pulled back into Laos. As the enemy settled into a wait-and-see strategy, heavy incoming fires and limited ground probes nevertheless continued to plague the marines. But this waiting game proved disastrous because clear skies dominated the area for all but five days in March and the air strikes were stepped up considerably. The observers had unrestricted visibility and were able to ferret out artillery positions and bunker complexes. The clear skies and accurate supporting fires formed a potent combination, and the number of confirmed enemy dead recorded in March increased approximately 80 percent over the number recorded in February.

On 31 March, the 1st Cavalry Division took control of the 26th Marine Regiment, signalling the start of PEGASUS, a fifteen-day air assault operation that ended the battle of Khe Sanh. The 1st Cavalry Division, along with the 1st Marine Regiment and the South Vietnamese 3d Airborne Task Force, began a push from Ca Lu, located east of Khe Sanh, to reopen Route 9 and relieve the pressure on Khe Sanh. The siege, in effect, was over.

The basic plan of Operation PEGASUS called for the 1st Marine Regiment, with two battalions, to attack west toward Khe Sanh while the 1st Cavalry Division air assaulted onto the high ground on either side of Route 9 and moved constantly west toward the base. On D plus 1 and D plus 2, all elements would continue to attack west toward Khe Sanh. Then on the following day the 2d Brigade of the 1st Cavalry Division would land three battalions southeast of Khe Sanh and attack northwest. The 26th Marine Regiment, holding Khe Sanh, would attack south to secure Hill 471. The linkup was planned for the end of the seventh day.

Fire support involved a multitude of units, requiring detailed planning and co-ordination for the two phases of the operation—reconnaissance and attack. The objective of the reconnaissance phase was the destruction of the enemy antiaircraft resources between Ca Lu and Khe Sanh and the selection of landing zones for use by the advancing airmobile assault force. The 1st Squadron, 9th Air Cavalry, assumed this mission and was supported by an abundance of air and artillery. Additional artillery was moved into the area during the reconnaissance phase and automatically came under the control of a forward division artillery fire direction center located at Landing Zone STUD and manned by personnel of the 1st Battalion, 30th Artillery. The additional artillery included one Marine 4.2-inch mortar battery at Ca Lu and two 105-mm. batteries (one Marine and one Army) at the Rockpile. On 25 March an 8-inch battery and a 105-mm. battery moved from Quang Tri to Ca Lu and STUD, respectively. This move brought the total to 15 batteries available to support the 1st Squadron, 9th Air Cavalry, in its reconnaissance. All batteries in the area began answering calls for fire from the 1st Squadron, 9th Cavalry, on D minus 6 and commenced attacking planned targets that night. Prior co-ordination between the 3d Marine Division; the 108th Artillery Group; and the 1st Battalion, 13th Marines (Artillery), insured that all available target information would be in the hands of the forward fire direction center and that lateral communication would be established. Throughout this phase, air and artillery fire destroyed enemy automatic weapons, mortars, and troop positions. The attack phase consisted of the preparation of landing zones, suppression of enemy fires, and on-call support of committed ground forces. For this phase, ten 105-mm. howitzer batteries, four 155-mm. howitzer batteries, one 8-inch howitzer battery, and one 4.2-inch mortar battery joined the already overwhelming artillery force. Each cavalry battalion drew support from the battery with which it was habitually associated. Each cavalry brigade had reinforcing fire from a medium battery, and the 1st Marine Regiment could count on support from two 105-mm. batteries, one 155-mm. battery, and one 4.2-inch battery. The additional heavy battery with the mission of general support of the 1st Air Cavalry Division moved from Camp Evans to Landing Zone STUD. Thirty-one batteries supported the relief of Khe Sanh—the largest array of artillery ever to support a single operation in Vietnam to that time.

Counterbattery fire contributed significantly to the success of Operation PEGASUS. For some time, North Vietnamese forces had been able to shell Khe Sanh at will with 152-mm. and 130-mm. artillery plus rockets and mortars positioned to the southwest and northwest of the base. When the 1st Cavalry Division Artillery came within range of the enemy guns, rapid and massive counterbattery fires achieved superiority. From that point enemy artillery ceased to be a serious deterrent to maneuver.

On 6 April at 1350, six days after Operation PEGASUS had begun, the initial relief of Khe Sanh took place. A lead company of the South Vietnamese 3d Airborne Task Force airlifted into Khe Sanh and linked up with the South Vietnamese 37th Rangers. Two days later the 2d Battalion, 7th Cavalry, had completed its sweep along Route 9 and the official relief took place. The command post of the 3d Brigade, 1st Cavalry, airlifted to the base at 0800 and became its new landlord. By the evening of 8 April, all elements of the PEGASUS task force were in position on the Khe Sanh plateau. The North Vietnamese 304th Division faced entrapment and destruction as a great vise closed about the enemy daily. American and South Vietnamese units soon uncovered grisly evidence of how badly the North Vietnamese had been beaten. They found hundreds of North Vietnamese bodies in shallow graves and hundreds more that lay where they had fallen. The allies destroyed or captured 557 individual weapons, 207 crew-served weapons, and two antiaircraft pieces. In addition, they confiscated 17 vehicles ranging from PT76 tanks to motor scooters, tons of ammunition and food, and numerous radios and items of individual equipment. The mountain of captured or abandoned enemy stores indicated either that PEGASUS had caught the enemy flatfooted or that the remnants of the enemy divisions had been unable to cart off their equipment and supplies.

On the morning of 14 April, PEGASUS officially ended. The operation was successful, Route 9 opened, the enemy routed, and the base itself relieved. The North Vietnamese lost 1,304 killed and 21 captured. The battle of Khe Sanh established that, with sufficient fire power, an encircled position could be successfully held and the enemy devastated.

A Shau

With the exception of the defense of Khe Sanh, post-*Tet* operations were similar to past counterguerrilla actions. The enemy, badly shaken, again eluded massed allied forces. It was necessary to hunt him in search and destroy operations conducted over large land areas. The two largest of such operations took place in the III Corps area and were known as QUYET TONG (Resolve To Win) and TOAN THANG (Complete Victory). Both took place in and around Saigon and were aimed at destroying enemy forces that had participated in the *Tet* attacks and were hiding in the area. Operation TOAN THANG involved 42 U.S. and 37 Vietnamese maneuver battalions and was the largest operation of the Vietnamese war. Artillery support was provided by 81 batteries of U.S. artillery and all Vietnamese artillery in the area.

Though not the largest, perhaps the most significant operation of the period immediately following *Tet* was DELAWARE–LAM SON 216. This operation, in April 1968, took friendly forces into the A Shau Valley, which had been controlled by the enemy since 1966. The operation, like PEGASUS, was preceded by intelligence acquisition by the 9th Cavalry. Antiaircraft weapons were pinpointed and destroyed by artillery, tactical air, and B–52 strikes. Two battalions of the 3d Brigade air assaulted into the northern portion of the A Shau Valley on 19 April. Hampered by extremely bad weather in the objective area, the brigade did not close until 23 April. On 24 and 25 April the 1st Brigade was deployed in the central portion of the valley. On 29 April, one battalion of the South Vietnamese 3d Regiment was airlifted into the southern part of the valley and, by the end of the month, most elements of the regiment were operating in the south central portion.

Artillery support for Operation DELAWARE–LAM SON 216 was provided by two organic battalions of the 1st Cavalry Division Artillery—the 2d Battalion, 19th Artillery, and the 1st Battalion, 21st Artillery. In addition, two batteries of the attached 1st Bat-

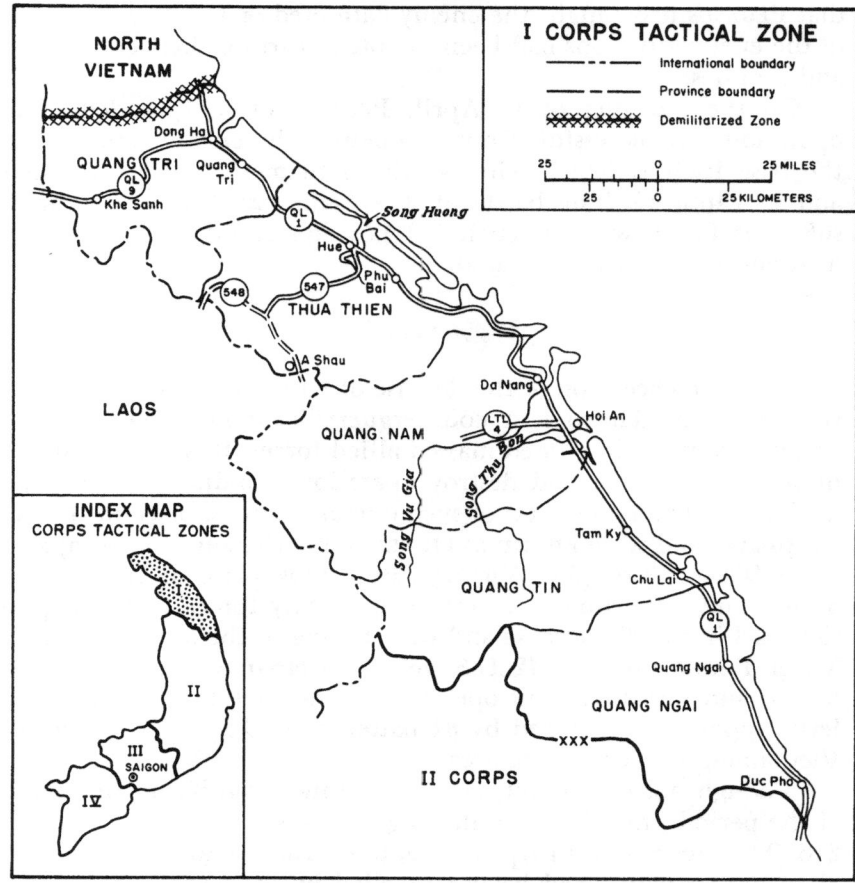

MAP 16

talion, 30th Artillery (155, towed), reinforced the two direct support battalions, and the 2d Battalion, 20th Artillery (Aerial Field Artillery), were in general support. Heavy artillery was provided by six 175-mm. guns of the 1st Battalion, 83d Artillery, and 8th Battalion, 4th Artillery. One battery of the 1st Battalion, 21st Artillery, moved into the valley on 19 April 1968. Plans called for moving another battery; however, hazardous flying conditions prevented the move. No additional artillery was moved into the valley until 23 April. By 29 April, however, all the supporting artillery was in position. (*Map 16*)

Movement into the A Shau Valley was much slower than planned because of enemy antiaircraft fire. The enemy air defense was composed of relatively sophisticated weapons and fire distribution means, served by well-trained and disciplined crews, and an effective communication system. Despite attacks by tactical aircraft and artillery, the air defense weapons took a heavy toll of U.S. aircraft on the first day of the operation.

The entire operation by the 1st Cavalry Division was conducted by air. Positioning and supporting the artillery were hampered not only by enemy antiaircraft fires but also by difficult weather conditions. The operation was successful only because of feats of airmanship performed under instrument flight rule conditions by aviators of the 11th Aviation Group, the 9th Cavalry Squadron, and the 2d Battalion, 20th Artillery. Despite their efforts, however, careful management of ammunition and supplies by all supporting artillery units was necessary. On one occasion, water to swab the tubes of the 155-mm. howitzers was even in short supply.

The success of Operation DELAWARE can be measured principally by the amount of supplies and equipment captured, not by the number of enemy killed:

Type	Total	
Small arms	2,342	
Machine guns	36	
Antiaircraft guns	13	
Recoilless rifles	10	
Mortars	2	
Rocket launchers	11	
Flame throwers	31	
Explosives	2,182	pounds
Plastic caps	5,994	
Small arms ammunition	134,757	rounds
Recoilless rifle ammunition	796	rounds
Assorted ammunition	75,653	rounds
Mines	35	
Grenades	2,486	
Bulldozers	2	
Wheeled vehicles	75	
Radios	6	
Tracked vehicles	3	
Road stores	71,805	pounds

Later in the year, another operation was conducted into the A Shau Valley. Intelligence indicated that the enemy had rebuilt his defenses in the valley following the withdrawal of the 1st Air Cavalry Division. The enemy was actively clearing and improving access to and along Route 548 while moving large amounts of supplies and replacements in Thua Thien Province and southern

I Corps Tactical Zone. Accordingly the 101st Airborne Division was directed to conduct a follow-up operation into the valley and, during the period 19–26 July 1968, built bases to support the operation. Before D-day, eight batteries of field artillery were moved into the bases. Each 105-mm. battery stockpiled 3,000 rounds of ammunition; each 155-mm. battery, 2,000 rounds. Two 175-mm. batteries were within supporting range.

The amounts and types of preparatory fires were impressive. Fourteen B–52 strikes were directed against the hard targets. Eleven of the strikes were within twenty-four hours of H-hour, the last at 0850 on D-day. Following the strikes, a tactical preparation of four flights dropped Daisy Cutter bombs to neutralize any enemy in the landing zones. When the last aircraft cleared the landing zones, the artillery preparation began. Each 105-mm. battery fired 1,000 rounds, each 155-mm. battery fired 600 rounds, and each 175-mm. battery fired 200 rounds on two landing zones. Approximately 8,000 rounds of artillery were fired before H-hour by the ten batteries supporting the operation.

Enemy resistance was light on one landing zone and moderate to heavy on the other. Four gunships were damaged or destroyed during the initial phase of the operation, but no troop-carrying ships were lost.

By 6 August, all elements of the 101st and the Vietnamese task force had been moved into the A Shau Valley and were conducting reconnaissance-in-force (RIF) operations in their assigned areas, with very light contact. Withdrawal of the forces began on 17 August 1968 and was completed on 19 August. Results of the operation were 181 enemy killed and 4 captured, 45 individual weapons and 13 crew-served weapons seized, and the following miscellaneous enemy equipment captured or destroyed:

Equipment	*Quantity*
2-ton trucks destroyed	7
Rice captured	12 tons
122-mm. rockets	11
Crew-served weapon ammunition	1,142 rounds
12.7-mm. heavy machine gun ammunition	18 cases
Small-arms ammunition	32 cases
Mines	54
Medicine	51 pounds
Medical kits	4
Communication wire	11 kilometers
Switchboard	1
Field telephones	2
Huts destroyed	215

Actions at Fire Bases and Lessons Learned

Fire bases throughout Vietnam sustained numerous attacks in this period of maximum U.S. troop commitment. The fire base concept surpassed the most optimistic expectations. Occasionally the enemy was able to penetrate the defenses and take a heavy toll of personnel and equipment, but he never was able to take an American fire base. At the same time, lessons learned in countering enemy attacks during this period suggested further refinements of procedures for establishing and defending a fire base. For instance, actions at Fire Support Bases MAURY I and PIKE VI provided valuable insights on the proper positioning of artillery when several batteries occupied the same fire base.

Batteries B and C (105-mm.), 7th Battalion, 11th Artillery, and Battery A (155-mm.), 3d Battalion, 13th Artillery, were occupying MAURY I, a 25th Infantry Division Artillery fire base. Although the base was located in what was probably the best available area, bamboo thickets and wood lines surrounded the clearing. The three field artillery batteries had been arranged within the perimeter in a triangle, with one battery at each point. The 155-mm. battery was to the west and the 105-mm. batteries to the northeast and southeast.

On the night of 9 May, MAURY I came under heavy attack. (*Map 17*) The enemy began his attack at 0200 with an intense mortar and RPG (Russian-made antitank grenade) barrage. He launched a diversionary attack against the northeastern and southwestern portions of the perimeter followed by the main attack directed against the western portion of the triangle, where the 155-mm. battery was located less than 200 meters from the tree line.

The 155-mm. battery, between the two 105-mm. batteries and the attacking enemy, took the brunt of the attack. The RPG fire had a devastating effect on the 155-mm. howitzers. At 0330 an attempt was made to move two 105-mm. howitzers to the southwestern side of the perimeter to aid the medium battery. By this time, only one of the 155-mm. howitzers was serviceable; of the others, three had been completely destroyed, as had two M548 ammunition trucks. Flareships and gunships arrived by 0330 and Air Force fighter aircraft by 0500. At 0530 a relief element of the 4th Battalion, 23d Infantry (Mechanized), arrived and battered its way into the beleaguered base. The attack was finally repulsed.

All Beehive ammunition had been expended but, because of the speed and accuracy of the assault against the medium battery, less than 10 rounds of 155-mm. ammunition had been fired before

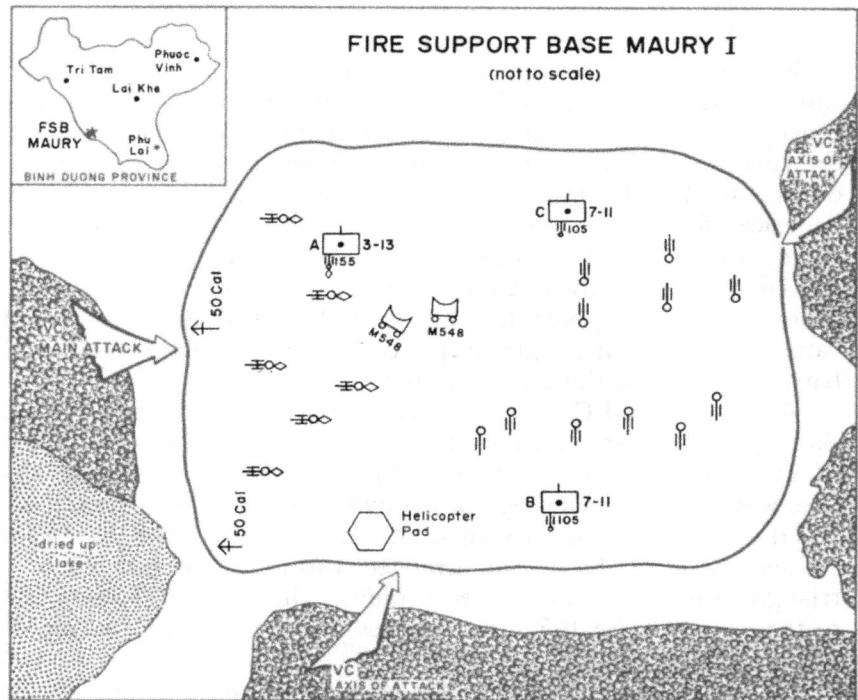

MAP 17

the destruction of the howitzers. Eighteen Viet Cong were confirmed dead, and friendly losses numbered 10 killed and 66 wounded. Four men died of wounds received in battle. These, along with 7 others killed and 39 wounded, were artillerymen. Five M109 howitzers were destroyed; one serviceable howitzer was later pieced together from two damaged howitzers. Two M548 trucks were destroyed, and one 5-ton truck was severely damaged. Fourteen M16 rifles were either lost or destroyed.

The defenders had been aggressive and determined in withstanding a heavy enemy attack. Despite their success, as with any actions, there were lessons to be learned. An analysis of the battle suggested techniques that might reduce American losses and increase enemy casualties in a similar situation. No bulldozer had been available to construct berms around the howitzers; ammunition was protected on the sides only; the medium battery situated at the point of the triangle should have been more centrally located within the perimeter and away from a tree line; and poor fields of fire reduced the effectiveness of the Beehive rounds. Positions that would have allowed maximum use of the Beehive round should have been chosen early in the occupation of the fire support base.

On the morning of 11 May, Fire Support Base PIKE VI was occupied by Battery B, 6th Battalion, 77th Artillery (105-mm.); Battery A, 1st Battalion, 8th Artillery (105-mm.); and Battery C, 3d Battalion, 13th Artillery (155-mm., self-propelled). (*Map 18*) The commander set up the base using the valuable experience gained from the attack on MAURY I. The batteries entered the fire support base early in the afternoon, and a bulldozer began constructing berms for the 155-mm. howitzers immediately. By nightfall only the turrets of the howitzers were exposed. The 105-mm. batteries had been carefully positioned to allow maximum use of Beehive, and two 105-mm. howitzers, one from each battery, had been placed at strategic points along the perimeter some distance from the rest of the battery positions. Although the terrain was much the same as that at MAURY I, the nearby wood lines were covered by two attached Dusters. The light batteries enjoyed excellent fields of fire. The medium battery was positioned between the two light batteries and thus was able to support equally well in all directions.

At 0130 on 12 May 1968 the enemy attacked with a mortar barrage of approximately 400 rounds, all falling within 30–60 minutes. Once again, the enemy began a diversionary attack from the south. The Duster position on the southern tip of the base took 60–70 Viet Cong under fire with its M60 machine gun and 40-mm cannon. The crew managed to fire only 12 rounds of 40-mm. ammunition, however, before the Duster was silenced by an RPG round. Leaving 16 enemy bodies in their wake, the crew fell back to a 105-mm. howitzer pit directly to their rear. The enemy managed to reach the Duster, but small arms and a few well-placed Beehive rounds from the 105-mm. turned him back.

As the main attack was starting from the west, artillery shells from adjacent units were already impacting around the perimeter. Support was called for and received from 155-mm. howitzers of Battery B, 3d Battalion, 13th Artillery, near Saigon. The entire western approach was covered by a 105-mm. battery which fired round after round of Beehive and time rounds, all with a very short fuze setting, into the attacking enemy. The defense was entirely successful and the attack ended just two and one-half hours after it began. Mop-up operations in daylight produced a body count of 110. Friendly force losses amounted to 5 killed and 30 wounded, of which 1 killed and 5 wounded were artillerymen. No equipment was lost. The damaged Duster was easily repaired, and two vehicles sustained minor damage.

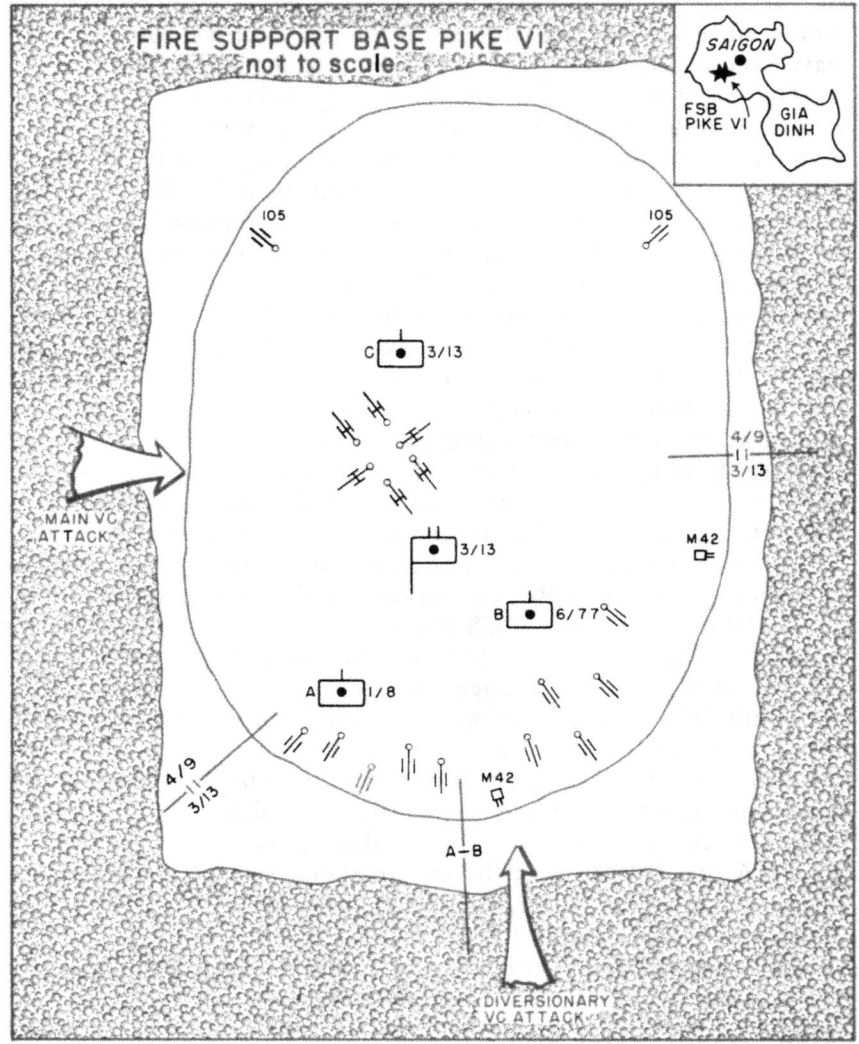

MAP 18

Actions MAURY I and PIKE VI offered an excellent example of how techniques could be improved by observing lessons learned. The Killer Junior technique, for instance, was developed during this period and used profitably in defense of fire bases. The technique was expanded to include projectiles of improved conventional munitions as well as high explosive projectiles. Killer Junior was employed in the defense of PIKE VI as well as on numerous later occasions. The following are a few instances when the technique proved particularly effective:

1. On 13 September 1968, Battery C, 2d Battalion, 13th Artillery, expended 1,305 rounds in defense of Fire Support Base BUELL and killed 76 enemy.

2. On 25 September 1968, a platoon of Battery C, 6th Battalion, 15th Artillery, expended 288 rounds in defense of Katum and killed 47 enemy.

3. On 25 September 1968, a platoon of Battery B, 6th Battalion, 15th Artillery, expended 220 rounds in defense of a position at Thien Ngon and killed 142 enemy.

The 25th Infantry Division conducted an appraisal of its fire support bases in late 1968, after many of the bases in the Tay Ninh area had been attacked, and made two major recommendations. First, commanders were to insure that insofar as possible fire bases be constructed in a circle and small enough for one rifle company to defend. Both these recommendations were in accord with what were already considered correct procedures. Apparently there were sufficient deviations from correct practice to warrant further emphasis. The circular shape permitted equal fire power in all directions and allowed for faster emplacement. The reduction in construction time became essential because the enemy began to deviate from his normal two- or three-day reconnaissance and to attack bases on the first or second night after the base was occupied. The smaller size of the bases also freed more companies for night ambushes and mobile patrols and reduced the number of enemy shells that landed in the area. These modifications proved highly successful in a series of engagements fought along the Cambodian border in early 1969. Each base was manned by one rifle company and one howitzer platoon. The apparent vulnerability of these small positions was tempting, and the enemy seized the opportunity to try to destroy them. But his forces ran into a storm of carefully preplanned fire power, which not only broke the assault but also shifted to attack the enemy and his supporting weapons as he retreated.

The second major recommendation was that the activities of fire bases be viewed as offensive operations. The base was considered the anvil and the maneuver force the hammer. Fire support or "offensive fires" were planned for the entire battle area. Enemy troops, attack positions, supporting weapon positions, and command centers were struck simultaneously, and then when activity declined, the routes of withdrawal and likely assembly areas were attacked. This system of deep, simultaneous, and continuous fires was employed at Fire Support Base CROOK on the night of 5–6 June and served to test the validity of the fire support base evaluation.

Perhaps the best example of the damage that could be inflicted on the enemy by the determined defenders of a well established fire support base occurred in late 1968 during Operation FISH HOOK. The operation, along the Cambodian border, was in an area astride a primary infiltration route running through War Zone C into the Saigon complex. Two fire support bases, RITA and DOT, and one night defensive position were established to obstruct and interdict enemy movement south from Cambodia. They were so located that each fire support base could mutually support the other with artillery fire and both could support the infantry position.

Headquarters and Battery B of the 1st Battalion, 5th Artillery (105-mm., towed), commanded by Lieutenant Colonel Charles C. Rogers, and Battery C, 8th Battalion, 6th Artillery (155-mm., self-propelled), were located at Fire Support Base RITA. This base, with two batteries and the artillery tactical operations center (TOC), was the key position. The base was also occupied by one cavalry squadron and one infantry company. Battery D, 1st Battalion, 5th Artillery, was at Fire Support Base DOT. During the period 25–30 October, there were enemy mortar and ground attacks on all three bases. Artillery support called in on all these attacks resulted in a Viet Cong body count of 105.

On 1 November 1968 at 0330, the west-northwest perimeter of Fire Support Base RITA was attacked by a North Vietnamese Army force of an estimated 800 men. (*See Map 13.*) The attack immediately followed a "mad minute" reconnaissance by fire by the friendly forces. The enemy, initially surprising the friendly forces with the intensity of his attack, penetrated the defensive perimeter and was inside the position of the 155-mm. howitzer battery. A counterattack was mounted and the bunkers were retaken. A second attack and penetration was made at 0515 by the enemy against the southwest perimeter. Again, the enemy was beaten back by an aggressive counterattack and the defensive positions were re-established. When the enemy attempted to regain the initiative by attacking the northern perimeter with a third charge, the 105-mm. howitzers were swung to the north and lethal barrages were fired into the massed assaulting enemy.

During the battle, the U.S. forces suffered 12 men killed and wounded. The enemy body count could not be obtained, but it was estimated that at least 200 bodies lay in the woods around the fire support base. The ferocious intensity of the battle, which raged from 0330 until 0645, with frequent concentrations of mortars impacting the fire support base until 0800, was attested to by the massive quantity of ammunition expended by friendly forces. The field artillery fired 1,300 rounds in direct fire and 800 rounds in indirect fire. In addition, the defense was supported by air strikes and innumerable strikes by helicopter gunships and fire teams from the 1st Infantry Division. Colonel Rogers directed the defense of the base with such heroism as to be awarded the Medal of Honor.

Peak Strength and Beginning of Redeployment

On 4 May the enemy launched another wave of nationwide attacks against 109 cities and military installations, including 21 airfields. These attacks lacked the intensity and co-ordination of the *Tet* offensive. Bien Hoa Air Base was the hardest hit installation; strong attacks occurred in Binh Duong and Hou Nghia Provinces. The enemy also tried to seize the Saigon-Bien Hoa highway bridge near Saigon. Heavy fighting continued near Dong Ha in northern I Corps on 6 May, and moderate to heavy fighting persisted around Saigon. Because of the attacks on Saigon, another task force was formed to control U.S. units in the Capital Military District. The task force was commanded by Major General John H. Hay, Jr., deputy commander of II Field Force, Vietnam.

The buildup of U.S. forces continued through most of 1968. Between February and July, four additional artillery battalions arrived. Two were 155-mm. towed battalions, which were assigned to the 41st Artillery Group and the 54th Artillery Group. One was a 105-mm. towed battalion which was assigned to the 108th Artillery Group. The fourth was a 155-mm. towed and 8-inch self-propelled battalion which was assigned to the Americal Divison as its general support battalion. During July the 1st Brigade of the 5th Mechanized Division arrived with its 155-mm. self-propelled direct support battalion. The 1st Brigade was the last major U.S. Army maneuver unit to be deployed to Vietnam.

Later in the year, two additional artillery battalions arrived together with more support units and infantry battalions. These were National Guard units, the first to be deployed to Vietnam. The two artillery battalions were the 3d Battalion, 197th Artillery, from New Hampshire, and the 2d Battalion, 138th Artillery, from Kentucky. They were assigned to the 23d Artillery Group and the Provisional Corps, Vietnam, respectively. The 4th Battalion, 77th Artillery (Aerial Rocket Artillery), arrived in December 1968 and was assigned to the 101st Airborne Division (Airmobile). With its arrival, the field artillery was at its maximum strength of the war.

During the latter part of 1968, some major troop realignments took place. In September the 1st Brigade, 101st Airborne Division, moved to I Corps to rejoin the rest of the division, and the 3d Brigade, 82d Airborne Division, moved to III Corps from I Corps. In October, over the objections of the Commanding General, XXIV Corps, and Commanding General, III Marine Amphibious Force, the 1st Cavalry Division began the move from I Corps to III Corps. The move was completed in November 1968 and the division began to operate in III and IV Corps areas. With these operations the 1st Cavalry added another first to its list, that of being the first division-size unit to operate in all four corps tactical zones.

On 8 June 1969, President Richard M. Nixon announced plans for returning 25,000 U.S. troops from Vietnam. One month later, a C–141 Starlifter jet left Bien Hoa Air Base with members of the 3d Battalion, 60th Infantry. On 12 June the 9th Infantry Division received notification of its selection as the first major U.S. Army unit to leave the Republic of Vietnam. The first field artillery unit to redeploy was the 3d Battalion, 34th Artillery, which left Vietnam on 26 July 1969. It was followed in mid-August by the 1st Battalion, 11th Artillery; 1st Battalion, 84th Artillery; and the 9th Infantry Division Artillery. Since the 3d Brigade, 9th Division, was remaining in Vietnam, the 2d Battalion, 4th Artillery, also remained as its direct support battalion. The next redeployment of artillery units took place in September and October, when the 3d Battalion, 197th Artillery, and the 2d Battalion, 138th Artillery, the two National Guard units, were returned to the United States. The 2d Battalion, 12th Artillery, and 1st Battalion, 39th Artillery, were activated in Vietnam as replacements.

The enemy *Tet* offensive and the allied counteroffensive propelled the artillery toward increased sophistication. During the period, the artillery was exposed to essentially three types of major operations, each with its own peculiar demands. Because of the proximity of friendly forces and civilians, solving clearance problems was crucial in Hue and Saigon. The defense and relief of Khe Sanh resembled a conventional situation with requirements for large volumes of supporting fires concentrated in a relatively small area. Operations into A Shau were highlighted by movement and supply by air and by support of dispersed ground forces. The period thus offers an interesting study of the actions taken by field artillerymen to optimize the effectiveness of supporting fires in all situations.

Artillery Organizations

Various organizations were adopted for the field artillery in Vietnam during this period to meet both the peculiarities of certain short-term operational requirements and long-term needs. Artillery commanders at all levels were flexible and innovative in organizing their subordinate units to provide the best possible support.

At the start of the *Tet* offensive 34 U.S. Army artillery battalions were in Vietnam. They were organized for the most part to provide dedicated support to divisions or separate brigades or to provide area coverage. *(Chart 2)* Units in I and II Field Force Artilleries served primarily in the latter role. I Field Force Artillery, with two artillery groups—the 41st and the 52d—and two separate battalions, provided force artillery in the II Corps areas. II Field Force Artillery, with two groups—the 23d and 54th—provided force artillery for both III and IV corps areas. The 108th Artillery Group was not assigned to either field force. Before *Tet* it had been placed under the operational control of III Marine Amphibious Force to provide artillery support in the I Corps area. The group was reinforced with the 1st Battalion, 83d Artillery (8-inch and 175-mm.), from the 54th Artillery Group.

This organization served U.S. maneuver forces and augmented South Vietnamese artillery when needed during *Tet;* however, some reorganization took place thereafter. During the first half of 1968, General Westmoreland created two new headquarters to coordinate the actions of U.S. forces in I Corps and in the Capital Military District. In March the Provisional Corps, Vietnam (later changed to XXIV Corps), succeeded Military Assistance Command Forward, which had been operational since 9 February; and in June, the Capital Military Assistance Command re-established the co-ordination which existed during the brief existence of Task Forces WARE and HAY. The command paralleled that of the newly established Military Governor of the Capital Military District, who controlled all South Vietnamese Army forces, National Police, Regional and Popular Forces, and General Reserve in the district. This reorganization prompted, in turn, a reorganization of artillery. *(Chart 3)* In I Corps a provisional Corps Artillery, Vietnam, was formed. No separate U.S. artillery command was formed to serve the needs of the Capital Military Assistance Command, but artillery units around Saigon could look to a single centralized clearance and co-ordination activity.

Despite the amount of artillery in Vietnam, the old cry that there were not enough artillery units to support the maneuver elements was heard again and again. The creation of a fourth firing battery in some artillery battalions, particularly with the division artillery direct support battalions, dramatized the requirements and response. There were generally two reasons for the extra battery. First, in a brigade, it was not uncommon to have a fourth maneuver element resulting from the use of the divisional armored cavalry squadron as a separate maneuver force. A fourth firing battery was essential to insure the timely delivery of fire to this fourth maneuver element. Second, the large areas of operations assigned to division were often difficult to cover by division or field force

CHART 2—FIELD ARTILLERY TASK ORGANIZATION, JANUARY 1968

I Field Force Artillery
  41st Artillery Gp
    7th Bn, 3d Arty (105, T)
    7th Bn, 15th Arty (8-in/175)
    2d Bn, 17th Arty (105-155, T)
    1st Bn, 30th Arty (155, T)
  52d Artillery Gp
    3d Bn, 6th Arty (105, SP)
    6th Bn, 14th Arty (8-in/175)
    5th Bn, 22d Arty (8-in/175)
    1st Bn, 92d Arty (155, T)
    5th Bn, 27th Arty (105, T)
    6th Bn, 32d Arty (8-in/175)
II Field Force Artillery
  23d Artillery Gp
    2d Bn, 11th Arty (155, T)
    2d Bn, 13th Arty (105, T)
    1st Bn, 27th Arty (155, SP)
    6th Bn, 27th Arty (8-in/175)
    2d Bn, 32d Arty (8-in/175)
  54th Artillery Gp
    7th Bn, 8th Arty (8-in/175)
    7th Bn, 9th Arty (105, T)
    2d Bn, 35th Arty (155, SP)
    1st Bn, 83d Arty (8-in/175)
    6th Bn, 77th Arty (105, T) [1]
    6th Bn, 15th Arty (105, T) [2]
  Military Assistance Command,
    Vietnam, Forward [3]
  108th Artillery Gp
    1st Bn, 40th Arty (105, SP)
    8th Bn, 4th Arty (8-in/175)
    2d Bn, 94th Arty (175)
1st Infantry Division Artillery
  1st Bn, 5th Arty (105, T)
  1st Bn, 7th Arty (105, T)
  2d Bn, 33d Arty (105, T)
  8th Bn, 6th Arty (155/8-in, SP)
25th Infantry Division Artillery
  1st Bn, 8th Arty (105, T)

25th Infantry Division—continued
  7th Bn, 11th Arty (105, T)
  2d Bn, 77th Arty (105, T)
  3d Bn, 13th Arty (155/8-in, SP)
173d Airborne Brigade
  3d Bn, 319th Arty (105, T)
199th Light Infantry Brigade
  2d Bn, 40th Arty (105, T)
11th Armored Cavalry Regiment
  3 Sqdn How Btrys (155, SP)
1st Cavalry Division Artillery
  2d Bn, 9th Arty (105, T)
  1st Bn, 77th Arty (105, T)
  1st Bn, 21st Arty (105, T)
  2d Bn, 20th Arty (ARA)
4th Infantry Division Artillery
  6th Bn, 29th Arty (105, T)
  4th Bn, 42d Arty (105, T)
  2d Bn, 9th Arty (105, T)
  5th Bn, 16th Arty (155/8-in, SP)
23d Infantry Division Artillery
  6th Bn, 11th Arty, 11th Inf
    Bde (105, T)
  1st Bn, 14th Arty, 198th Inf
    Bde (105, T)
  3d Bn, 82d Arty, 196th Inf
    Bde (105, T)
  3d Bn, 18th Arty (8-in/175)
  3d Bn, 16th Arty (155, T)
101st Airborne Division Artillery
  2d Bn, 319th Arty (105, T)
  2d Bn, 320th Arty (105, T)
  1st Bn, 321st Arty (105, T)
9th Infantry Division Artillery
  2d Bn, 4th Arty (105, T)
  1st Bn, 11th Arty (105, T)
  3d Bn, 34th Arty (105, T)
  1st Bn, 84th Arty (155, T/8-in, SP)

---

[1] Attached 25th Infantry Division.
[2] Attached 1st Infantry Division.
[3] Provisional Corps, Vietnam, activated and replaced Military Assistance, Vietnam, Forward on 10 March 1968, later redesignated XXIV Corps, Vietnam.

Chart 3—Field Artillery Task Organization, July 1969

I Field Force Artillery
  41st Artillery Gp
    7th Bn, 13th Arty (105, T)
    7th Bn, 15th Arty (8-in/175)
    2d Bn, 17th Arty (105-155, T)
    6th Bn, 84th Arty (155, T)
  52d Artillery Gp
    3d Bn, 6th Arty (105, SP)
    6th Bn, 14th Arty (8-in/175)
    5th Bn, 22d Arty (8-in/175)
    1st Bn, 92d Arty (155, T)
    5th Bn, 27th Arty (105, T)
    6th Bn, 32d Arty (8-in/175)
  XXIV Corps Artillery
  108th Artillery Gp
    1st Bn, 40th Arty (105, SP)
    8th Bn, 4th Arty (8-in/175)
    2d Bn, 94th Arty (175)
    6th Bn, 33d Arty (105, T)
    1st Bn, 83d Arty (8-in/175)
    2d Bn, 138th Arty (155, SP) [1]
  1st Cavalry Division Artillery
    2d Bn, 19th Arty (105, T)
    1st Bn, 77th Arty (105, T)
    1st Bn, 21st Arty (105, T)
    2d Bn, 20th Arty (ARA)
    1st Bn, 30th Arty (155, T)
  25th Infantry Division Artillery
    1st Bn, 8th Arty (105, T)
    7th Bn, 11th Arty (105, T)
    2d Bn, 77th Arty (105, T)
    3d Bn, 13th Arty (155/8-in, SP)
II Field Force Artillery
  23d Artillery Gp
    2d Bn, 14th Arty (105, T)
    1st Bn, 27th Arty (155, SP)
    6th Bn, 27th Arty (8-in/175)
    2d Bn, 32d Arty (8-in/175)
    3d Bn, 197th Arty (155, T) [2]
    6th Bn, 15th Arty (105, T)
  54th Artillery Gp
    7th Bn, 8th Arty (8-in/175)
    7th Bn, 9th Arty (105, T)
    2d Bn, 35th Arty (155, SP)
    5th Bn, 42d Arty (155, T)
    6th Bn, 77th Arty (105, T) [3]

1st Brigade, 5th Mechanical Division
  5th Bn, 4th Arty (155, SP)
173d Airborne Brigade
  3d Bn, 319th Arty (105, T)
199th Light Infantry Brigade
  2d Bn, 40th Arty (105, T)
3d Brigade, 82d Airborne Division
  2d Bn, 321st Arty (105, T)
11th Armored Cavalry Regiment
  3 sqdn how btrys (155, SP)
1st Infantry Division Artillery
  2d Bn, 4th Arty (105, T)
  1st Bn, 11th Arty (105, T)
  3d Bn, 34th Arty (105, T)
  1st Bn, 84th Arty (155, T/8-in, SP)
9th Infantry Division Artillery
  2d Bn, 4th Arty (105, T)
  1st Bn, 11th Arty (105, T)
  3d Bn, 34th Arty (105, T)
  1st Bn, 84th Arty (155, T/8-in, SP)
4th Infantry Division Artillery
  6th Bn, 29th Arty (105, T)
  4th Bn, 42d Arty (105, T)
  2d Bn, 9th Arty (105, T)
  5th Bn, 16th Arty (155/8-in, SP)
23d Infantry Division Artillery
  6th Bn, 11th Arty, (105, T) 11th Inf Bde
  1st Bn, 14th Arty (105, T) 198th Inf Bde
  3d Bn, 82d Arty, (105, T) 196th Inf Bde
  3d Bn, 18th Arty (8-in/175)
  3d Bn, 16th Arty (155, T)
  1st Bn, 82d Arty (155, T/8-in, SP)
101st Airborne Division Artillery
  2d Bn, 319th Arty (105, T)
  2d Bn, 320th Arty (105, T)
  1st Bn, 321st Arty (105, T)
  2d Bn, 11th Arty (155, T)
  4th Bn, 77th Arty (ARA)

---

[1] Arrived Oct 68, redesignated 1st Bn, 39th Arty, Oct 69.
[2] Arrived Sep 68, redesignated 2d Bn, 12th Arty, Sep 69.
[3] OPCON Senior Adviser, IV Corps.

artillery under conventional organization. A fourth firing battery alleviated this condition. Otherwise, the desire to keep maneuver elements within the range of a 105-mm. battery restricted operations.

The requirement for additional firing batteries could be satisfied in a number of ways. In one instance Headquarters, U.S. Army, Vietnam, authorized a fourth battery for the 3d Battalion, 319th Artillery, 173d Airborne Brigade. The battalion in this case supported five maneuver elements and badly needed the additional artillery. Additional firing batteries in all other cases were organized from existing assets. Typical was the artillery reorganization in the Americal Division. Each of the division's direct support battalions was reorganized into two five-tube and two four-tube batteries. The 1st Infantry Division had a more unusual solution. One or two 4.2-inch mortar platoons were attached to each of the division's direct support artillery battalions and designated Batteries D and E. Although attached to the headquarters battery for administration, these platoons functioned tactically as separate fire units. The range of the mortars limited their employment in the direct support role. Consequently, they defended base camps or covered fire support bases that were out of range of other field artillery. The particular situation of many artillery battalions did not require the formation of a fourth battery. Even so, contingency plans were often developed to permit the reorganization on a moment's notice if the situation were to change. II Field Force Artillery, for instance, required all light and medium battalions to have contingency plans for forming a fourth battery from organic assets. None of these reorganizations made the support rendered less effective. The nature and size of targets most frequently encountered in Vietnam (six or less personnel) could be effectively engaged with four howitzers rather than six per battery. In fact, four-tube batteries were frequently more compatible with the small position areas available.

One of the most interesting organizations was that of Battery D, 2d Battalion, 13th Artillery. This was a composite 105- and 155-mm. battery which was formed temporarily on two occasions for a specific purpose. Battery A, 2d Battalion, 13th Artillery, provided three 105-mm. tubes and Battery B, 3d Battalion, 197th Artillery, provided three 155-mm. towed weapons toward the formation of the battery. The regular gun crews were transferred along with weapons. Other battery personnel and equipment requirements to flesh out Battery D were filled by both contributing batteries. The unit capitalized on the advantages of both calibers for jungle operations. Whereas the 155-mm. howitzer was more effective for firing in the triple-canopy jungle, the 105-mm. was more effective for close-in defense and for delivering fire at high rates. Battery D, known as the Jungle Battery, operated in direct support of the 3d Mobile Strike Force, a joint U.S.–Vietnamese Special Forces command during operations in War Zone D.

Safety

Artillery units at all levels took every reasonable precaution to insure the safety of allied forces and noncombatants. The requirement that artillery units obtain both political and military clearance was but one of many rules that the artillery was required to observe in engaging the enemy. The rules were published in a directive entitled *MACV Rules of Engagement,* cited below. They are evidence of the unusual care that was required of all soldiers and commanders to insure that friendly casualties were held to an absolute minimum:

1. UNINHABITED AREAS.
   a. Fire may be directed against VC/NVA forces in contact in accordance with normal artillery procedures.
   b. Unobserved fire may be directed at targets and target areas, other than VC/NVA forces in contact, only after approval by Province Chief, District Chief, Sector Commander, or Subsector Commander and US/FWMAF Military Commander, as appropriate, has been granted.
   c. Observed fire may be directed against targets of opportunity which are clearly identified as hostile without obtaining Province Chief, District Chief, Sector Commander, or Subsector Commander and US/FWMAF Military Commander's approval.
   d. Approval by Province Chief, District Chief, Sector Commander, or Subsector Commander and US/FWMAF Military Commander, as appropriate, is required, before directing fire on targets of opportunity not clearly identified as hostile.
2. VILLAGES AND HAMLETS.
   a. Fire missions directed against known or suspected VC/NVA targets in villages and hamlets occupied by noncombatants will be conducted as follows:
      (1) All such fire missions will be controlled by an observer and will be executed only after approval is obtained from the Province Chief or District Chief, as appropriate. The decision to conduct such fire missions will also be approved by the attacking force battalion or task force commander, or higher.
      (2) Villages and hamlets not associated with maneuver of

ground forces will not be fired upon without warning by leaflets and/or speaker system or by other appropriate means, even though fire is received from them.

(3) Villages and hamlets may be attacked without prior warning if the attack is in conjunction with a ground operation involving maneuver of ground forces through the area, and if in the judgment of the ground commander, his mission would be jeopardized by such warning.

b. The use of incendiary type ammunition will be avoided unless absolutely necessary in the accomplishment of the commander's mission or for preservation of the force.

3. URBAN AREAS.

a. Fire missions directed against known or suspected VC/NVA targets in urban areas must preclude unnecessary destruction of civilian property and must by nature require greater restrictions than the rules of engagement for less populated areas.

b. When time is of the essence and supporting weapons must be employed to accomplish the mission or to reduce friendly casualties, fire missions will be conducted as follows:

(1) All fire missions will be controlled by an observer and will be executed only after GVN/RVNAF/US approval. The decision to conduct fire missions in urban areas will be retained at corps/field force or NAVFORV level. Approval must be obtained from both the corps commander and the US field force level commander. This approval is required for the employment of any US supporting weapons in urban areas to include those US weapons in support of RVNAF.

(2) Prior to firing in urban areas, leaflets and loudspeakers and other appropriate means will be utilized to warn and to secure the cooperation and support of the civilian populace even though fire is received from these areas.

(3) Supporting weapons will be used only on positively located enemy targets. When time permits, damage to buildings will be minimized.

(4) The use of incendiary type munitions will be avoided unless destruction of the area is unavoidable and then only when friendly survival is at stake.

(5) Riot control agents will be employed to the maximum extent possible. CS agents can be effectively employed in urban area operations to flush enemy personnel from buildings and fortified positions, thus increasing the enemy's vulnerability to allied firepower while reducing the likelihood of destroying civilian property. Commanders must plan ahead and be prepared to use CS agents whenever the opportunity presents itself.

4. THE ABOVE STATED PROCEDURES WILL NOT BE VIOLATED OR DEVIATED FROM EXCEPT, WHEN IN THE OPINION OF THE RESPONSIBLE COMMANDER, THE SITUATION DEMANDS SUCH IMMEDIATE ACTION THAT THESE PROCEDURES CANNOT BE FOLLOWED. SUCH SITUATIONS INCLUDE PRESERVATION OF THE FORCE OR THE RIGHT OF SELF-DEFENSE.
5. RVN/CAMBODIAN BORDER AREA.

a. Fire missions within 2000 meters of the RVN/Cambodian border will be observed, except under circumstances where fires are in defense of friendly forces and observation of such fires is not possible. These requirements are in addition to applicable control procedures stated elsewhere in this directive.

b. Fire missions with intended target areas more than 2000 meters from the RVN/Cambodian border may be unobserved, subject to applicable control procedures stated elsewhere in this directive.

c. Fire missions will not be conducted where dispersion could result in fire being placed on or over the RVN/Cambodian border.

d. Commanders will review and comply with the provisions of MACV Rules of Engagement—Cambodian when planning for operations near the Cambodian/RVN border.

Major commands subordinate to Military Assistance Command frequently published directives that interpreted the MACV rules, expanded them in greater detail, and often added qualifications which made them even more restrictive.

Field artillery units adopted the following procedures in the employment of their weapons to insure accuracy and preclude friendly casualties:

1. Firing a smoke shell set for a 200-meter height of burst as the first round for most observed missions. Smoke was relatively safe; thus, if the target location was improperly reported, supported ground troops would not be hurt. The forward observer made any correction necessary to insure that subsequent high explosive rounds fell in the intended locations.

2. Double-checking or triple-checking all data at each echelon from the forward observer to the howitzer. This procedure created a problem for some units because of personnel requirements. In many cases, especially in force artillery units, a battalion did not control its batteries. When the battalion controlled the batteries and retained a technical fire direction center either the battery or the battalion computed the mission and the other checked the data. When the batteries operated separately, each battery center had to be augmented so that it would have two shifts or two com-

1ST BATTALION, 8TH FIELD ARTILLERY, FIRE DIRECTION CENTER. *Note primary plotting chart with check chart.*

puters and two chart operators for the double-check system. Data sent from the fire direction center by one computer were monitored by the other computer. The executive officer post received the data and read them back. Data then were passed to the guns through the executive officer post. One practice called for placing an AN/GRA–39 remote radio set at each gun. This permitted all members of the section to hear the data being transmitted to the guns. One section then read back the data received.

    3. Conducting periodic gunner (firing) inspections and drills for subordinate units.

    4. Separating and segregating, by lot, projectiles and powder for separate-loading ammunition.

    5. Insuring that howitzers were boresighted at least twice daily and that batteries registered twice weekly.

    6. Conducting frequent staff inspections of subordinate units to see that safety policies were being complied with.

    Friendly casualties resulting from misplaced artillery fires were thoroughly investigated whenever the combat situation permitted. Often the mistake was unavoidable, and, for that reason, investigation first determined whether the mistake was an accident or an

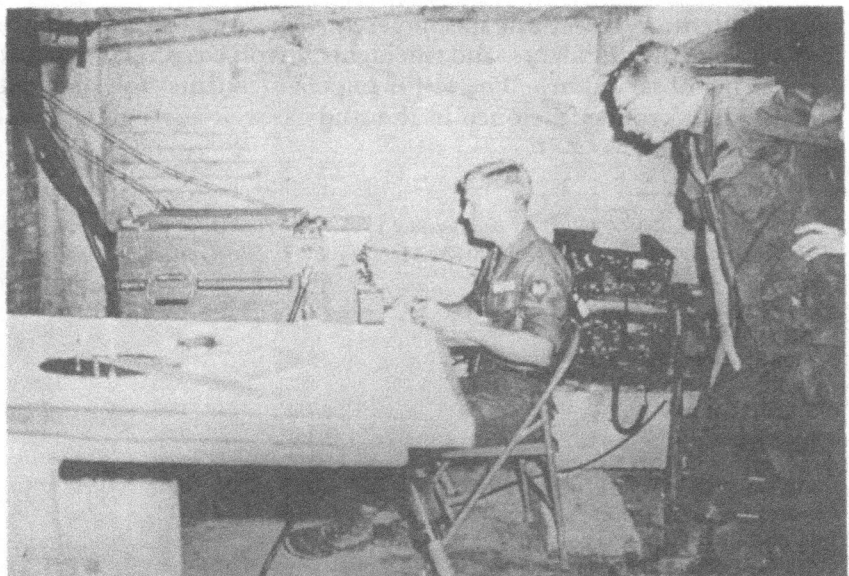

FADAC Computer With Backup Chart and Radio Communications

incident. A firing accident was defined as an occurrence not caused by human error or neglect. Malfunction of ammunition or equipment, civilian casualties in previously cleared areas, and personnel hit by debris or secondary fragments were classified as accidents. A firing incident, on the other hand, resulted from human error or neglect. Plotting errors by the forward observer or fire direction center, crew errors in setting quadrant elevation or deflection, and errors in transmitting unit locations or firing data, in obtaining proper clearance, in following the rules of engagement, or in identifying friendly units contributed toward firing incidents. If the firing error resulted in an incident, its precise cause was determined and necessary action was taken at all levels to prevent similar errors in the future.

The investigation of artillery accidents brought to light a problem in illumination missions. The impact point of the baseplate and the projectile body could not be accurately determined because of the erratic trajectory after fuze function. Consequently, it became necessary to establish a buffer zone around the grids of illumination and impact. Clearance to fire into these buffer areas was required before illumination could be fired.

A study conducted in 1969 by U.S. Army, Vietnam, into the causes of artillery, mortar, and aviation incidents and accidents set out to determine if incidents and accidents followed any discernable patterns so that commanders might be forewarned to give careful attention to certain specific areas. The study showed that a majority of the accidents and incidents involved direct support units firing observed fire. The following chart outlines the incident and accident profile developed in the study as well as recommended corrective action:

Section I
Incident/Accident Profile

Occurrence—Time of Day	Artillery	Mortar	Aviation
Morning	20%	13%	27%
Afternoon	23%	20%	40%
Night (before midnight)	31%	47%	21%
Night (after midnight)	26%	20%	12%
Clearance Causes	15%	15%	7%
Materiel Causes	15%	25%	8%
Fire Direction Center Causes	26%	18%	
Firing Battery (Mortar Platoon) Causes	21%	19%	
Forward Observer Causes	11%	11%	
Location Errors	11%	11%	
Indefinite Target Location			21%
Fire Too Close to Friendly Locations			18%
Improper Employment by Ground Element			13%

Section II

Most Frequent Causes	Recommended Corrections
Improper Clearance	In the transmission of cleared and uncleared grids, address each grid individually specifying its cleared or uncleared status. Do not clear targets in groups.
Fire Direction Center 1. Plotting Error 2. Deflection Computation Error 3. RTO/Computer Read Wrong Data 4. Friendly Locations not Plotted	1. Use FADAC as the primary source of firing data when possible. When not possible, use FADAC for firing data check. 2. Maintain firing charts in pairs. Use one as independent check of the other. 3. Require slow, distinct read backs. 4. Require fire direction officers to pass a qualifying examination before assumption of duty in battalion or battery FDC. 5. Plot fire bases and frequented locations on firing chart overlays. Continuously update overlay or mobile patrols and operations.
Firing Battery 1. Deflection Error 2. Quadrant Elevation Error 3. Wrong Charge	1. Require gunners to pass a qualifying practical examination before assumption of duty. 2. Chiefs of section check quadrants with gunner's quadrant. 3. Prohibit chief of section participation as a crew member.
Forward Observer 1. Misorientation 2. Incorrect Observer-Target Azimuth	1. Upon entering a new area of operation, conduct familiarization with terrain-map relationships for that area. Conduct practical tests. 2. When making large lateral shifts in adjust-

Location Error	ment, observers report a corrected azimuth to the target. Require infantry platoon and squad leaders to attain terrain-map proficiency described above for forward observers.

Artillery units were concerned not only with the safety of friendly forces and noncombatants on the ground but also with that of aircraft. Aircraft safety was assured by the establishment of aircraft warning centers. These centers normally were set up and operated by field artillery liaison sections at maneuver battalion and brigade. The liaison section was notified by artillery units in the area before firing and given the direction of fire, the maximum ordinate of the trajectory, and the point of impact of the projectile. Aircraft entering the area could then be advised of artillery firings and provided with recommended safe routes through the area.

In most cases Army control of air space over the battle area was not contested by the Air Force. Where it was contested, local agreements were made between representatives of both services. The most common agreement was that air space below 5,000 feet would be controlled by the Army and that above 5,000 feet by the Air Force. In certain areas such as Bien Hoa, Tan Son Nhut, and Da Nang, where the activity of the Air Force aircraft was the greatest, the Air Force controlled all air space.

Target Acquisition

Targets must be found and their location pinpointed if field artillery is to be effective. In Vietnam, as in past wars, forward observers augmented by aerial observers were the principal means to identify artillery targets. Despite the development and improvement of other target acquisition means, observers were, and promise to be for some time to come, more reliable, flexible, and responsive than any other system. This does not say that other target acquisition means are not valuable. Radars, sound and flash ranging, and sensors were all employed profitably in Vietnam.

Three target acquisition batteries were deployed to Vietnam. They were Battery F, 2d Target Acquisition Battalion, 26th Artillery, and the headquarters batteries of the 8th Target Acquisition Battalion, 26th Artillery, and the 8th Target Acquisition Battalion, 25th Artillery. Each of the headquarters batteries was assigned to a field force headquarters to co-ordinate field force level target acquisition activities. Battery F established sound and flash bases in the XXIV Corps area to monitor the Demilitarized Zone. This was the only sound ranging equipment employed, and though the equipment failed to detect a large number of targets, all sound located targets that were engaged resulted in secondary explosions.

Two field artillery radars—the AN/MPQ-4 countermortar radar and the AN/TPS-25 ground surveillance radar—were deployed throughout the country. The AN/MPQ-4 was assigned to every direct support battalion and the AN/TPS-25 was assigned to every division artillery. Both radars were also assigned to field force radar detachments.

Most units believed that the AN/TPS-25 did a good job and was a valuable piece of equipment. The AN/MPQ-4, however, caused mixed reaction. Units identified two major shortcomings: the radar had a small sector of scan, and it could not locate low-trajectory weapons, specifically rockets. The first shortcoming could be significantly alleviated where several radars were available to provide mutual and overlapping coverage. The second could not be corrected because the radar had been designed solely to detect high-trajectory weapons.

An evaluation of the effectiveness of the AN/MPQ-4 was conducted in 1969. The study revealed that in 1,759 attacks over a six-month period the radar determined only 342 confirmed launch locations for an over-all effectiveness average of 19.44 percent. For the months of May and June, the study singled out the limited sector of scan as the foremost disadvantage. The set could scan only a 445-mil sector at a time, which accounted for many nonsightings. Of 537 attacks by fire during these two months, 253 occurred out of sector, 56 during normal offtime for the crews, and 20 while the set was down because of mechanical failure. In the remaining 208 attacks in which sightings were possible, 89 sightings were made, for an over-all operator efficiency of 42.8 percent. The enemy, aware of these limitations, initiated mortar and rocket attacks from positions outside the scan of the radar. He first noted the orientation of the radar and then selected the axis of his attack. In order to cope with this handicap, U.S. troops employed a screen to conceal the direction in which the radar was oriented.

As with any sophisticated equipment, the value of the Q-4 was directly related to the degree its use was emphasized by commanders. When careful consideration was given to its positioning and employment to realize its maximum effectiveness, command interest aroused in radar crews a feeling that their work was important. They, in turn, strove to obtain maximum effectiveness from their radars. On the other hand, lack of command interest often resulted in a radar being positioned on the corner of some installation where it was ignored, its crews bored and indifferent.

The radar was found to be valuable in fulfilling certain tasks for which it was not specifically designed. Such tasks included registering batteries, locating the limits of friendly villages, determining the battery center when survey was not available, and directing friendly aircraft in bad weather or at night. Hamlets within range of an AN/MPQ–4 radar were located by hovering a helicopter over the hamlet while the radar computed an eight-place co-ordinate. On frequent occasions the 2d Battalion, 9th Artillery, used its Q–4 to establish the location of firing units within range. After the base piece had fired a round with charge 1, high angle, the Q–4 because of the low muzzle velocity of the round could compute an accurate location within 50 meters. A good example of the radar's use in directing aircraft occurred during Operation WHEELER in October 1967.

Sensors were employed extensively in Vietnam to determine targets. The sensor was not part of field artillery target acquisition equipment, but the intelligence elements responsible for their employment and the artillery worked closely together. Pre-positioned field artillery was the only fire support means that could respond immediately to sensor activations. The first family of sensors sent to Vietnam featured air and land emplaced types. They sensed intrusion by enemy vehicles or foot troops either seismically, acoustically, or magnetically. The sensors, planted in strings, had several important advantages. The direction of movement, the size of force, and the length of the columns could be determined. Once the direction of movement was determined, mortars and artillery were prepared to fire on another sensor further along the string when that sensor was activated. A mixture of sensors eliminated erroneous readings and verified readings for more accuracy; alone, readings of the basic seismic sensor could be of questionable value, but acoustic and magnetic sensors mixed in the sensor string produced more valid data. Sensors first gained notoriety when they were used in the creation of the so-called McNamara Wall, a forty-kilometer-long barrier system extending across the Demilitarized Zone and into Laos. The system consisted of sensors to detect enemy intrusion, physical barriers to impede enemy movements, and tactical troop units to strike at enemy incursions. Most of the fire power to support the system came from artillery, tactical air, and naval gunfire. The system aimed at cutting down the need for costly search operations in an area constantly subjected to enemy artillery and mortar fire from adjacent sanctuaries. Work on this project began in mid-1967 and continued until early 1968, when the buildup of U.S. forces in I Corps pre-empted the logistical support needed to supply the construction material.

Although the physical barrier was never completed, certain portions of it were sufficiently developed to permit use. South Vietnamese forces manned the complete static defense positions and thereby freed the American troops for mobile operations. A part of the early warning system operated during the siege of Khe Sanh and proved to be effective. Although in themselves no deterrent to enemy movement, sensors enabled friendly forces to bring the enemy under fire by providing targeting data for bombing and artillery strikes.

Once the McNamara Wall was shelved, sensors were made available to units in Vietnam. The experiences of the 25th Infantry Division provide two examples of their value.

On the morning of 15 March 1969, sensors near Fire Support Base MALONE, a relatively secure troop recuperation area near Dau Tieng, were activated. (*See Map 13.*) The monitor alerted the command group and the fire support element to the possibility of enemy presence. The command group soon determined that an enemy force had assembled in a bamboo thicket several hundred yards from the base. Artillery and mortar barrages covered the area. At daylight a patrol searched the area and found 21 enemy dead and 4 wounded, 129 rounds of heavy weapons ammunition, 3 rocket-propelled grenade launchers, a mortar, and a flamethrower. A pending attack had been thwarted.

The attack against Fire Support Base CROOK on the evening of 5–6 June 1969 serves as a second example. (*Map 19*) The base, established in April 1969 northwest of Tay Ninh city, hampered enemy operations and served as a springboard for American operations near the Cambodian border. Anticipating an attack, U.S. forces emplaced sensors along all possible approaches. On 5 June the sensors exposed enemy activity 950 meters east and 550 meters northwest of the base. Simultaneously, a tower-mounted radar picked up enemy movement along the wood line. Artillery and small-arms fire engaged the enemy. The North Vietnamese forces responded with a fierce mortar barrage and several probing attacks but never managed to reach the perimeter. At dawn the enemy withdrew and left 75 dead. The Americans suffered 1 killed from an enemy mortar round. The next night sensors heralded a renewed attack in greater strength. This time the American defenders, alerted by the sensors and aided by their night vision devices, accounted for 323 enemy dead and 10 captured without a single American loss. On the night of 7 June the Viet Cong launched another, much weaker, attack but then withdrew and left 3 dead on the battlefield. The early warning provided by the sensors on these occasions had stripped away the element of surprise.

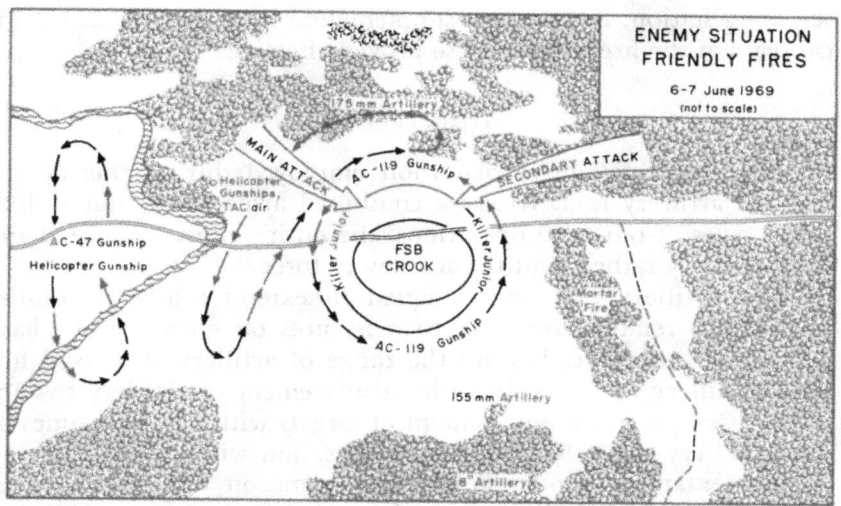

MAP 19

Ground surveys and meterological data determination have traditionally been considered by the field artillery to be target acquisition activities, though in the strictest sense they are not. Ground survey and meteorological data provide accuracy to fires on targets that have already been acquired.

Survey increases accuracy by determining the exact location of firing units in relation to other firing units, and, where possible, in relation to the forward observer and the target. The Vietnam environment made survey difficult. Survey control points were scarce and those that were available had often been disrupted; distances which survey parties were required to cover were often excessive and areas insecure; and field artillery often displaced so frequently that there was no time for survey. The most common method for determining position location consisted of a sun shot taken by survey personnel at the battery location which would provide accurate direction. The position location was then determined by resection or map spot.

If local meteorological data are available, weapons accuracy can be further improved, because weather effects can be applied by fire direction centers to the computation of fire missions. Accordingly, meteorological stations were established throughout Vietnam. Station sites were continuously evaluated and sections were relocated when necessary to provide optimal coverage. Where a large difference in altitude existed between a fire base and the servicing station, the use of a supplemental mountain meteorological team at the fire support base proved effective.

Artillery Raids

A principal offensive operation employed during this period was the artillery raid. It was a combined arms effort, but unlike other types of offensive operations, the entire effort supported the field artillery rather than the maneuver force.

The artillery raid was designed to extend available combat power into remote areas and to mass fires on enemy units, base areas, and cache sites beyond the range of artillery at a fixed fire base. Artillery raids involved the displacement of artillery to supplementary positions, engagement of targets with heavy volumes of field artillery and other supporting fires, and withdrawal from the supplementary positions. The entire operation was conducted as rapidly as possible to achieve surprise and took maximum advantage of the airmobility and the aerial observation and target acquisition capabilities of the division. The majority of the raids were conducted with 105-mm. and 155-mm. howitzer units of division artillery; however, field force artillery, particularly 155-mm. towed batteries, was frequently employed in raids or in support of divisional artillery raids.

Experience demonstrated that artillery raids were best conducted and controlled by a brigade headquarters. The decision to conduct a raid was normally made at division level. Target area selection was based on all available intelligence, and a specific area of operation for the raid was assigned to the brigade headquarters. Divisional or nondivisional artillery supported the operation with the requested or available number of firing batteries. The controlling brigade headquarters tasked a subordinate battalion to provide security, and the division made the required aviation lift available. A typical package included one 105-mm. howitzer battery, one understrength 155-mm. howitzer battery (three howitzers), one rifle company for security, aerial observers from division artillery, and, when available, air cavalry assets for target acquisition and damage assessment.

In order to conduct artillery raids on short notice, divisions developed and published standing operating procedures in the form of operations plans. Contingency loads, assembled to support all quick reaction operations, were immediately available to support artillery raids. Particularly during the monsoon period, raids served the important secondary purpose of maintaining airmobility expertise in artillery units that would otherwise remain static for extended periods. As troop strength declined, Americans were defending increasingly larger areas with fewer forces. This, in turn, resulted in the increased use of artillery raids as a method of making U.S. combat power more widely felt and denying the enemy the unrestricted freedom of movement he would otherwise have enjoyed beyond the range of guns.

Logisticians were kept busy delivering ammunition and supplies to field artillery units and providing required maintenance support. From the logisticians's point of view, the preferred method of supplying field artillery units was by truck convoy, augmented by helicopter delivery. Truck convoys were more economical, more dependable, and could move more supplies at one time than those helicopters normally available for resupply. The enemy situation and operational needs, however, dictated the manner in which units were supplied. Light firing batteries which moved frequently were often supplied entirely by helicopter. Other units which moved less frequently were generally supplied by helicopter on initially occupying a fire base, and later by truck if roads were available and could be cleared of mines and secured. Heavy units moved by road and could thus bring initial supplies with them and continue to be supplied by convoy thereafter.

Supply by road in insecure areas was frequently accomplished every two or three days. On those days the road was swept for mines in advance and secured by ground forces long enough for the convoy to complete its run. Daily needs such as rations, water, and ice could then be supplied by helicopter.

All firing batteries carried sufficient supplies and ammunition with them during their move to permit them to start construction and fire supporting missions immediately upon occupying a fire base. Stocks were increased or replenished in subsequent supply deliveries. No generalizations can be made as to the amounts and types of bunker and barrier material a unit would carry or receive later. Ammunition requirements, on the other hand, were established in written directives. Firing units were required to carry a basic load with them at all times. Basic loads varied somewhat depending on the area of operation and location of the ammunition supply point. The following basic load is representative:

a. *105-mm. Howitzer Battery*
   (1) High Explosive (HE) .... 1,600 meters
   (2) Illumination (ILL) .... 320 rounds
   (3) White Phosphorus (WP) .... 60 rounds
   (4) Antipersonnel or "Beehive" .... 36 rounds
   (5) Improved Conventional Munitions (ICM) or "Firecracker" .... 24 rounds

b. *155-mm. Battery*
- (1) HE ... 1,200 rounds
- (2) ILL ... 400 rounds
- (3) WP ... 48 rounds
- (4) ICM ... 18 rounds

c. *8-Inch Howitzer Battery*
- (1) HE ... 600 rounds
- (2) ICM ... 8 rounds

d. *4.2-Inch Mortar Platoon (Infantry)*
- (1) HE ... 1,200 rounds
- (2) ILL ... 300 rounds
- (3) WP ... 50 rounds

While occupying a position a firing unit was continuously supplied at a rate which allowed it to maintain a prescribed stockage objective. The stockage objective was established above the basic load and was used as an aid in ammunition supply management. A typical stockage objective for high explosive ammunition is as follows:

Ammunition	*Number of Rounds*
105–mm.	2,000
155–mm.	1,600
8–inch	800
4.2–inch	1,600

Maintenance support requirements varied with the type of unit and were satisfied in several ways. Units with towed howitzers generally experienced no unusual maintenance problems because the weapons had relatively few moving parts to malfunction. On those occasions when towed weapons needed to be repaired, they could quickly be picked up by helicopter from the fire base, brought to the repair facility and returned quickly when repairs were completed. Self-propelled weapons were more troublesome. They were more sophisticated, more likely to break down, and too heavy to move by helicopter. It was necessary to make arrangements to evacuate the equipment by road. Either a separate convoy for that purpose was formed or the weapon was held until it could be linked up with a convoy of some other unit. If the malfunction of the weapon was in its mobility system, additional arrangements were made to secure a tank retriever to tow the weapon.

Whenever possible, maintenance contact teams were sent by helicopter to the fire base to attempt repairs on inoperative weapons. The teams were alerted by the unit requesting their support of the nature of the problem and were, therefore, able to limit their load to only those tools and spare parts required to make

AMMUNITION RESUPPLY BY CH–54 *on Fire Support Base 6 near Kontum.*

the repair. Still, all repairs could not be made on site, and though the efforts of maintenance contact teams alleviated the problem, they came far from solving it.

In 1968 U.S. Army, Vietnam, recognized that user level and direct support maintenance was difficult to perform on site and was often neglected because of operational needs. As a result U.S. Army, Vietnam, established a repair and return program for 8-inch and 175-mm. units. A weapon and its crew stood down in a direct support maintenance facility for complete maintenance service of the weapon.

Harassing and Interdiction Fires

One topic of much discussion in Vietnam was the effects of harassing and interdiction (H&I) fires. These were unobserved fires placed on likely or suspected enemy locations or routes. Targets were most often chosen from aerial and map reconnaissance.

Lieutenant General Frank T. Mildren, Deputy Commanding General, U.S. Army, Vietnam, stated, "In my estimation, pure H&I fires in Vietnam environment have little, if any, value while doing practically no damage to the enemy. I have requested that tactical commanders reduce their H&I fires." There were many who agreed with General Mildren, but there were many who did not. Numerous reports indicated that the Viet Cong feared the artillery firing at night and that this firing was inflicting damage and casualties. Even so, no one could deny that if not employed judiciously, harassing and interdiction fires could result in extremely large ammunition expenditures.

During General Mildren's tour, the use of harassing and interdiction fires was reduced and a program of intelligence and interdiction (I&I) fires was instituted. Whereas targets for the former were often based on map reconnaissance alone, the latter were less arbitrary in that some type of enemy intelligence had to justify the firings.

The 4th Division set the example in executing the intelligence and interdiction program. The largest portion of the unobserved fires delivered by the artillery with the 4th Division was fired on targets acquired by one or more intelligence means. Interdiction fire was used successfully in conjunction with the road security missions of the division. The division developed a road firing program that covered likely approaches to areas in which repeated mining incidents had occurred and approaches to key bridge and culvert crossings along Highways 14N and 19E. The fires, which were delivered periodically throughout the night and early morning, resulted in the reduction of mining and bridge incidents along these major highways.

Intelligence and interdiction fires were effectively employed using the time-on-target technique. Instead of firing single rounds on a target over a period of time, a battery or several batteries would time the rounds so that all arrived on the target at the same time. These fires created shock and achieved maximum surprise.

Civic Action

Field artillery units throughout South Vietnam supported the government's pacification program through a number of civic action programs. Short-term projects included food and clothing distribution, rodent and pest control, and medical assistance. Long-term projects included construction and follow-up support of schools, markets, hospitals, and orphanges.

Firing batteries normally carried out only short-term projects. They generally moved too frequently to do otherwise. Their usual contribution was in connection with the Medical Civic Action Program (MEDCAP). Battery aidmen supervised by the surgeon of the parent battalion visited local hamlets daily to treat the sick and to educate local medical personnel. The seriously ill or injured were evacuated to civilian hospitals or, sometimes, to U.S. military hospitals. On one occasion the 1st Battalion, 44th Artillery, assisted an eight-year-old girl and her grandmother, each of whom had a missing leg. The two were evacuated to the German hospital ship *Helgoland* where they were fitted for artificial limbs.

Long-term civic action projects were accomplished by the headquarters and service batteries of field artillery battalions and higher. Their accomplishments were impressive. The civic action project in Vietnam recognized as the most outstanding was Gadsden Village, accomplished by a field artillery unit—the 23d Artillery Group. The citizens of Gadsden, Alabama, adopted the 23d as their sponsored unit in Vietnam. They offered financial assistance to the group for any project to help the men. Instead of accepting the Alabama goodwill for themselves, the artillerymen decided to channel the aid to the homeless refugees in the Phu Loi area.

With land donated by the Vietnamese government and the more than $21,000 contributed by the citizens of Gadsden, the artillerymen set out to help the refugees build a village. Houses were built with self-sufficiency in mind. There was enough space between the houses for a vegetable garden for each family. But the Redlegs did not stop with building houses. They constructed a six-room schoolhouse and hired trained teachers, built a community center building, and established a co-operative sewing center, a large dispensary, a soccer field, a hog-raising complex, and a water distribution system. Gadsden Village was exemplary of the goal of civic action—to help the people help themselves.

CHAPTER VI

Vietnamization, November 1969–February 1973

President Richard M. Nixon, in November 1969, officially established the goal of the American effort in the Vietnam conflict as being that of enabling the South Vietnamese forces to assume the full responsibility for the security of their country. Although Vietnamization was a new word, the concept was neither new nor revolutionary but was, in fact, a return to an earlier policy—one that had all but disappeared in the feverish escalation from aid and advice to combat support to active participation. As early as the summer of 1967, the first tentative steps toward Vietnamization were being taken. Concerned about the effectiveness of Vietnamese Army, Regional Forces, and Popular Forces units, General Westmoreland directed that a conference be held to air views, consider proposals, and make recommendations through which assistance could be provided the Vietnamese military in order to mold it into an aggressive and responsible fighting force.

Field Artillery Assistance Programs

Senior American commanders met at Pleiku on 12 August 1967 and, on the basis of their conclusions, the Commanding General, I Field Force, Vietnam, directed that the Commanding General, I Field Force Artillery, "establish liaison with Vietnamese units and . . . isolate problems to be alleviated through U.S. training support." I Field Force Artillery immediately assigned a liaison officer to II Corps (Vietnamese) Artillery to "provide a channel for the request of supporting U.S. artillery for ARVN operations in II CTZ." This officer was recalled when the necessary procedures had been established, and his duties were assumed by the artillery officer of II Corps Advisory Group. To provide further assistance, an "on-call" liaison officer from the 52d Artillery Group was designated.

Even as this co-ordination was being established, a decentralized assistance program was developing. On 28 September 1967, Brigadier General William O. Quirey directed that all field force artillery battalions establish forward observer teams specifically to train

Regional and Popular Forces units in the techniques of fire adjustment. Further, battalions were to provide any assistance necessary to assist Vietnamese artillery units to achieve maximum technical proficiency. This guidance, however, proved to be too general. Field force battalions provided only sporadic aid in the II Corps area, and effectiveness depended on the willingness of the Vietnamese participants in the program and the ability of the U.S. units to do the job.

Meanwhile, I Field Force Artillery had initiated a four-month study of Vietnamese Army artillery operations in order to evaluate the effectiveness of their support. Total assets in II Corps were 103 105-mm. howitzers and 41 155-mm. howitzers. Of these, 6 155-mm. and 15 105-mm. tubes were committed to support training centers, 6 155-mm. and 13 105-mm. tubes were located at Duc My in support of the South Vietnamese Army Artillery Center and School, and 2 105-mm. pieces were situated in Da Lat in support of the South Vietnamese Military Academy. Although all school support weapons had the secondary mission of supporting the Duc My complex and Da Lat city, their primary function of school support prevented their effective utilization in support of operations. In addition 18 105-mm. pieces were positioned in platoons at Special Forces and Civilian Irregular Defense Group camps. The remaining guns—55 105-mm. and 30 155-mm. pieces—had primary responsibility for supporting Army and Regional and Popular Forces maneuver elements. Because this artillery also had to provide fire support for road security and the various political headquarters throughout II Corps, platoon and split-battery configurations were the prevalent formations employed. The size of II Corps Tactical Zone, some 30,000 square miles, and the magnitude of the mission proved the artillery incapable of providing even marginal fire support to maneuver forces during offensive operations.

The study examined ten long-term operations and seventy-two short-term operations. Long-term operations were defined as those performed within the framework of the normal mission of the maneuver force and short-term operations as those in response to specific and immediate needs such as those based on special intelligence. Findings showed that artillery supported slightly less than half of the short-term operations. Of those operations which were listed as being supported by artillery, each maneuver battalion was shown to have received artillery support which averaged slightly more than one platoon (two guns). The average support was less than one platoon of artillery per battalion when all short-term operations were taken into consideration. The study also showed that although South Vietnamese Army artillery units were thoroughly grounded in the fundamentals of gunnery, they were severely hampered by poor maintenance practices, slipshod repair parts support, and inadequate communications equipment. Further problem areas were encountered in the meteorological support and survey capabilities of the Vietnamese. Based on this study, specific programs were initiated to upgrade the ability of Vietnamese artillery to support maneuver forces in the field. This aid was aimed at increasing the responsiveness of the firing units in answering calls for fire and the ability of the ground soldier to request and adjust fire. Because the mission of Vietnamese batteries continued to be security of roads and strategic installations, no attempts were made to increase the fire-massing capacity of these units.

To remedy the problems exposed by the study, American artillery units in early 1968 initiated four assistance programs. Task Force DAI BAC I (Cannon I) was formed by the 1st Battalion, 92d Artillery, to assist Vietnamese artillery units in the Kontum area. This program was short-term, lasting only 23–27 February 1968. Its primary mission was to ascertain the condition of the Vietnamese weapons and to demonstrate the responsiveness of Vietnamese and U.S. artillery to calls for fire from Vietnamese, Regional and Popular Forces, and U.S. units in the Kontum area. To accomplish this mission, the 92d Artillery established a fire direction center, collocated with the Vietnamese 221st Artillery Battalion at Kontum, that could control all artillery fire in the area. The objective was to create a working Vietnamese fire direction center. Another team with interests in logistics and maintenance was to examine and correct hardware deficiencies. Additional teams were designated to assist in firing battery operations, communications, and survey. Because of the short duration of the program, specific objectives were established for each day to insure that all areas were examined and upgraded. The program revealed that significant shortcomings in fire direction procedures were caused primarily by a lack of logistical support and by poor understanding of sophisticated gunnery procedures. Firing battery deficiencies were closely tied to logistical or maintenance support. Tubes ranged in age from thirteen to twenty-seven years and averaged 10,000 rounds per tube. The task force provided the necessary logistical support to upgrade the weapons and instructed Vietnamese in advanced fire direction procedures. The task force also pointed out that the remaining problem areas were founded in the weak Vietnamese logistical system and recommended that artillery advisers spend more time with their units and actively establish liaison with neighboring American units so that assistance could be made more readily available.

At the same time that Task Force DAI BAC I was being established, another program began to provide assistance to Civilian Irregular Defense Group and Special Forces artillery platoons. Responsibility for the program was given to the major artillery commands in II Corps. These commands provided technical assistance to the Civilian Irregular artillery platoons. Classes were conducted in fire direction, firing battery operations, and maintenance. Initial success resulted in the continuation of the program on a regular basis.

Perhaps the most important of the four projects was the I Field Force and Army of the Republic of Vietnam Associate Battery Program, which commenced on 14 March 1968. The idea behind the program was to augment the existing advisory effort, improve the effectiveness of Vietnamese forces, and open channels for better co-ordination of fire support and mutual understanding. Under this concept, U.S. artillery units sponsored selected Vietnamese battalions in their locale and provided them with a responsive American headquarters from which to request technical, maintenance, and training assistance.

Finally, I Field Force Artillery developed a program of instruction to train Vietnamese artillerymen in the use of antipersonnel (Beehive) ammunition in preparation for the time when Vietnamese firing units would be issued the special rounds. This program, however, never became functional because the Vietnamese Joint General Staff had not authorized their units to draw and employ the ammunition.

The initial success of these programs, coupled with the disastrous defeat suffered by the Communist forces during their ill-fated *Tet* offensive earlier in the year, allowed the embryonic Vietnamization program to grow. During the fall of 1968 military leaders in Vietnam studied after-action reports, intelligence estimates, and staff studies pertinent to the *Tet* campaign and its immediate aftermath. From these evaluations a parallel course—one that would merge with President Nixon's some eight months later—began to germinate. On the basis of an over-all evaluation of the Army of the Republic of Vietnam, it became evident to these leaders that if Vietnamese forces were eventually to assume the burden of the ground war, a test of their ability to operate semi-independently would be necessary. The stress on semi-independence rather than complete autonomy was in recognition of the inherent weakness of these forces in fire support and air assets. To this end, a suitable testing ground had to be found. The area had to be secure enough to allow for unhampered transfer of forces before Vietnamese units became actively engaged but at the same time had to have potentially significant enemy activity to provide the Vietnamese with a viable test. Further, the testing ground had to be in an area of minimal danger to the pacification program. An ideal area was found in northern Kontum Province, with its sparse population, potential enemy threat from Laos and Cambodia, and relative isolation from the psychologically important population centers of the country.

Preliminary discussions between American and Vietnamese leaders began in late 1968, and a verbal agreement was reached in January 1969 between Lieutenant General William R. Peers, Commanding General, I Field Force, Vietnam, and Major General Lu Mong Lan, Commander, II Corps. However, this agreement was not written, and the designated Vietnamese force, the 42d Regiment, and its command headquarters, the 24th Special Tactical Zone, failed to assume responsibility for the area by 1 February 1969, as had been agreed. Further, negotiations were hampered by the natural confusion of a change of command at I Field Force, Vietnam, and it was not until 12 April 1969 that General Lu Lan indicated general agreement with a new proposal. A draft memorandum of agreement was drawn up and signed by American and Vietnamese officials on 24 April 1969. On the same day the exchange of forces neared completion and the Army of the Republic of Vietnam assumed responsibility for northern Kontum Province.

In deference to the weakness of Vietnamese artillery (six 105-mm. howitzers and six 155-mm. howitzers) the agreement specifically provided that the 4th Infantry Division Artillery units would assume effective artillery coverage of National Highway 14, the major north-south artery in the highlands, and that the Commanding General, I Field Force Artillery, would provide general support artillery as required; support operations within the 24th Special Tactical Zone with a minimum of two light or medium artillery batteries; and maintain the fire support co-ordination center to co-ordinate all fire support means available, including operation of air advisory stations.

I Field Force assigned the mission of providing the specified support to the 52d Artillery Group headquarters in Pleiku. The 52d immediately provided six light, twelve medium, and five heavy artillery pieces to the 24th Special Tactical Zone to augment organic Vietnamese batteries. Battery C, 4th Battalion, 42d Artillery, a 4th Division Artillery unit, provided road coverage. Automatic weapons were allocated from Battery B, 4th Battalion, 60th Artillery (Automatic Weapons). With the assumption of responsibility for northern Kontum Province by the 24th Special Tactical Zone, the first major Vietnamese ground operation began. Dubbed DAN QUYEN by the Vietnamese, it grew out of special agent reports indicating a major buildup of enemy units southwest of the Ben Het Civilian Irregular Defense Group camp, which sat precariously at the convergence of the Laotian, Cambodian, and Vietnamese borders.

In order to head off Communist plans to execute a strong offensive effort in the highlands, the 24th Special Tactical Zone was tasked to conduct operations to spoil Communist plans, protect Ben Het, and compel enemy forces to retire to their Cambodian sanctuaries. The operation was conducted in three phases: Phase I (5–15 May) involved forces of three Vietnamese and two mobile strike force battalions screening the tri-border area west of Ben Het; Phase II (16 May–3 June), based on intelligence produced during the initial phase, was a six-battalion (plus) offensive operation conducted southeast of Ben Het and targeted against elements of the North Vietnamese 66th Infantry, 28th Infantry, and 40th Artillery Regiments; and Phase III (3–5 June) consisted primarily of bomb damage assessments by multibattalion Vietnamese forces and the establishment of a defensive screen around the Dak To, Tan Canh, and Ben Het areas. By operation's end the South Vietnamese had succeeded in mauling the Communist forces and establishing a favorable 7-to-1 kill ratio. In support of the operation, the 52d Artillery Group provided 29 tubes of artillery—12 105-mm. howitzers, 12 155-mm. howitzers, 1 8-inch howitzer, and 4 175-mm. guns—and assigned the 1st Battalion, 92d Artillery, to establish the forward command post for U.S. support forces. This command post was later expanded into a fire support co-ordination center for all American artillery in the area. From their own assets, Vietnamese forces utilized 8 155-mm. and 6 105-mm. howitzers in support of the operation. A total of 73,016 rounds was expended by friendly firing units. Enemy soldiers captured during the campaign expressed a fear of first-round volley fire employed by both South Vietnamese and U.S. units in the form of random time-on-target missions.

Although the operation, was deemed a success, a number of weaknesses became apparent. The magnitude and complexity of co-ordinating, integrating, and controlling available fire support means virtually overwhelmed the 24th Zone staff at the Dak To tactical operations center. Some of the blame for this failure was attributable to an inexperienced staff and the inadequate manning structure of the headquarters, but specific shortcomings were apparent as well. When the 92d Artillery established the U.S. fire support co-ordination center at Dak To, South Vietnamese commanders were encouraged to send representatives, but only one did so. Fire support activities thus were not properly co-ordinated, so flexibility was lost, resources were wasted, efforts were duplicated, and frequently targets were not attacked with the appropriate means at the proper time. This problem originated with the failure of the force commanders in organizing for combat to understand or appreciate the need to integrate closely maneuver plans and fire support plans and to collocate the tactical operations and fire support co-ordination centers. The problem was finally rectified two weeks after the operation started when the commander of the 1st Battalion, 92d Artillery, was tasked to establish an integrated fire support co-ordination center. This agency quickly matured into an effective organization capable of providing timely and accurate fire support.

Additional problems were encountered in fire clearances, co-ordination of fire support assets at company level, and requests for and adjustment of artillery fire. It became apparent that these deficiencies were a result of the dependence of the South Vietnamese commanders on American advisers. These weaknesses were not corrected satisfactorily and it was clear that additional stress in training would be required to upgrade the fire support co-ordination ability of Vietnamese units.

Despite the weaknesses noted during the campaign, the performance of the Vietnamese forces proved that they could plan and successfully execute semi-independent ground operations against Communist main force units. The significance of this fact would not be apparent for another five months, when the policy of Vietnamization became the stated objective of the American command in Vietnam.

By 1968, Military Assistance Command had submitted its plans for Phase II of the Republic of Vietnam Armed Forces Improvement and Modernization Plan. Phase II planning was based on assumptions that North Vietnamese intervention would increase and that the missions of the allied forces would remain substantially unchanged from those that had been stated for fiscal year 1968; that is, U.S. and allied forces were assigned to destroy Viet Cong and North Vietnamese Army forces and base areas, and South Vietnamese Army and Regional and Popular Forces units were to support the pacification program. Because of these assumptions, the improvement plan was rather methodical and cautious. The proposal was submitted to the Secretary of Defense, who disapproved and returned it to the Saigon planners for substantial revision. In early 1969 the plan was resubmitted as Phase IIa, which assumed the same basic premises as those of the initial Phase II plan but substantially increased the speed and scope of the modernization. On 28 April 1969, the Deputy Secretary of Defense gave final approval of the Military Assistance Command program as modified by the Joint Chiefs of Staff and in his approving memo stated: "Vietnamizing the war should have the highest priority. Providing needed equipment for the RVNAF is therefore of greatest importance. To assure that equipment turned over to the RVNAF can be used effectively, it must be supported by (1) training and (2) logistic support."

Phase IIa of the Improvement and Modernization Plan recognized that major shortfalls existed in the fire power capabilities of the Vietnamese forces, and a substantial portion of the plan was devoted to rectifying this weakness. The equipment ceilings established by the plan were intended to increase substantially the artillery capability of the Vietnamese. These proposed figures were further modified when Presidents Nixon and Thieu met at Midway in June 1969. President Thieu presented the requirements as seen by the Vietnamese to President Nixon, who in turn gave them to General Abrams for study, comment, and possible inclusion in the program. One of the requirements, as seen by the Vietnamese, was heavy artillery in the form of four 8-inch field artillery battalions. After this proposal was scrutinized by Military Assistance Command, only portions of requests were approved. Three additional battalions of artillery, two 105-mm. and one 155-mm., were added to the fiscal year 1970 activation schedule. By the end of 1969, the artillery improvement plan had undergone a number of revisions but delivery of field artillery weapons was being accomplished smoothly and ahead of schedule.

EQUIPMENT DELIVERY STATUS, 1969

Item	Phase I Accelerated Fiscal Year 1969	Phase II Fiscal Year 1970	Approved Midway Fiscal Year 1970	MACV Revised November 1970	Total Shipped as of 31 December 1969
Howitzer, 105-mm. M101A1	602	776	731	731	730
Howitzer, 105-mm. M102	60	61	0	60	60
Howitzer, 155-mm. M114A1	701	274	290	289	294

At the same time the master plan for Vietnamization was taking shape, the required training base to prepare the South Vietnamese Army to assume a more proportionate share of the action immediately and the entire combat role in the future was receiving careful consideration from the appropriate American commands throughout the country. I Field Force Artillery, which had a substantial jump on the other headquarters in the establishment of a training assistance program for Vietnamese forces, reviewed its existing programs, found them to be valid, and, on the basis of additional studies, added two plans through which it intended to improve the capabilities of Regional Forces and Popular Forces units to call for and adjust artillery fire in defense of their positions and in support of their operations. In addition, basic fire planning was taught to the Regional Forces so they could support their own operations. Based on this program, a comprehensive defensive target list was developed throughout II Corps and, if a target fell within range of an artillery unit, fire was adjusted onto it. This program increased hamlet and village security. Before the initiation of the plan, only 684 of the existing 4,208 defensive targets planned at various times during the war had been fired on. By August 1969, with the emphasis applied by I Field Force Artillery, each of the 52 districts in II Corps had a fire plan, 5,869 targets had been developed, and 32 percent of the targets had been fired in. The effectiveness of the program was demonstrated during the week of 11 August 1969, when eight friendly hamlets drove off Viet Cong attacks by simply calling for previously fired-in defensive targets.

In III Corps Tactical Zone, II Field Force Artillery was also examining the Vietnamization of artillery support. Until the summer of 1969, assistance to Vietnamese artillery had been limited to small contact teams concerned primarily with assisting the Vietnamese to solve maintenance and logistics problems by making American supply channels available for immediate, pressing needs. However, during the summer of 1969, through the efforts of the commanders of II Field Force Artillery and III Corps Artillery, the need for a co-ordinated assistance program was examined. Such a program would complement the II Field Force and III Corps Operation DONG TIEN (forward together). A combined working committee was formed to develop a plan for the program, define its concepts, and establish policies and procedures for co-ordinating all mutual support projects, which would increase the capabilities and effectiveness of the combined artillery team in III Corps. The objectives of the program, as seen by the committee, were to improve co-ordination and mutual understanding between allied artillery units; to improve fire support effectiveness by combining planning and co-ordination of fire support, standardizing techniques, and improving quality of training; and to increase artillery firing capabilities.

To accomplish the program objectives, the planning committee developed nine mutual support projects:

Project 1: Exchange visits of battery personnel
Project 2: Combined fire support co-ordination centers
Project 3: Procedures and co-ordination requirements for planning combined fire support
Project 4: Standardized operational readiness evaluations
Project 5: Combined unit refresher training program
Project 6: Standardization of tube calibration procedures
Project 7: Standardization of registration policy
Project 8: Combined use of meteorological data
Project 9: Combined survey control plan

The proposed projects were translated into concrete programs and initiated in a low key through the associate battery concept. Key personnel from both U.S. and Vietnamese units visited their "sister" batteries to gain a better understanding of each other's problems, observe battery operations, and exchange views. This exchange of ideas led naturally to the establishment of the standardized operational readiness evaluations (ORE's) as outlined in Project 4. A denotative checklist was developed to measure the effectiveness of artillery units. The checklist was particularly effective because it matched performance against an established standard rather than against another unit, minimizing the threat of embarrassment or loss of face—an important consideration with the Vietnamese. To prepare units for operational readiness evaluations, unit refresher training was initiated. Mobile training teams were created and dispatched to isolated areas to give instruction. Classes were kept small so that thorough instruction could be given to key personnel and specialists, and on-the-job training was conducted whenever possible.

In order to standardize procedures and improve the accuracy of Vietnamese artillery fires, the committee developed a plan to insure that all weapons were calibrated annually. Second, a standardized registration policy was adopted throughout III Corps and emphasis placed on persuading Vietnamese units to accept American registration practices.

To refine artillery accuracy further, teams provided assistance to Vietnamese units to develop the capability to use meteorological data. All U.S. meteorological stations in III Corps began to conduct dual-language broadcasts four times daily in order to provide Vietnamese artillery units with the requisite data. Finally, a combined effort was initiated to extend survey control to all artillery units in III Corps.

By May 1970, the DONG TIEN Program was well under way and had scored a number of successes. Over 88 percent of the howitzers employed by Vietnamese artillery in III Corps were calibrated; survey was brought in to 67 of 122 Vietnamese firing positions, an increase of 55 percent in six months; meteorological data were received and employed by the majority of the Vietnamese units; and a substantial number of the Vietnamese artillery units were employing American registration techniques.

With the refinement and improvement of Vietnamese fire support, the necessity to control these fires became apparent. Combined fire support co-ordination centers were created in various provinces throughout III Corps. These centers included Vietnamese, U.S. and Free World forces artillery representatives, U.S. Air Force representatives, and, where necessary, U.S. Navy personnel. In addition to planning fire support and clearing fires, they provided a readily accessible means for the interchange of fire requests between Vietnamese and American units. These agencies significantly increased mutual support and reduced primary reliance on U.S. artillery.

In addition to DONG TIEN, three other significant programs were initiated. The Civilian Irregular Defense Group Artillery School was opened at Trang Sup on 1 September 1969. It was created to train CIDG artillerymen to assume the fire support of seven Special Forces camps. The school was staffed and operated by the 23d Artillery Group, which designed a compact but thorough ten-week course. The school conducted three sessions during which 186 Civilian Irregular artillerymen were trained and deployed to designated camps. With the irregulars assuming artillery duties at these outposts, Vietnamese Army artillerymen were relieved to return to their regular force structures. In September 1969, III Corps Artillery began training a Vietnamese Army artillery battery in air movement techniques and jungle operations. Training was completed in December 1969, and the battery assumed direct support of the 3d Mobile Strike Force, a mission that had been the responsibility of the U.S. Jungle Battery, a composite battery of three 105-mm. and three 155-mm. howitzers. This III Corps training program enabled six guns to be returned to force artillery assets. Finally, the Fire Direction Officer's School, conducted by Field Force Artillery for its own officers, was made available to Vietnamese personnel. This week-long course assisted in standardizing artillery procedures in III Corps by providing comprehensive instruction in the latest gunnery techniques employed by U.S.

artillery. By May of 1970, 56 Vietnamese officers had been graduated from this school.

At about the same time, considerations for Vietnamization were being examined in Military Region I. With the impending redeployment of the 3d Marine Division, the Vietnamese role would increase significantly. From November 1969 until 9 March 1970, the primary exchange of ideas and programs took place between XXIV Corps Artillery and Vietnamese 1st Division Artillery because, until its redeployment in March 1970, III Marine Amphibious Force was the principal American headquarters in the northern provinces. This interplay between the Americans and Vietnamese consisted of decentralized programs initiated at all levels through personal contact and co-ordination established by the U.S. commanders.

In early 1970, XXIV Corps Artillery, in anticipation of the impending departure of the Marines, began to study the feasibility of a more intensive and centralized Vietnamization program. A XXIV Corps regulation was prepared by corps artillery to outline the minimum requirements for insuring effective co-ordination of U.S. and Vietnamese fires. The regulation also included provisions for establishing liaison between supporting artillery elements and territorial force headquarters down to subsector level. At the same time, work was initiated to revamp the artillery and air strike warning system since, at the time, a dual system existed within the Vietnamese and U.S. chains of command. As American withdrawals continued, inordinate difficulties might be experienced by both U.S. and Vietnamese pilots unless the system was effectively Vietnamized. After careful study, the collocation of the respective warning agencies was adopted at the most practical solution—one that would allow for the most orderly eventual transfer of responsibility to the Vietnamese when U.S. strength in Military Region I no longer justified the combined effort.

During March 1970, XXIV Corps Artillery initiated an artillery instructor training program in support of the Vietnamese artillery refresher training project. Representatives of all artillery battalions in the Vietnamese 1st Division and the Quan Da Special Zone underwent three weeks of instruction to prepare them to conduct training in their own organizations. Separate courses were presented in fire direction procedures, firing battery operations, and maintenance. Upon completion of the instructor training phase, each battalion formed a mobile training team which was augmented by one U.S. officer and one U.S. noncommissioned officer. These teams then moved to the field to conduct refresher training at battery locations. Early indications were that the program was successful and that the proficiency of the firing units was clearly improved.

One month later a team of officers from XXIV Corps Artillery and I Corps Artillery (Vietnamese) conducted a survey to determine the proficiency of Regional Forces and Popular Forces personnel in artillery adjustment procedures and the desirability of conducting training in the subject. The team interviewed Vietnamese officials and U.S. advisers in all five provinces; all agreed on the necessity for forward observer training and agreed to support a combined U.S. and Vietnamese program to provide such training. Two programs were instituted, one for Regional Forces and one for Popular Forces. XXIV Corps directed that the 23d Infantry (Americal) Division incorporate the Regional Forces training into its Regional Forces and Popular Forces leadership and orientation course. The goal of the course was to train observers from sector headquarters (1 each), subsector headquarters (1 each), battalion headquarters (2 each), company group headquarters (2 each), and company (3 each).

The first class started on 10 June 1970, and 889 Regional Forces officers were scheduled to undergo training.

Training for the Popular Forces was assigned to I Corps Artillery, which designed a comprehensive three-day course stressing basic essentials and live firing. A total of 3,138 Popular Forces leaders was scheduled to learn adjustment procedures in an eight-week period beginning 15 June 1970.

Further, agencies responsible for existing programs that had been established to support American units were directed to shift their emphasis to Vietnamese artillery batteries. In February 1970, the corps artillery firing battery inspection team began providing technical assistance to Vietnamese units. Detailed technical checks of fire direction procedures, firing battery operations, maintenance, and safety were made at each battery visited. On-the-spot critiques were given during the inspections and formal reports were submitted to I Corps Artillery. Logistical support was limited primarily to technical assistance and emergency aid to insure that the Vietnamese supply system was exercised. Whenever emergency assistance was given in the form of supplies or repair parts, one of the contingencies under which it was granted was that the Vietnamese unit initiate parallel supply action in its logistics channels to insure that the demand was recorded.

Even as these programs were being initiated, Military Assistance Command was finalizing the Republic of Vietnam Armed Forces Improvement and Modernization Plan for fiscal year 1971. An analysis of Vietnamese combat capability conducted as part of this

FORMAL FIRE DIRECTION CENTER CLASS FOR ARVN FIELD ARTILLERYMEN

plan revealed that a primary shortfall existed in artillery. The study projected weaknesses in fire power for the coming three fiscal years in the following areas: medium, heavy, and long-range artillery for 1971; medium and heavy artillery for 1972; and medium artillery for 1973.

In addition, the rapid expansion of Republic of Vietnam Armed Forces cut drastically into their experienced manpower pool and, in turn, diluted the leadership and technical base of newly created artillery units. To offset this problem Military Assistance Command emphasized the improvement of instruction at the Vietnamese Artillery School and approved its expansion. During 1970 the Artillery School enrolled 2,327 students, well above the 1,715 initially planned for the year. Instruction was improved. New programs were prepared for the survey officer course and the survey instructor course. A copy of the program for the U.S. artillery advanced course was obtained from Fort Sill, edited to emphasize essential portions, and provided to the director of instruction for updating the battalion commanders course. Several new gun emplacements with concrete ammunition and personnel bunkers were built in the school demonstration area.

In June 1970 the most significant training improvement occurred when the school began to co-ordinate service practice, fire direction, and gun crew training during live fire exercises. This arrangement saved ammunition and training time and released support troop gun crews to perform maintenance. Their training improved noticeably after the commandant directed that classes be inspected daily and written reports submitted.

In consonance with the American Vietnamization plan, the Republic of Vietnam Armed Forces Artillery Command implemented a new training program entitled the Reorganization Technique Plan. The program was to operate in an eleven-month time frame and was to raise the technical proficiency level of all Vietnamese artillery units. During Phase 1, January and February 1970, the Artillery Command developed the concepts and disseminated instructions and lesson plans to the artillery units, which in turn formed mobile instruction teams. In Phase II, March 1970, the various division artillery and corps artillery headquarters consolidated the mobile training teams, issued instructions, and conducted instructor training. In Phase III, April–November 1970, two-week training programs were presented at all firing positions and a proficiency test was administered. To insure the adequacy of the training, the corps or division artillery headquarters administered a unit test thirty days after the mobile training teams had completed the training and individual testing of all firing elements.

Once Military Assistance Command had established the added emphasis necessary to create a strong training base, it examined the problems of the projected artillery shortfalls. It became apparent that the fragmented positioning of artillery, as practiced by South Vietnamese Army units to secure lines of communication and strategic centers of population, detracted from the artillery's support of offensive operations. Even with the activation of new artillery battalions, the ratio of tubes to maneuver battalions did not increase significantly. Further, the requirement to man artillery platoons in static locations cut into the manpower pool of Vietnamese forces and created difficulties during new unit activations. To offset this weakness, Military Assistance Command approved the addition of 176 two-gun fire support platoons to replace Vietnamese artillery in fixed sites. Each platoon was authorized 29 spaces to be provided from Regional Forces assets. By year's end 100 of the 176 platoons were activated, and of these 53 were deployed throughout Vietnam. Training of the territorial artillerymen varied from military region to military region. In Military Region I, contingency plans, which had been formulated by XXIV Corps Artillery to train these forces, were activated. In Military Region II, training was accomplished at the Artillery School and the Vietnamese division training centers; II Field Force Artillery reoriented the Civilian Irregular Defense

Group Artillery School to prepare territorial forces to assume the artillery mission. In Military Region IV, the Vietnamese Corps Artillery established a training center for the Regional Forces artillerymen. With at least part of the light artillery problem solved, planners in Saigon attacked the Vietnamese long-range fire power weakness. After thorough investigation, Project ENHANCE was promulgated. This plan authorized the activation and deployment of five 175-mm. gun battalions. Three of these battalions were scheduled for deployment in Military Region I. The remaining two battalions were projected for Regions II and III. Two battalions were to be trained, equipped, and deployed along the demilitarized zone in 1971 to replace withdrawing American units.

Operations Into Cambodia

Although commanders throughout Vietnam were placing primary emphasis on Vietnamization and the structure of the program was taking shape, the American effort and the ability of Vietnamese forces to absorb it had not had a significant test. The vehicle through which the Vietnamese fighting potential could be tested and its progress more reliably gauged was rapidly approaching in the spring of 1970.

The sanctuaries and base areas established by the Communist forces along the South Vietnam-Cambodia boundary had long been a frustrating irritant to both American and Vietnamese military leaders. (*Map 20*) Although the occupation of these areas by the North Vietnamese was a flagrant violation of Cambodian neutrality, the position taken by Prince Sihanouk and his government made it impossible to conduct operations across the border in an effort to deny the enemy the free use of these sanctuaries. Sihanouk's neutrality was flexible, ranging from open hostility toward South Vietnam and her allies to a more agreeable tolerance of the North Vietnamese and the Viet Cong. Over the years, this tolerance permitted the establishment and maintenance of these base areas.

In the spring of 1970 the political atmosphere in Cambodia changed drastically and erupted into violence, which culminated in the overthrow of the Sihanouk regime. With the formation of the Lon Nol administration, the attitude of the Cambodian government changed completely; its hostility was directed away from the South Vietnamese and against the Communists. This reversal of position made possible the subsequent incursions into Cambodia.

Intelligence reports had been indicating a massive logistics buildup in the Cambodian sanctuaries in the Military Region III area for some time. Evidence was strong that the Communists were

ARVN 155-MM. HOWITZER STATIC POSITION

planning a major offensive—possibly similar in intensity to the 1968 *Tet* offensive. In addition, military intelligence had pinpointed the location of the Central Office of South Vietnam (COSVN), the major North Vietnamese headquarters for South Vietnam, in the "Fish Hook" region of Cambodia. The intent of the Cambodian incursion was to forestall an enemy offensive, despoil the sanctuaries, and, if possible, capture the Central Office. At the same time, the achievement of these objectives would so disrupt Communist plans and capabilities that the Vietnamization program would greatly benefit from the added time gained.

South Vietnamese operations into Cambodia commenced on 14 April 1970 with several limited penetrations into the "Angel's Wing" area. These penetrations were followed by a major Vietnamese thrust launched on 29 April 1970. Operation TOAN THANG 42 (Rock Crusher) was initiated by the Vietnamese III Corps attacking with three task forces into the Angel's Wing area and then south into the "Parrot's Beak" area of Cambodia. (*Map 21*) Each task force was supported by one battery of mixed 105-mm. howitzers and augmented by U.S. self-propelled medium artillery as needed. II Field Force Artillery supported the attack with six batteries of medium and heavy artillery, intially deployed to the north and east

ARVN 103D FIELD ARTILLERY BATTALION IN TRAINING

of the area of operations in order to provide maximum support for the maneuver units. Liaison to further insure timely support was established with all Vietnamese task forces, III Corps, and IV Corps. All U.S. artillery fires in TOAN THANG 42 were co-ordinated and controlled by a forward element of the 23d Artillery Group, which was collocated with the Vietnamese III Corps tactical operations center at Go Dau Ha and later at Tay Ninh. During the latter phases of this operation, two medium and two heavy batteries displaced into Cambodia to keep pace with the rapidly moving Vietnamese forces. These batteries provided close and continuous support to the maneuver elements but were not allowed to displace west of Svay Rieng, the westernmost limit of the politically imposed U.S. operational boundary. As the operation progressed, two of the task forces turned north to Prey Vang and the Chup Plantation.

On 27 April 1970, the 1st Cavalry Division was given the mission of planning and executing a campaign to eliminate the North Vietnamese base areas in the Fish Hook region of Cambodia adjacent to Military Region III. (*Map 22*) To accomplish this mission, elements of the 11th Armored Cavalry Regiment and the Vietnamese 1st Airborne Division were placed under the operational control of the 1st Cavalry Division. Task Force SHOEMAKER was formed to carry out the attack.

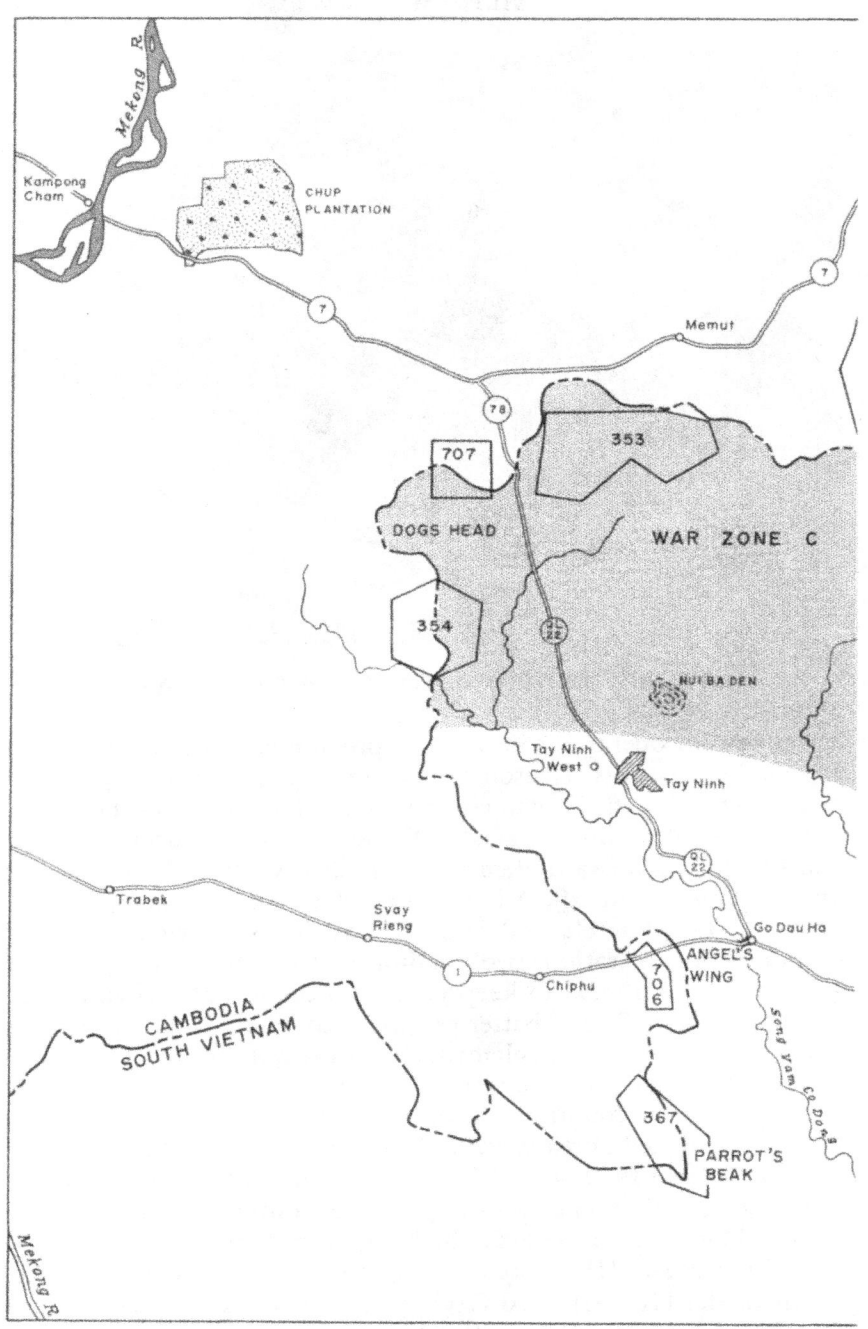

MAP 20

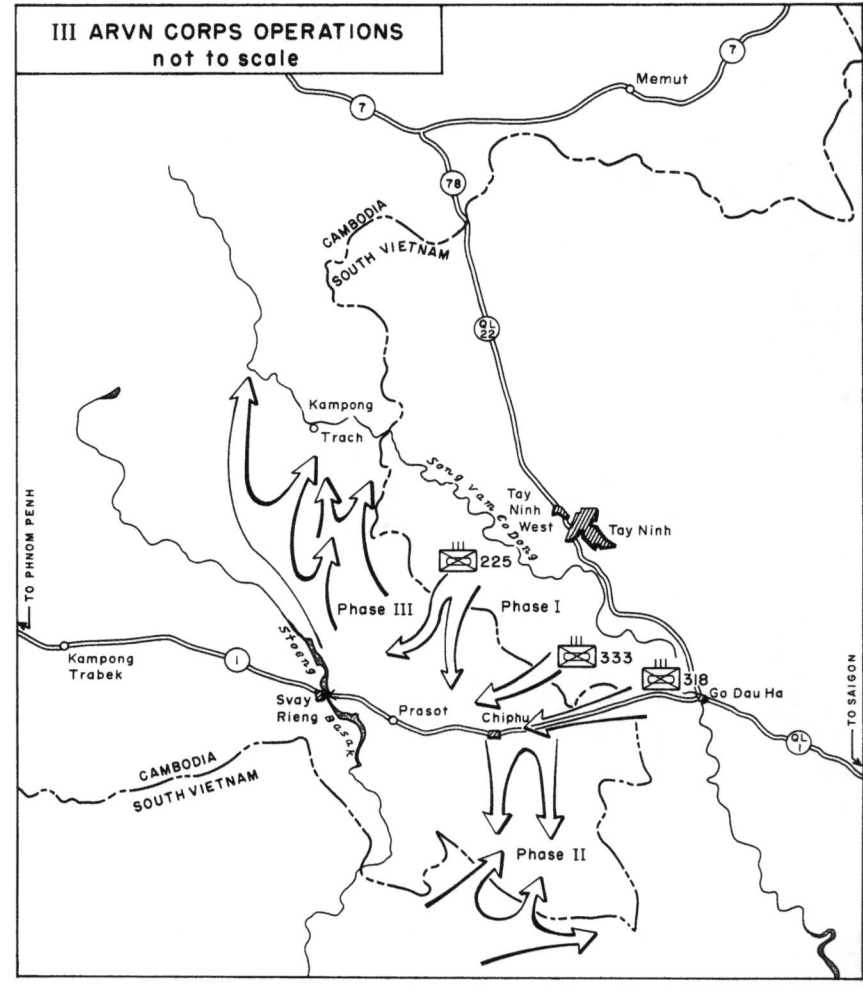

MAP 21

The maneuver plan was simple and direct. The 3d Brigade of the Vietnamese 1st Airborne Division would occupy blocking positions north of the objective area, and elements of the 1st Cavalry Division and the 11th Armored Cavalry Regiment would make a four-pronged attack from the south. Artillery would be provided from all the elements involved in the attack, and additional fire support would come from II Field Force Artillery units.

The fire support available was formidable and included the largest concentration of artillery, tactical air strikes, and B–52

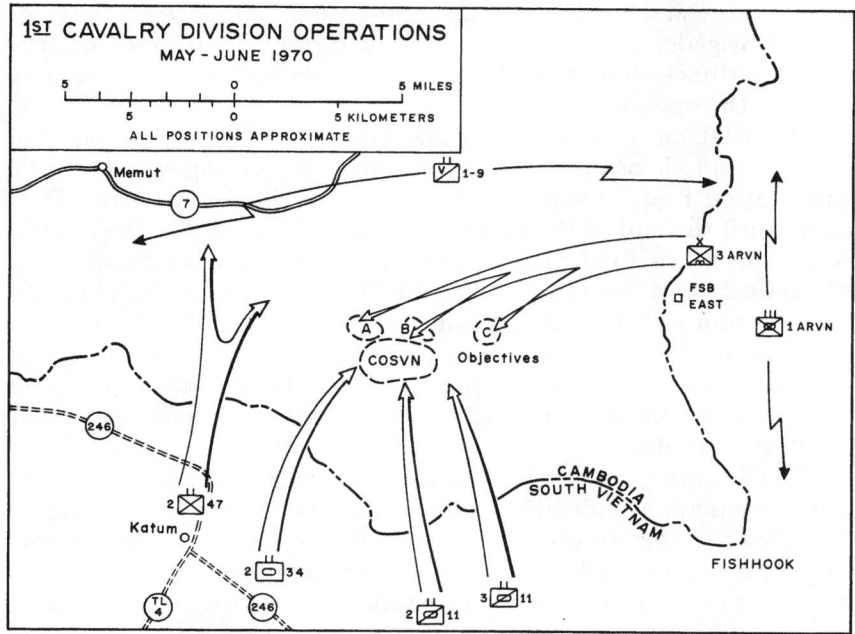

MAP 22

strikes committed in support of an operation of this size by the Free World Military Assistance Forces in the Republic of Vietnam. The fire support co-ordination planning required to support the operation was extremely complex and detailed. Initially, targeting information was limited; however, after the operation was approved, additional information became increasingly available from II Field Force and Military Assistance Command sources. The bulk of the fire planning was conducted during 27–29 April 1970. After the basic fire support annex and artillery fire support appendix were prepared, detailed co-ordination of fires with other fire support assets was conducted. Care was taken to insure that the various fire supports did not interfere with each other, times on target were adjusted to insure flight safety for ordnance-carrying aircraft, and definitive air corridors were established. The annex and appendix with target lists and overlays were distributed on 29 April for the D-day H-hour fires and on 30 April for the planned fires in support of subsequent phases of the operation.

Ninety-four cannon artillery pieces were positioned to support the initial phases of the attack: thirty-six 105-mm. howitzers, forty-eight 155-mm. howitzers, four 8-inch howitzers, and six 175-mm. guns. The initial positioning of artillery took place during the period 29 April–1 May 1970. By 30 April (D minus 1), the II Field

Force heavy and medium artillery, the direct support artillery for the 3d Brigade, 1st Cavalry Division, and one Vietnamese airborne artillery direct support battery were in position and prepared to support the operation.

At 0600 on 1 May, D-day, an extensive 390-minute planned artillery and air preparation was initiated. Beginning with the 0600 preparation fires, in support of elements of the 1st Airborne Division, until the end of the preparation at 1245, a total of 2,436 artillery rounds was fired. These fires were effectively integrated with 48 tactical airstrikes to complete the D-day preparations. Throughout the morning tactical air and cannon and aerial field artillery were simultaneously employed in the attack on multiple target complexes. The total fire support delivered for D-day operations included 185 tactical air sorties, 36 arc light missions, and 5,460 artillery rounds.

During the period 2-5 May, the detailed fire support planning paid handsome dividends as many lucrative targets were engaged. The heavy concentration of cannon artillery and flexible fire support co-ordination allowed fires to be massed again and again with relative ease. Artillery moves to support advancing friendly forces began on 2 May and were subsequently made whenever necessary to insure continuous artillery coverage. II Field Force Artillery units alone moved 198 times during the sixty-day operation to maintain pace with the maneuver forces.

On 5 May plans were initiated for an expansion of operations in Cambodia. As a result of the planned expansion, Task Force SHOEMAKER was dissolved and the responsibility for fire support co-ordination was passed from the task force to the 1st Cavalry Division.

With the initiation of Operation TOAN THANG 45 northeast of Bu Dop by the 2d Brigade of the 1st Cavalry Division, in Base Area 354 by elements of the U.S. 25th Infantry Division, and in Base Area 350 by the Vietnamese 9th Regiment, fire support co-ordination activities were expanded but did not change significantly from the smooth-functioning procedures previously established. Positioning II Field Force Artillery units centrally and well forward had facilitated the support of the additional maneuver units as they attacked into Base Areas 354, 707, 350, and 351. Except for a few batteries located in critical areas of III Corps, virtually all remaining units of II Field Force Artillery were moved to the Cambodian border or across it. During one three-day period, 32 artillery moves were conducted to place the firing elements in the best positions to support the expanded operations.

During the withdrawal phases of both TOAN THANG 43 and

TOAN THANG 45, extraction support plans were formulated to derive maximum benefit from all available fire support. The purpose of these plans was to deny the enemy access to the extraction sites and air corridors. Like the fire plans that had been developed for the conduct of the operation, the extraction support plans were comprehensive and effective. Each direct support artillery battalion planned the extraction fires for the supported brigade, and the division fire support co-ordination center co-operated closely with the Vietnamese airborne division artillery commander to establish the fire scheme for the withdrawal of the Vietnamese forces. These plans were so effective that continuous fire was maintained around the extraction sites and air corridors during the entire operation. By 1800 on 29 June 1970, all American units were withdrawn from Cambodia.

At the same time that the well-publicized campaign across the Cambodian border was kicking off in the Military Region III area, the 4th Infantry Division, located in the central highlands of II Corps Tactical Zone, received a warning order to be prepared to conduct operations across the border into Base Area 702 to locate and destroy enemy resources, installations, and command facilities. Planning was initiated immediately for the two-brigade assault. Fire support was provided by division artillery units reinforced by medium and heavy elements of the 52d Artillery Group. Division artillery established a forward tactical command post at New Plei Djereng and, in conjunction with a permanent liaison party provided by the 52d Artillery Group, developed the fire support plan for the operation, called BINH TAY I. Because South Vietnamese elements were involved in the operation, it was necessary to form the additional liaison parties to support Vietnamese units. A special fire support team was established with the Special Forces and Civilian Irregular Defense Group unit at New Plei Djereng to insure timely clearance of fire requests. Firing units were positioned in forward areas on 4 May 1970 to facilitate joining the maneuver forces and reduce the time required to lift the units into the selected fire support bases. After the planned occupation of the fire bases by the light and medium artillery batteries, only one battery was relocated within the base area. This move was required because of a decision to increase the troop density in the 1st Brigade area of operation. With this one exception, all artillery units remained in their initial positions throughout the Cambodian operation. Although artillery support of the operation was adequate, ammunition resupply problems hampered the total effectiveness of the firing units. A temporary ammunition supply point was established at New Plei Djereng; however, its stockage was not in accord with the recommended stockage objective. A critical shortage was avoided only because the initial combat assaults of the maneuver forces were delayed one day.

Although significant amounts of material were captured and destroyed, Operation BINH TAY I was less than a total success. Because of other commitments and operational requirements in II Corps, 4th Division elements were withdrawn ten days after the operation started and substantial areas were left unexploited. The lack of air assets, both Army and Air Force, artillery resupply problems, and heavy initial contact severely hampered the efficiency of the operation. Although Vietnamese forces continued to operate in Base Area 702 until 25 May 1970, the major tactical effort was complete with the withdrawal of the 1st Brigade units on 16 May.

The Cambodian incursion was an overwhelming success both in materiel captured or destroyed and the artillery rounds expended in support of the operation. During the two-month assault, friendly units expended 847,558 rounds of which 261,039 were fired by Vietnamese artillery units. Reported surveillance credited artillery units with 253 killed and 70 bunkers and 20 tunnel systems destroyed. Surprisingly, all artillery kills were reported by Vietnamese sources and 230 were reported as a result of the preparation fires that initiated the operation. The 1st Cavalry Division, in whose area of operations 708,965 rounds were fired by both U.S. and Vietnamese field artillery, did not credit the artillery with any kills or any bunker or tunnel destructions.

The Cambodian operation measured in terms of Vietnamization showed that weaknesses in Vietnamese fire support techniques still existed. Vietnamese artillery was not employed to its full effectiveness by task force commanders. Repeatedly, these commanders waited too long for tactical air, gunships, and light fire team support when direct support artillery was within range and ready to provide immediate fire. Throughout the operation, task force commanders called for tactical aircraft and light fire team strikes without regard to the nature of the target being engaged. Often, light fire teams were called to engage well-fortified positions—targets better suited for artillery engagement. This failure to expeditiously engage the enemy materially reduced the effectiveness of the combat mission. Often, Vietnamese artillery liaison officers and forward observers were not properly utilized. On numerous occasions the maneuver element commanders personally adjusted artillery fire and Vietnamese Air Force air strikes although trained observers were available. On several occasions, Vietnamese fire support officers were intimidated by their supported unit commanders to the extent that they would not approach the commanders with recommendations on the use of artillery. These failings resulted in lowering the effectiveness of the fire support and removed the commanders from their more immediate responsibilities of command. In addition, some co-ordination and liaison problems emerged between U.S. and Vietnamese forces. These problems were most acute whenever U.S. units were under the operational control of Vietnamese commands, and the difficulties manifested themselves in displacement, emplacement, and security arrangements. At times, slow reaction by the responsible Vietnamese headquarters in target clearance matters hampered the ability of the American artillery units to provide responsive fire support to elements in contact.

One of the most significant successes of the Cambodian incursion was really a byproduct of the action. With Vietnamese troops committed in such large numbers to the operation, territorial security became the primary responsibility of the Regional and Popular Forces. Their reaction to the challenge was surprisingly good and, more important, the confidence they gained from their successes served as a valuable psychological boost.

Toward Vietnamese Self-Sufficiency

With the termination of the Cambodian operation, primary attention was returned to Vietnamization. The performance of Vietnamese units during the recent campaign was carefully scrutinized, their strengths and weaknesses were analyzed, and emphasis was placed on those areas in which improvement was necessary. It also became apparent that the ability of ARVN artillery units to support maneuver forces adequately was substandard. Although the deployment of territorial artillery, as projected and approved by Military Assistance Command, was considered the ultimate answer, it was evident that, because of the physical limitation of training and equipping them, these platoons could not deploy rapidly enough to release Vietnamese artillery units to provide standard tactical support. At the same time, the redeployment of American artillery was progressing so rapidly that the "repositioning tactic" employed earlier in the year was losing its validity. It became apparent that immediate stopgap measures were required. More and more senior artillery commanders admitted that the platooning of American artillery for extended periods of time to increase area coverage was the best solution. Though it had been common practice in Vietnam to separate U.S. batteries into platoon positions, the practice had been viewed as a short-term expedient only. In the fall of 1970, Brigadier General Thomas J. McGuire, I Field Force Artillery commander, summed up the feeling of most artillery commanders when he said, " . . . even though US artillery is prepared to respond rapidly by moving and shooting to destroy the enemy, we are prepared to replace ARVN artillery platoons and batteries which are on LOC [lines of communication] missions so that these ARVN batteries may move with the ARVN maneuver elements and support them on operations."

This tactic became standard procedure for American artillery units during the latter phases of the war. It also magnified the myriad problems that had plagued Vietnamese artillerymen when they platooned their guns. U.S. commanders found that the problems—command and control, technical proficiency, maintenance, and apathetic personnel—they had attributed to the "personality" of the oriental were, in fact, the result of the fragmented employment of artillery units. Diminishing assets made logistical support of these subunits difficult, the lack of qualified fire direction personnel limited the efficiency of the platoons, the absence of well-defined missions caused morale problems, and battery commanders were often out of touch with major parts of their units.

To offset diminishing long-range fire capabilities, heavy artillery raids were planned and conducted frequently. These raids normally were co-ordinated: the targets were carefully planned, the ammunition was quickly fired, and the guns were returned to their normal positions.

By the end of the year, the Vietnamese artillery posture had increased substantially and further deployments were planned. A total of 1,116 tubes were providing artillery support throughout the country.

ARVN Artillery Posture, 31 December 1970

Units	Authorized	Activated	Deployed
105–mm. battalion (divisional)	30	30	30
105–mm. battalion (airborne)	3	3	3
105–mm. battalion (separate)	7	7	7
155–mm. battalion (divisional)	10	10	10
155–mm. battalion (separate)	5	5	5
175–mm. battalion (separate)	2	0	0
Sector artillery platoon (105–mm.)	176	100	53

With the approval of Project ENHANCE in the fall of 1970, XXIV Corps was directed to prepare a comprehensive training program for presentation to cadre personnel of the 101st Artillery Battalion, the first Vietnamese 175-mm. gun unit scheduled for activation.

Corps artillery began this mission by carefully scrutinizing the composition of the proposed unit to insure that each facet of 175-mm. gun employment received sufficient coverage in the program of instruction. Added emphasis was placed on maintenance, since this was to be the initial experience of ARVN forces with self-propelled artillery. Meteorological training received special consideration because, by tables of organization and equipment, the Vietnamese gun battalions were assigned meteorological teams. In early 1971 the program of instruction was approved, and the schooling of sixteen Vietnamese cadres began on 15 March 1971. On 19 April cadre training was completed and the general instruction of troops initiated. Fire direction and firing battery procedures were taught at Fire Support Base CARROLL, meteorology was taught at Fire Support Base NANCY, and driver and maintenance procedures were taught at numerous locations throughout Military Region I. Although instruction was conducted by the newly trained cadres, American experts were available to supervise and advise as necessary. Deployment of the first 175-mm. gun unit was scheduled for July–August 1971.

The year 1971 brought another shift in the Vietnamization concept. Since the promulgation of the Vietnamization program in November 1969, the basis for Vietnamization had been training programs and combined operations conceived and controlled by Americans. By 1971, the American troop strength in Vietnam had been halved and it became apparent that the capability of U.S. units to directly support training programs was fast diminishing. At the same time, American commanders felt that if Vietnamese forces were to become self-reliant, they would have to provide the training impetus for themselves. Assistance was offered only as needed and required. This shift in policy produced some hopeful indications as the Vietnamese began to assume the initiative in meeting most of their requirements.

In 1971, Military Assistance Command reviewed the Vietnamization program and divided it into three phases:

Phase I—Turn over ground combat responsibilities to the Republic of Vietnam Armed Forces.

Phase II—Develop air, naval, artillery, logistics, and other support capabilities of the Republic of Vietnam Armed Forces to the degree that effective independent security can be maintained.

Phase III—Reduce the American artillery presence to a military advisory mission and, finally, withdraw as the South Vietnamese become capable of handling the Communist threat without U.S. military assistance.

Although these phases were rather definitively stated, work was being done in both Phases I and II because it was impossible to achieve any success in the first phase without substantial gains in the second.

Having examined and approved the feasibility of providing self-propelled 175-mm. guns to Vietnamese forces, Military Assistance Command began studies relative to the turnover of self-propelled 155-mm. howitzers. The concept called for the activation of three battalions armed with the M109 howitzers. The study was continued until 23 August 1971, when General Abrams informed General Vien, Chief of the Vietnamese Joint General Staff, that the activation of the three new battalions was not feasible and that " . . . introduction of this new weapon into ARVN will overtax the training base and the logistics system, which is not now prepared to cope with the maintenance difficulties presented by this weapon . . ."

Meanwhile, in January 1971 U.S. and ARVN commands planned an operation across the border into Laos from Quang Tri Province in northern Military Region I. Both U.S. and South Vietnamese intelligence estimates had strongly indicated that the enemy was preparing to conduct an intensified resupply and reinforcement operation in southern Laos as well as to build up supplies and equipment in Military Region I. Sources estimated enemy strength across the Quang Tri Province border to be 13,000 line and 9,000 support troops. In view of the successful Cambodian sanctuary operations of 1970, the logical tactical follow-up would be an effort to disrupt North Vietnamese supply and reinforcement operations.

The operation, termed LAM SON 719 and commanded by the commanding general of the Vietnamese I Corps, did not call for the employment of American ground forces in Laos. However, U.S. air assets augmented the South Vietnamese Air Force in supporting ground operations. To permit a greater Vietnamese effort, American ground units provided extensive ground support in northwestern Quang Tri Province.

U.S. and Vietnamese forces estimated a four-phase offensive:

Phase I—U.S. units would open fire bases in Khe Sanh Plateau and secure Route 9 as well as staging areas and artillery positions from which to support subsequent operations.

Phase II—Vietnamese forces would attack into Laos on three axes, with the major axis along Route 9. Attacks would carry no further west than Tchepone, about thirty kilometers into Laos.

Phase III—Gains would be consolidated.

Phase IV—Friendly forces would be extracted.

Planning for the employment of U.S. artillery to support Phase I was extensive. Although ARVN maneuver units had their own light and medium artillery, they needed augmentation by heavy U.S. artillery operating from the border. To this end, fire support was planned between the I Corps fire support element and the XXIV U.S. Corps fire support element through I Corps Artillery, the I Corps G–3, and the I Corps Artillery adviser. In addition, plans included co-ordination with the 108th U.S. Artillery Group, the control headquarters for heavy U.S. artillery.

The 108th Artillery Group consisted of the 8th Battalion, 4th Field Artillery, and the 2d Battalion, 94th Field Artillery, each with four 8-inch howitzers and eight 175-mm. guns, as well as Battery B, 1st Battalion, 39th Field Artillery, with four 175-mm. guns. The 4th Battalion, 77th Aerial Field Artillery, 101st Airborne Division, was also available to support the operation and, being an air asset, was not restricted by borders. Three 175-mm. batteries and one 8-inch battery were situated along the Laos-Vietnam border. The remaining batteries were set up in the Khe Sanh area.

Phase I, dubbed Operation DEWEY CANYON, proceeded without a significant hitch. However, subsequent phases, which were to be conducted primarily by Vietnamese forces, went awry. Plans called for the Vietnamese 1st Airborne Division to conduct an airmobile attack all the way to Tchepone. At the same time, the Vietnamese 1st Armored Brigade was to attack along Route 9 and link up with the airborne division to open up necessary supply lines. Unfortunately, the armored brigade did not fulfill its mission. It could neither advance with sufficient speed to provide a timely linkup nor keep the route to its rear open. Supplies to the airborne force had to be moved by air against intensive enemy antiaircraft fires. The consolidation phase ended quickly and extraction began in haste. Enemy pressure forced the abandonment of equipment, including artillery pieces. Notwithstanding the loss of equipment, statistics were quite impressive in favor of Vietnamese forces. Over 19,360 enemy were killed in action whereas ARVN forces sustained 1,749 killed.

In terms of Vietnamization, LAM SON 719 again pointed out Vietnamese weaknesses, particularly the inability of units to co-ordinate fire support. Without the assistance of U.S. advisers, who had been left behind, the South Vietnamese displayed a marked deficiency in requesting and controlling artillery and tactical air. Weapons were poorly matched to targets, air strikes were often requested for targets more suitable for artillery, and aerial field artillery was often requested to attack targets beyond its capabilities. So inefficient was the fire support co-ordination system that in most cases maneuver units abandoned the procedures and sent fire requests directly to fire support elements.

1972 Enemy Offensive

In mid-1971, shortly after the conclusion of LAM SON 719, Military Assistance Command redeployed the 1st Brigade of the 5th Infantry Division and thus removed the last American maneuver unit from the demilitarized zone. Artillery units of the 108th Artillery Group, however, remained because Vietnamese forces still desperately needed artillery assets. To fill the void created by the withdrawal of the American forces, the Joint General Staff activated the Vietnamese Division. This unit was a conglomeration of independent units already operating in Military Region I and newly created units still being trained and outfitted. Artillery elements taken from I Corps Artillery assets and redesignated the 30th and 32d Artillery Battalions supported the newly created division. Of these, the 30th Artillery Battalion was a 155-mm. howitzer unit. The third direct support element, the 33d Artillery Battalion, was activated on 1 December 1971. Unit training was to start 17 January 1972, and field deployment was scheduled for 1 April 1972.

Over-all, 1971 was a wait-and-see year. More and more responsibility was given to Vietnamese units, and their performance was evaluated. Although operationally their performance was spotty, there were some hopeful indicators. Territorial artillery assumed greater fire support responsibilities, and by year's end 100 platoons had been deployed; the Artillery School continued to revamp and upgrade its program to include initiation of the artillery officer's advanced course in August; and in some divisions, the artillery began to assume traditional support roles and develop habitual support relationships with the maneuver regiments. By December, deployed Vietnamese artillery strength had increased to 1,202 tubes of various calibers, including twelve 175-mm. guns.

ARVN Artillery Posture, 31 December 1971

Unit	Authorized	Activated	Deployed
105–mm. battalion (divisional)	33	33	32
105–mm. battalion (separate)	5	5	5
105–mm. battalion (airborne)	3	3	3
155–mm. battalion (divisional)	11	11	11
155–mm. battalion (separate)	4	4	4
175–mm. battalion (separate)	2	2	1
Sector artillery platoon (105–mm.)	176	135	100

By mid-December 1971, intelligence sources were beginning to note increased enemy activity along the Ho Chi Minh Trail and in the demilitarized zone area of Vietnam. As this buildup continued and a pattern of sorts developed, American and Vietnamese commanders began warning their commands to prepare for a major enemy offensive commencing with the *Tet* holidays in mid-February. As the pulse of enemy movements picked up through January 1972, commanders increased vigilance and expected heavy action to erupt with the Vietnamese new year. American leaders believed that the expected offensive would be the greatest test of Vietnamization, perhaps with the preservation of the entire nation at stake. Wary eyes studied the demilitarized zone. If a major attack materialized, the untested 3d Division would have to bear the brunt of the fighting.

Tet passed with no significant increase in enemy action. Allied commanders continued to expect an attack, but the vigilance and readiness established for the holidays could not be maintained. As the days after *Tet* slipped by without action, the nervous edge of the troops faded and daily routine returned to normal. Then on 30 March 1972 the North Vietnamese launched an infantry-armor attack through the east central portion of the demilitarized zone against the fire bases defended by elements of the 3d Division. With this attack, the Nguyen Hue offensive started. The North Vietnamese units quickly routed the defending forces and slashed forward toward Dong Ha. South Vietnamese forces fled in the face of the onslaught, and Dong Ha fell with little resistance. Farther south in Military Region I, the North Vietnamese attacked east from Laos and by 14 April had captured Fire Support Base BASTOGNE and were threatening Hue. Meanwhile, in Military Region III, Communist forces launched their An Loc campaign on 1 April by overrunning Fire Support Base PACE, 35 kilometers northwest of Tay Ninh city. On 5 April, the North Vietnamese attacked Loc Ninh and controlled the city by the next morning. The withdrawing South Vietnamese forces suffered continual attacks and sustained heavy casualties as they moved south on Route 13. By this time General Minh, commander of III Corps, realized that the main enemy effort would be in Binh Long Province and quickly reinforced An Loc. On 10 April, the anticipated offensive began. The North Vietnamese 9th Division, supported by armor elements, attacked An Loc.

In Military Region II, the initial enemy action was limited to increased harrassing tactics, interdiction of Route 14 at the Kontum Pass, and the successful closing of the An Khe Pass on Route 19 on 11 April 1972.

Action in the Mekong Delta was negligible.

Early in the offensive, some of the objectives of the co-ordinated attacks throughout the Republic of Vietnam became apparent:

1. To divide the national reserves and force piecemeal and, therefore, indecisive commitment of these forces.

2. To give the impression of greater strength by attacking on several "fronts."

3. To promote a lack of decisiveness on a South Vietnamese command structure faced with few clearcut options and several ominous potential situations.

4. To encourage widespread dissatisfaction with the government of Vietnam by demonstrating its inability to protect its people.

The strategy of the enemy in attaining these objectives centered on the provincial capitals. These cities or towns were focal points because of, first, their governmental prominence; second, their relative isolation; and, third, their comparatively weak defenses. It also became clear that the ultimate objective of the North Vietnamese was the capture of Quang Tri, Qui Nhon, Kontum, An Loc, Tay Ninh, and, because of its psychological importance as the historical and cultural center of Vietnam, Hue. The loss of these cities could well have precipitated the collapse of the South Vietnam government.

The first two weeks of the offensive were disastrous for the South Vietnamese forces. Throughout the country they experienced heavy personnel losses, had to face infantry and armor attacks in significant numbers for the first time, and, often, especially in Military Region I, found themselves outgunned by enemy artillery. During the first ten days of the Nguyen Hue offensive, South Vietnamese units lost 81 105-mm. howitzers, 32 155-mm. howitzers, and 4 175-mm. guns. Most of their losses were due to reliance on aircraft for fire base evacuation and the inability of the aircraft to do the job because of enemy artillery. In Military Region I, the 30th and 31st Artillery Battalions of the 3d Division lost all their guns and the 33d Artillery Battalion escaped similar fate only because it was still in training and only partially deployed. Still, the 33d managed to lose 2 of its guns. All the fire support bases north and west of Dong Ha were overrun and the artillery positioned there was captured or destroyed. Artillery losses throughout the remainder of South Vietnam were fewer only because units were more widely deployed.

Throughout April and May the North Vietnamese Army continued to apply pressure along all the fronts. In Military Region I, enemy units attacked and captured Quang Tri in early May. In Military Region II, the drive in the highlands began on 23 April. In quick succession Fire Support Bases 5 and 6, Tanh Canh, and

ARVN Artillery Losses, 31 March–10 April 1972

Weapon Caliber	Unit	Military Region	Number
105–mm.	Marines	I	16
105–mm.	31st Field Artillery Battalion	I	18
105–mm.	33d Field Artillery Battalion	I	2
105–mm.	14th Field Artillery Battalion	I	5
105–mm.	22d Field Artillery Battalion	I	6
155–mm.	30th Field Artillery Battalion	I	18
175–mm.	101st Field Artillery Battalion	I	4
155–mm.	220th Field Artillery Battalion	II	2
155–mm.	37th Field Artillery Battalion	II	2
105–mm.	51st Field Artillery Battalion	III	2
105–mm.	53d Field Artillery Battalion	III	12
105–mm.	52d Field Artillery Battalion	III	4
105–mm.	182d Field Artillery Battalion	III	6
105–mm.	Ranger Border Camp	III	2
155–mm.	50th Field Artillery Battalion	III	8
105–mm.	91st Field Artillery Battalion	IV	1
105–mm.	211th Field Artillery Battalion	IV	2
105–mm.	213th Field Artillery Battalion	IV	1
105–mm.	419th Field Artillery Platoon	IV	2
105–mm.	449th Field Artillery Platoon	IV	2
155–mm.	90th Field Artillery Battalion	IV	2

Dak To fell and northwestern Kontum Province was in enemy hands. In Military Region III, An Loc remained under pressure, Dau Tieng suffered attacks, and the interdiction of Route 13 continued.

As these actions occurred, South Vietnamese forces began to regroup. They stiffened their resistance to enemy pressure and, with the aid of massive air support, including large numbers of B–52 arc light strikes, slowed the momentum of the enemy thrust. During May the action began to stabilize as ARVN forces established a defensive line along the My Chanh River in Military Region I, stopped the enemy at Kontum, and stubbornly resisted at An Loc. Although enemy pressure remained great throughout May, the thrust of the offensive had been blunted. Once checked, the North Vietnamese attack never regained its force. Throughout the counteroffensive that followed, opportune application of artillery and air power prohibited enemy buildups and attacks.

The late May stabilization permitted South Vietnamese commanders to scrutinize carefully the over-all situation and take appropriate actions. When it became apparent that An Loc and Kontum would not fall, they turned their attention to planning a counteroffensive in Military Region I to recapture Quang Tri Province.

Whereas the actions around both Kontum and An Loc were monuments to air power, the counterattack out of the My Chanh River line proceeded along conventional lines. The purpose of the counterattack, dubbed Operation LAM SON 72, was to provide a defense for Hue, secure the Quang Tri and Dong Ha area, and destroy enemy forces and restore government control to Quang Tri Province.

Republic of Vietnam Armed Forces limited their operations during most of June to repositioning of forces, probing attacks to test enemy strengths, and cover and deception activities. Then, on 28 June, the counterattack began. The Airborne Division conducted the main attack west of Route 1 in the direction of La Vong and Quang Tri. The Marine Division conducted the supporting attack along Route 555 in the direction of Trien Phong and Quang Tri. Initial progress was slow but steady. South Vietnamese forces met only moderate resistance. As they approached the Thach Han River, however, enemy reaction stiffened. By the time the Airborne Division had reached the outskirts of Quang Tri city on 7 July, it was clear that the enemy intended to hold the city at all costs. The counterattack ground to a halt. Although the initial plan called for Quang Tri to be bypassed, recapture of the city now became an emotional national objective. On 27 July, the boundary between the Airborne and Marine Divisions was shifted and the more heavily equipped marines were given the mission of taking the city. The airborne troopers were ordered to secure the Thach Han River line, seize Fire Support Base BARBARA, block enemy supply routes from the west, and secure Route 1—the corps main supply line.

Success during August continued to be limited, and it was not until early September that the final phase of the Quang Tri battle began. Then the marines launched the final push against the citadel within the city. Progress was slow and costly in the face of determined enemy resistance, but on 11 September 1972 the marines succeeded in breaching the citadel wall. After heavy fighting at close quarters for five days, the marines gained control of the citadel on 16 September and by nightfall on the 17th the city belonged to the Marine Division. Activity now shifted to the area of operation of the Airborne Division as they drove to capture Fire Support Base BARBARA. Their efforts were hampered by heavy attacks by fire and deteriorating weather as the October monsoon began to bring its heavy rains. However, by the end of October the fire support base was recaptured and the major tasks of the counteroffensive were accomplished.

The employment of artillery in support of the counteroffensive in Military Region I gradually evolved from the fire base concept to conventional tactics. This change resulted from the introduction of 122-mm. and 130-mm. artillery weapons by the enemy and the effective use of these weapons against fixed fire bases. Although artillery contributed extensively to the success of the combat operations, poor artillery procedures were evident in all units. The failure to survey, register, and apply meteorological data and the use of improper ammunition-handling procedures reduced the accuracy of artillery fire. Further, a tendency to substitute massive unobserved fires for less intense observed fires resulted in excessive ammunition expenditure rates. At the same time, the development of the I Corps fire support element at Hue during May 1972 enabled the corps, for the first time, to integrate all U.S. and Vietnamese fire support means. The fire support element worked extremely well and contributed substantially to the success of the corps operation.

Problems During Phase-Down of U.S. Forces

The massive emphasis given so suddenly to Vietnamization caused a variety of feelings among the Republic of Vietnam Armed Forces leaders. These feelings became more and more verbal in early 1970. In connection with an assessment of the Vietnamization effort, II Field Force, Vietnam, indicated:

> To most senior ARVN Commanders, Vietnamization has provided the motivation . . . to assume the responsibility for the defense of their country in as short a time as possible. Many of these responsible individuals also express concern lest the Vietnamization process move too rapidly, leaving them to face a determined and waiting enemy before they are fully ready. Other responsible ARVN officers are optimistic about ARVN combat units taking over now . . . but they emphasize the continued need for U.S. combat support (helicopter, artillery, etc.) and logistics support . . . until these ARVN capabilities are fully built up.

Even as Vietnamese leaders were expressing anxiety over the relatively high speed of the Vietnamization programs, American commanders began experiencing operational difficulties caused by redeployments, stand-downs, and space reductions. To counter these problems, comprehensive studies were conducted to discern the most efficient utilization of the remaining assets. These studies revealed gaps in artillery coverage, poor utilization of heavy artillery capability, and unsatisfactory positioning of light artillery. The best example of the results of such a study was Operation METRO MEDIA executed by I Field Force Artillery. Between January and March 1970, over seventeen sequential and co-ordinated complete relocations of artillery battalion headquarters and subordinate elements were conducted. The moves resulted in I Field Force Artillery assets being positioned most effectively to accomplish the required support mission. Better utilization of the long-range capability of heavy artillery was realized and a quick reaction artillery force was created in the central portion of Military Region II.

Further problems were generated by the actual redeployment of artillery units. Since withdrawal plans and Vietnamization programs did not emanate from the same source, more often than not the administrative considerations of stand-down clashed with the tactical requirements of the commands affected by redeployment. Often, artillery coverage was not immediately available to replace that provided by the recalled elements and a short-fuzed shuffle of the remaining artillery assets ensued. This tended to lower the effectiveness of offensive operations because of the lack of adquate fire support. The withdrawal of the 9th Infantry Division from Military Region IV is a good example of this loss of fire power. The movement of the division from the Mekong Delta caused an immediate loss of three artillery battalions. Even when all the artillery with the Vietnamese 7th Division became operational, there was a net loss of two artillery battalions, and the addition of two battalions to IV Corps assets was insufficient to upgrade the artillery posture of the upper delta without affecting other portions of IV Corps Tactical Zone. Additional hardships resulted from the lack of experience by which to gauge the time requirements of stand-down. The effort to insure optimum artillery coverage for the longest time often placed inordinately heavy administrative requirements on the redeploying units.

The time squeeze was most apparent in personnel matters, in which transfers within the country and tour completion requirements posed difficulties. In addition, early stand-down cut into the active artillery posture, forced hasty repositioning, and at times affected offensive operations in progress. At the same time, early stand-down caused administrative problems by leaving units with no equipment, no mission, and no motivation—a situation ready made for racial tensions, drug incidents, and morale problems.

An additional problem that affected artillery units was the far-flung deployment of some firing elements. This widespread positioning prevented the battalion headquarters from effectively controlling the stand-down of their batteries. To overcome this situation, higher headquarters directed battalions in the same locale as the isolated unit to assist the battery during stand-down operations. The assisting battalion was not staffed to absorb the added work load.

As redeployment progressed the experience factors were established, most of the administrative hardships were overcome, and a general system was developed. The tactical difficulties, however, remained and often grew. Because of the technical and personnel limitations, Vietnamization in certain areas of the country lagged behind the pace of the American withdrawal programs.

With the introduction of tube artillery by the enemy during the Nguyen Hue offensive, the weakness of South Vietnamese target acquisition means and counterbattery techniques became apparent. This inability to produce lucrative artillery targets was compounded by the consistent ability of enemy artillery to outrange South Vietnamese artillery and thus make counterbattery fires almost impossible. To offset this weakness the Field Artillery School at Fort Sill sent target assistance teams to Vietnam to aid in "target acquisition, with emphasis on the counterbattery program." The teams arrived in Vietnam on 21 May 1972 and deployed to the field two days later. Their success depended on the specific needs of each South Vietnamese division: its mission, its degree of involvement with the North Vietnamese offensive, and the attitude of its commanders. The teams were fairly successful in helping to establish counterbattery intelligence centers, especially in I Corps where units were heavily committed to combat operations against North Vietnamese forces.

ENEMY ARTILLERY EMPLOYED DURING NGUYEN HUE OFFENSIVE

Weapon	Supplying Country
M46 130–mm. field gun	Soviet Union, Peoples Republic of China
D74 122–mm. field gun	Soviet Union
M38 122–mm. howitzer	Soviet Union, Peoples Republic of China
A19 122–mm. corps gun	Soviet Union
M44 100–mm. field gun	Soviet Union
D44 85–mm. field gun	Soviet Union
ZIS3 76–mm. field gun	Soviet Union

The following results highlighted some of the target acquisition efforts of the target assistance teams and South Vietnamese units: the 18th Division acquired 178 confirmed targets over a seventeen-day period; the 21st Division destroyed 6 howitzers; the 22d Division destroyed 2 howitzers; and I Corps destroyed 11 130-mm. guns, 2 122-mm. weapons, and ammunition storage.

However, the main source of targeting information concerning hostile armor and artillery weapons continued to come from airborne visual and electronic observation conducted by U.S. Army and Air Force resources.

More telling of the state of Vietnamization was the report of the target assistance teams. The Vietnamese Artillery School, the report concluded, performed "its mission in an outstanding manner" and its curriculum incorporated sufficient instruction in target acquisition. "The inadequacies in the proper employment of counterbattery tactics and techniques appeared to be generated in the field." Units such as the Vietnamese 25th and 1st Divisions had personnel knowledgeable in counterbattery procedures but saw no need to employ counterbattery tactics and techniques. They entertained, the teams reported, "no real sense of urgency." This neglect led to deterioration and eventual inability to employ effective counterbattery programs. The teams observed that the units required "strong ARVN command emphasis with corresponding advisory followup." The solution, then, seemed to lie not with more instruction but with constant supervision. Here, in microcosm, was the dilemma of the entire Vietnamization program. U.S. Army, Vietnam, units had to support maneuver elements and simultaneously supply the drive behind Vietnamization. Personnel problems alone often destined the latter task to be secondary. And, without full-time support, the Vietnamese failed to perceive the necessity of certain procedures. Consequently, they remained dependent on American aid.

The teams also provided valuable information concerning North Vietnamese Army artillery employment methods. Their analysis indicated that the North Vietnamese artillerymen were extremely professional and capable. The gunners generally fired at optimum range and preferred to mass widely separate pieces in surprise fires. Their ability to utilize artillery in this manner indicated that they surveyed gun positions, established effective communication systems, and exercised centralized control of fires.

On the other hand, the target assistance teams found that South Vietnamese artillerymen still ignored basic requirements necessary for effective fire support. ARVN artillery units did not conduct registrations and limited survey functions to utilize the existing survey established by American units prior to redeployment. Moreover, all South Vietnamese units except the 1st Division ignored meteorological data. For these reasons, it became apparent that although artillery fires normally were available, Vietnamese commanders preferred to call on tactical air assets to neutralize targets.

Although the Nguyen Hue offensive remained in the forefront

throughout most of 1972, Vietnamization continued. During August, September, and October, the activation of three 175-mm. gun battalions marked the completion of the Project ENHANCE schedule. The Army of the Republic of Vietnam projected the employment of these battalions in Military Regions I, II, and III. Of these units, the 104th Artillery Battalion was the first to receive guns supplied directly from the United States rather than guns transferred within the country from departing American units.

The South Vietnamese Artillery School initiated a systems engineering approach in the structuring of programs of instruction. A thorough program of briefings and discussion insured that key personnel understood the systems engineering concept and that continuity would be maintained if key personnel were transferred. The school added classes in crater analysis and target acquisition for cadre personnel from the various branch schools and training centers throughout Vietnam. These classes were to be a base for similar courses at these various places.

Facilities at the Artillery School remained inadequate. There were only fourteen classrooms. When these were filled, classes were held in other facilities or on the parade field. The school submitted a compound improvement construction plan to V Area Logistics Command on four occasions, the last in October 1972, but received no replies.

A revised table of organization and equipment would have increased the instructor force level adequately to support the student population. Submitted some eighteen months before, the new table had still not been approved in late 1972.

Despite these shortcomings, the school managed to provide the basic training required to establish the foundation for South Vietnamese artillery. On 20–21 December 1972, the Field Liaison Directorate, Liaison and Inspection Team, evaluated the school and gave it a good rating.

From October 1972 until the cease-fire in early 1973, the entire scope of the war changed. As peace rumors increased, combat action rose. Both sides began final "land-grabbing and flag-raising operations." Vietnamization became primarily a logistical exercise in an attempt to stockpile as much equipment in Vietnam as possible. For all practical purposes, the active Vietnamization program had ended.

With the signing of the cease-fire on 25 February 1973 and its effective date on 28 February 1973, the United States involvement in Vietnam came to an end. During the last three years of that involvement, efforts were concentrated on preparing the Vietnamese to defend their country without active American participation. An assessment of that effort would show that despite the adoption of program after program to assist ARVN forces in becoming proficient in all phases of fire support, little improvement was to be seen in combat. The Ben Het–Dak To Campaign in 1969 pointed out weaknesses in fire support co-ordination, adjustment of fire, and clearance procedures. One year later the same weaknesses appeared during the Cambodian incursion. The LAM SON 719 operation in 1971 did not change the picture, and the Nguyen Hue campaign during 1972 added technical shortcomings to the fire coordination weaknesses noted in the earlier actions. In addition, surveys conducted throughout Vietnam during the period continued to show that Vietnamese forces ignored advanced gunnery procedures.

In retrospect, it is apparent that in almost all the field artillery programs that were cited as successful during the Vietnamization period, American units were actively involved, providing labor and material. The Vietnamese were merely recipients of a service. It can be argued that by providing the major impetus to the Vietnamization program the Americans doomed the program to marginal success at best. By providing services to the Vietnamese, the argument would go, the American command failed to involve the Vietnamese actively and therefore failed to teach them how to perform the work themselves or convince them of the program's value.

But the American command was in a quandary. Senior commanders were certainly intelligent enough to foresee the disadvantages of allowing American units to do the work while the Vietnamese sat idly by. On the other hand, much had to be accomplished in a short time. Any adviser could attest to the fact that it took time to convince ARVN commanders that an improvement was needed and to show them how to carry it out. If U.S. programs were to be successful, they would at least have to be implemented and, restricted by time, Americans would have to furnish the major impetus. Then the Vietnamese could at least be exposed to those techniques necessary to provide the best fire support possible. With American air power denied them, Vietnamese forces would turn more and more to their artillery to fill the gap in fire power. To provide this support, the artillery hopefully would be forced to utilize the techniques to which they were exposed during Vietnamization. Whether in fact they do is, of course, the question.

CHAPTER VII

An Overview

Work To Be Done

The U.S. Army's experience in Vietnam showed that developments and refinements in Army doctrine, organization, and materiel must help to realize the maximum effectiveness of American fire power in future conflicts. A major effort of the Army will continue to be devoted to fighting a conventional war because the greatest threat to national survival is recognized as coming from the Soviet bloc and Warsaw Pact countries. Priority must go to training, organizing, and equipping U.S. forces to fight on the terrain of fully developed countries against a sophisticated, armor-heavy enemy. But placing emphasis on preparing for one type of war will not necessarily preclude preparing for others, since many of the important needs of the Army in the areas of field artillery materiel and doctrinal development are equally applicable to the armor-heavy conventional war and to the counterguerrilla threat.

The primary emphasis of U.S. field artillery in training will be on survival on the modern battlefield, planning fires more quickly, and shooting faster because the gravity and intensity of future combat will require immediate response. To suppress enemy fires immediately will, in the long run, better accomplish the mission of close, continuous, and timely fire support to the maneuver forces. As discussed in Chapter V, the success of U.S. artillery fire at Khe Sanh, where rounds were "on the way" in forty seconds, is ample testimony to this fact. In Vietnam the field artillery, for reasons cited in earlier chapters, was not always responsive. While the Army may again be required to operate under strict rules of engagement, it is also developing new techniques, doctrine, target acquisition equipment, and extended range weapons, and is re-emphasizing the fire support mission as a vital part of the combined arms team. All of these new developments have one purpose—to make field artillery responsive. The field artillery was often accused of being too slow and unresponsive in Vietnam because to achieve the accuracy demanded in many cases, double and triple checks were cranked into the fire support process. The more checks, the more rules placed on the system, the longer it took to get a round off. Thus, some of these accusations were justified, but now training is designed to achieve the best of both worlds—faster response without degrading the concern for safety and accuracy. This training is applicable to a counterinsurgency or to the conventional, mid-intensity conflict.

Target acquisition is another excellent example of the meshing of U.S. Army needs in counterguerrilla and conventional warfare. Field artillery experiences in Vietnam underscored the fact that developments in target acquisition organizations and materiel through the 1960's had not kept pace with developments in weapons and mobility systems. Two general historical examples from Vietnam illustrate this point. First, American survey equipment was unequal to the task. In order to conduct a detailed survey with the means available, survey teams were required to bring control unusually long distances from questionable survey control points over insecure terrain. Even when these obstacles could be overcome, the means used were unresponsive to the needs of the many firing batteries that moved continuously, often two or three times in one day. As a result, survey personnel took shortcuts to obtain position and direction, although the shortcuts lessened accuracy. The requirement for similar rapid moves exists on the modern battlefield, conventional, armor-heavy, or otherwise. Second, the field artillery was deficient in locating enemy mortars, rockets, and artillery. The sector of scan of the 1950-era radar, the MPQ–4A, was unacceptably small. The Army had no radar designed to track low-trajectory projectiles, and the equipment available to vector on enemy firing positions by sound ranging was obsolescent and consequently never used effectively in Vietnam.

Much has been done to correct these target acquisition deficiencies. Advances in survey equipment and follow-up position determining systems indicate that the field artillery's requirement for fast, accurate survey is on the way to being solved. Needs have been stated for new countermortar and counterbattery radars, and the Army is in the advanced phases of the equipment development cycle for the new radars. Also being developed but not yet in the inventory is new sound ranging equipment that will be easier to emplace and will be faster and more accurate in determining enemy target locations.

Even while U.S. ground troops were still fighting in Vietnam, some promising developments occurred in target acquisition. A new moving target locating radar, the AN/TPS–58 (RATAC) was introduced to replace the AN/TPS–25. The RATAC, which has a longer range and a wider sector of scan and is easier to emplace than its predecessor, proved quite effective though its availability was limited. Perhaps more important than the RATAC was the employment of several types of unattended ground sensors. Though the over-all effectiveness of unattended ground sensors was difficult to assess, the concept proved workable and has prompted follow-up development.

While target acquisition systems are being developed and refined, the Field Artillery School has been conducting studies to determine those organizations that can best employ the systems. It is generally conceded that the present organization, which centralizes most of the target acquisition assets at corps artillery in the field artillery target acquisition battalion, is no longer adequate. While in some situations corps artillery will have a need to control a system whose coverage is wide and deep enough to serve the entire corps, in many other situations such centralization will inhibit the responsiveness of fire support. A sizable target acquisition capability at the division artillery and direct support battalion levels is needed in order to acquire and destroy targets at lower artillery levels in response to more localized needs on the modern battlefield.

In tactical operations planning Vietnam showed that the importance of the fire support co-ordinator and the forward observer to the success of a battle has expanded significantly over the past decade. The mobility of U.S. forces has advanced to a point that in any future conflict, whether a small-scale insurgency or a high-intensity war, the situation on the battlefield most likely will be fluid, with continuous night and day operations. No longer can the Army depend on the neat phasing of operations that permitted the luxury of detailed advance planning for employing maneuver forces and their supporting fires. Planning will be ongoing and in reaction to the circumstances of the moment. Moreover, the weapon systems available to support ground troops have proliferated over the years, as have the types of ammunition for each system. Fire support co-ordinators, particularly at the lower levels (maneuver battalion and brigade), will have to be chosen from the very best field artillery officers available. They and the forward observers with the maneuver units must bring decisive fire power of the right types and amounts to fulfill the needs of the ever-changing situation on the ground. On the modern battlefield they must know at once what fire support is available, how to get it, and how to employ it. They must be able to co-ordinate each of the various fire support means available to them so that they obtain the maximum effect from all. Through it all they must keep direct support battalions fully informed about what the supported maneuver forces are doing on the ground.

Despite the challenge that modern warfare presents to the fire support co-ordinator and the forward observer, neither can be given the training time required to learn their duties on the job. They must be trained and prepared to assume full duties immediately upon arrival in the combat theater. When the system is operating correctly the ground commander, knowing how to use fire support, can concentrate on the plan of maneuver, confident that his fire support co-ordinator and the forward observers will arrange the necessary fires to support the maneuver plan with minimum supervision.

The field artillery community has recognized the increased importance of fire support co-ordinators and forward observers and has taken action to insure that both will be fully qualified to assume their duties in the event of war. The program of instruction on fire support co-ordination for the field artillery officer advanced course and the instruction given lieutenants in the basic course on duties of the forward observer have been expanded to include more practical training in a more realistic environment. Fire planning is also being streamlined and will be realistically based on priority, not on quantity of targets.

We expect the high density of aircraft on the modern battlefield to require that air space usage be carefully co-ordinated. Vietnam exposed the overlapping control of usable air space, for the field artillery was given the mission of controlling air space over battle areas because it seemed a logical extension of its duty of co-ordinating fires. If the field artillery fire support officer co-ordinates the activities of all supporting fire in the target area, he is in fact co-ordinating the use of air space. The argument is valid so long as the air space co-ordination responsibilities of the fire support officer are limited to the target area. But this was not in fact the case. These responsibilities most often included a large area of operations and involved the issuance of advisories to administrative air traffic as well as all other air traffic entering or traversing the area. In Vietnam the artillery liaison sections, particularly at maneuver battalion and brigade levels, devoted a large portion of their efforts to controlling, or managing, air traffic, sometimes to the detriment of the primary duty for which they were organized and equipped—the co-ordination of supporting fires. At present, studies are being conducted to determine how this matter might best be resolved. Over the long term, air space management may be automated, and the Army is attempting to determine exactly what is required of an automated system before materiel is developed.

Overshadowing the whole problem of managing air space are service missions and functions that recognize the Air Force component commander as the air space manager in a combined environment. In practice, the Air Force has allowed the Army to manage air space over the battle area. Still, there is no assurance that the Air Force will be able to operate in future conflicts as it did in Vietnam.

In materiel, the requirements for upgraded artillery weapons in a conventional war conveniently overlap the requirements for artillery weapons in a counterguerrilla war. In Vietnam, weapons with longer ranges were needed to mass fires and to provide increased area coverage, just as they will be needed in a conventional war on the modern battlefield. Also, lightweight artillery contributes as much to the strategic mobility of airborne forces as it does to the tactical mobility of airmobile forces in either a conventional or counterguerrilla war. Both types of force will be well served by the new towed models of 105- and 155-mm. howitzers, which are in advanced stages of development. The new weapons will be close to the same weight and will have the same reliability but will shoot considerably farther than those they are to replace.

These, then, are the major areas on which the field artillery is concentrating its attention to prepare for future conflicts, regardless of the type of battlefield on which it is called to fight. In retrospect it is apparent that field artillery units initially sent to Vietnam were not always properly organized to accomplish the job before them. Major internal reorganizations and major changes to operating procedures were often required. This is no criticism of the state of preparedness to fight in Vietnam, for the U.S. Army was trained and its forces were organized to fight in a conventional war. There was no time to reorganize, and, even if time had been available, the Army had little counterguerrilla expertise within its ranks. Uncertainty of exactly what was to be done or how to do it resulted.

Vietnam provided valuable insight into how American forces might best fight and be organized to fight in future counterguerrilla operations, and detailed tactical field artillery lessons are available.

The challenges peculiar to counterguerrilla warfare for the field artillery may be addressed by doctrinal and organizational studies to determine how best to employ weapons effectively. These studies are relatively inexpensive, so the eventuality of another insurgency can be prepared for despite a redirection of priorities or budgetary restrictions.

The Field Artilleryman's Performance

Vietnam underscored certain doctrinal, organizational, and materiel insufficiencies that have been mentioned earlier. They are being corrected in the postwar period. It must be noted, however, that these insufficiencies did not prevent field artillerymen from carrying out their mission.

In every modern war the performance of the field artillery forward observer party has surpassed the most optimistic expectations. Vietnam was no exception. There an observer party generally consisted of only two men—the forward observer, who was most often a lieutenant but sometimes a junior noncommissioned officer, and a radio operator. Americans had in Vietnam the smallest forward observer party of any army in the Free World. Numerically, these parties represented a small part of the total field artillery force, but their number belied their importance. They were responsible for traveling with infantry rifle companies and calling for and adjusting indirect artillery fires in support of the companies. The forward observers were, therefore, the key to the proper functioning of the entire field artillery system—a responsibility that in many armies is fulfilled by the battery commander.

Vietnam presented unusual problems to the forward observer. Thick jungle foliage frequently obscured his observation and thus made difficult the adjustment of fires and determination of position. In the Mekong Delta, where observation was good, the land was often so flat and unvarying throughout that position determination was difficult. The forward observer used a number of tricks to support the infantry: he requested spotting rounds when his location was in doubt; he adjusted with smoke before firing high-explosive ammunition to insure the safety of ground troops; when in dense foliage, he adjusted by sound; and he continuously sought out vantage points—hills, rocks, trees—that would allow him to observe supporting fires.

There can be little doubt that the forward observer succeeded in supporting the rifle company. The very esteem in which he was held by the infantry is evidence enough that he got the job done. As in the past, the infantry valued artillery support so much that it was hesitant to move without its forward observer or beyond the range of its supporting cannons. If the forward observers had done nothing more than provide supporting fires, that would have been enough; most often, they did more. They commonly navigated for the company, directed the fires of organic infantry mortars, and assisted the company commander in numerous other ways. On occasion the forward observer, by virtue of his rank and the absence of other company officers, found himself second in command succession to the company commander. Vietnam reinforced the reputation of American noncommissioned officers and junior officers as the maneuver company commander's strong right arm.

Field artillery fire support co-ordinators at all maneuver levels from battalion up also deserve recognition for a job well done. The complexities of co-ordinating supporting fires on the modern day battlefield in general, and in Vietnam specifically, have been discussed earlier. There can be no doubt that tremendous demands were placed on fire support co-ordinators, especially those with the maneuver battalions and brigades. In addition, they were short on doctrine applicable to their situation, they were hampered by rules of engagement and necessary clearance procedures, and they were required continuously to co-ordinate air space usage. Yet they met the challenge superbly. They quickly learned the capabilities of each type of available weapon system, how to get it, and how to orchestrate its employment with other weapons on the battlefield.

During offensive operations, the fire support officer with a maneuver brigade or battalion often traveled with the maneuver commander. Most often the two, in addition to any subordinate commanders or staff officers the maneuver commander elected to take, orbited the battlefield in a command and control helicopter, a control method not likely to be used on the modern battlefield. The commander supervised and controlled the maneuver of his forces. The fire support officer, normally a field artillery captain, brought fire power to the battle area in support of the ground forces. He bore heavy responsibility for an officer of his rank. His job required that he think and act calmly and precisely, yet quickly, under intense pressure in response to the ever-changing situation below.

Artillerymen with firing units did a superlative job in providing continuous, and with the Military Assistance Command rules of engagement, responsive, support to ground forces. Their use both of existing mobility systems and of the fire base concept allowed firing units to follow and support forces with the same high quality support accredited to the field artillery in the past. Field artillerymen had experience in moving by road convoy and, as expected, did it well. Still, the environment increased the dangers to convoy movement and necessitated more detailed preparations than previously had been required. Roads had to be swept of mines and secured in advance, and personnel had to be thoroughly rehearsed in counterambush procedures. More impressive than their ability to move by convoy was the field artillerymen's ability to follow maneuver forces by helicopter and boat. A practiced direct support artillery battery could move by air quickly and efficiently. With only a few hours notice, battery personnel could break down their position and rig all their weapons, equipment, barrier materials, and ammunition for sling loads to be carried by helicopter. Combat loading was practiced so that when the first weapon arrived at its new position, equipment and ammunition would be ready to fire at once. The ability to move and support by boat was particularly noteworthy because the equipment used was simply never designed for that purpose. The development of U.S. riverine artillery involved a series of equipment and operational innovations, each one resulting in greater efficiency.

The most common term to come out of the Vietnam war was "fire base." The fire base was not a defensive outpost but an integral part of an offensive effort. Once the field artillery firing unit was moved and positioned, the establishment of a carefully planned fire base allowed the unit to stay in the position. The fire base provided protection for firing units, even in the most hostile regions. If a firing unit was brought into position in the morning, by nightfall overhead cover had been constructed, the infantry defenses had been prepared, infantry and artillery defensive fires had been integrated and rehearsed, and mutually supporting fires from distant fire bases had been planned and fired. These defensive preparations insured that the firing unit would always be effective when called upon to serve its function of supporting offensive operations with indirect fire.

Normally the fire base was the forward command post of the maneuver battalion. The men of the firing units were quick to adopt new schemes to bring responsive fire support to the infantry from their established fire bases. New procedures in the fire direction centers and at the weapons permitted the rapid shifting of fires with no loss of accuracy and little loss of time.

Field artillery commanders at all levels demonstrated flexibility and imagination in the performance of their mission. Much of the field artillery had been organized to fight conventionally. As a result, changes in organization and procedures had to be made at all levels to accommodate the situation. At the battery, fire direction centers were augmented with additional men and equipment to provide for decentralized operations and to permit firing units to occupy several separate positions. At direct support battalions, it was often necessary to organize additional firing batteries to provide the coverage required by maneuver brigades whose area of operations might cover hundreds of kilometers. At all battalions, many of the maintenance, supply, and administrative activities of the batteries were centralized and supervised so that battery commanders were relieved of many of those responsibilities. At higher levels, commanders were given new responsibilities such as base camp defense, which required internal reorganization of headquarters. Changes to operating procedures often required a corresponding organizational change, which could only be accomplished by use of assets authorized by tables of organization and equipment. Thus, when battery fire direction centers were increased in size and capability, personnel and equipment were taken from other sections within the battery or provided from the existing assets of the parent battalion. Or, when an additional firing battery was added to a battalion, it was organized from personnel and equipment taken from each of the other batteries. This ability of artillery commanders, restricted by tables of organization and equipment, to accomplish necessary internal reorganization to meet the situation was impressive.

The field artillery advisers in the early years of the war must also be recognized. Theirs was the lonely task of "advising" officers and men who had been in combat for years. They worked long and hard to teach the Vietnamese how to employ American weapons. They were often frustrated in the early years by the relative inefficiency of the Vietnamese artillery and the great reluctance with which their advice was sometimes accepted. That these were common complaints of the French advisers with the fledgling American army in the 1780's made them no less frustrating in the 1960's. Still, over the years the adviser's efforts achieved results and the South Vietnamese artillery at the time of the U.S. withdrawal had officers and men with the requisite knowledge and equipment to do the job.

Effective performance from individual field artillerymen is certainly required if the entire system is to be effective but offers no assurance that the system will be effective. An assessment of field artillery performance cannot be made in isolation from the rest of the Army. The field artillery was an integral part of total U.S. combat power, all working toward the successful completion of a single mission.

The most professional army that the United States has ever fielded was sent to Vietnam to help a faltering nation repel an insurgency. Time after time American soldiers met the enemy on the battlefield and defeated him soundly. They pushed him from hamlets and villages, pursued him across the countryside, drove him from the highlands, and finally followed him into his sanctuaries. They bought time for the South Vietnamese to build their armed forces and bring their government to their people. It is true that American forces did not destroy the enemy; he could not be destroyed, only repulsed, because of the boundary limitations and manpower restrictions that were imposed. But Americans left Vietnam a stronger nation with the requisite know-how and equipment to do the job.

In all of this, the field artillery contributed significantly to the successful completion of the Army's mission. It helped ground forces repel the enemy and followed the ground forces in pursuit. It aided in the protection of hamlets, government installations, and lines of communication and held the enemy at bay while the South Vietnamese government worked with the people to better their lives and gain their support. It also helped build and strengthen the South Vietnamese field artillery to a point where it is capable of providing the support needed by its army. That is what the field artillery set out to do.

Index

A Shau Valley: 157–60, 168
Abrams, General Creighton W.: 197, 218. *See also* United States Army, Vietnam; United States Military Assistance Command, Vietnam.
Accidents, prevention and investigation of: 176–79
Administration, conduct of: 23, 43, 226, 239
Advisers: 21–37, 190, 192, 219, 230, 239
Aerial observers: 83, 94, 96, 179, 228
Aerial rocket artillery: 50–51, 88, 90–96, 100–10, 118, 131, 141–42, 212, 219. *See also* Tactical air support.
Aerial supply. *See* Airlifts of troops and supplies.
Agriculture: 5–7
Air Assault Division, 11th: 53–54
Air assaults. *See* Airborne operations; Airmobility concept, development and application of; Parachute assaults.
Air defense: 47, 60, 219
Air defense, enemy: 31, 157–59
Air operations. *See* Strategic air support; Tactical air support.
Air space, co-ordinating usage of: 48, 179, 234–35, 237
Air strikes. *See* Strategic air support; Tactical air support.
Air supply. *See* Airlifts of troops and supplies.
Airborne Brigade, 173d: 38, 81–86, 110, 112–20, 131
Airborne Infantry Regiments
 327th: 121–24
 503d: 117
Airborne operations: 31, 117
Aircraft. *See also* Helicopters.
 B–52: 94–95, 120, 151–54, 157, 160, 210–11, 223
 C–47: 129
 C–123: 107
 C–124: 108
 C–130: 52, 107–08, 112, 117

Aircraft—Continued
 C–141: 168
 safety, assuring: 179
 transport by. *See* Airlifts of troops and supplies.
Aircraft warning centers: 179, 201
Airfields, construction of: 17, 112
Airlifts of troops and supplies: 34–35, 44, 52–56, 75, 81–83, 88–96, 101–04, 107–10, 133, 147, 156, 168, 185, 213, 219, 238
Airmobile Divisions
 1st Cavalry: 53–54, 75, 86–96, 108, 130, 142, 155–60, 168, 207–15
 101st Airborne: 54, 160, 167
Airmobile firing platform. *See* Fire support.
Airmobility concept, development and application of: 34, 53–54, 81–82, 84, 89–96, 101, 133, 155–60, 219
Ambush actions: 39, 90, 165
Ambush actions, enemy: 31, 75, 96, 107
Americal Division. *See* Infantry Divisions, 23d.
Ammunition
 antipersonnel projectile, XM546: 61, 79
 Beehive round: 61, 79, 108–10, 113, 120, 127, 129, 161, 163, 193, 213–14
 expenditures and resupply: 49, 75–76, 83, 95, 104–06, 118, 121, 129, 142, 146–47, 151, 159–60, 165, 167, 185–86, 195, 212
 improved conventional munitions: 148, 164–65
 incendiary rounds: 174
 in Republic of Vietnam Army: 27
 smoke rounds: 130, 175
 time-fuzed: 61
 white phosphorous: 85, 130
An Khe: 89, 92
An Khe Pass: 221
An Lao Valley: 101
An Loc: 144, 221–24
An My: 146

Anderson, Captain Charles C.: 117
Anderson, Staff Sergeant Webster: 122–24
Angel's Wing area: 206
Annamite Mountains: 5
Antiaircraft defenses. See Air defenses.
Antipersonnel projectile XM546. See Ammunition.
Ap Bac: 30
Arc Light. See Tactical air support.
Areas of operations: 42, 239
  CHIEF: 75
Armor support: 107
Armored Cavalry Regiment, 11th: 96, 110–17, 207–15
Armored personnel carriers: 31
Army Artillery: 42
Army Reserve units: 97
Artillery assistance programs: 190–205
Artillery Battalions. See also Artillery units.
  1st, 5th Artillery: 111–17, 166–67
  1st, 7th Artillery: 76, 86, 107–10, 112–17, 142
  1st, 8th Artillery: 61, 113, 163–65
  1st, 11th Artillery: 168
  1st, 21st Artillery: 49, 93, 140, 157–60
  1st, 30th Artillery: 104, 142, 155, 157–60
  1st, 39th Artillery: 168, 219
  1st, 40th Artillery: 147–48
  1st, 44th Artillery: 189
  1st, 77th Artillery: 106
  1st, 83d Artillery: 142, 147, 158–60, 169
  1st, 84th Artillery: 70, 168
  1st, 92d Artillery: 192, 195–96
  2d, 4th Artillery: 124–29, 168
  2d, 9th Artillery: 181
  2d, 11th Artillery: 111–17
  2d, 12th Artillery: 168
  2d, 13th Artillery: 107, 111–117, 143, 165, 172–73
  2d, 17th Artillery: 89–96
  2d, 19th Artillery: 89, 106, 110, 157–160
  2d, 20th Artillery: 118–20, 158–60
  2d, 26th Artillery: 179
  2d, 32d Artillery: 111–17
  2d, 33d Artillery: 107, 112–17
  2d, 35th Artillery: 111–17
  2d, 40th Artillery: 147
  2d, 77th Artillery: 111–17, 120–21
  2d, 94th Artillery: 219
  2d, 138th Artillery: 167–68

Artillery Battalions—Continued
  2d, 320th Artillery: 61, 86, 121–24
  3d, 13th Artillery: 111–17, 120–21, 161–65
  3d, 16th Artillery: 121–24
  3d, 34th Artillery: 77, 147, 168
  3d, 82d Artillery: 111–17
  3d, 197th Artillery: 167–68, 172
  3d, 319th Artillery: 81–86, 107, 112–17, 129, 172
  4th, 42d Artillery: 194
  4th, 60th Artillery: 194
  4th, 77th Artillery: 167, 219
  5th, 2d Artillery: 111–17
  6th, 15th Artillery: 165
  6th, 16th Artillery: 110
  6th, 27th Artillery: 108, 111–17
  6th, 77th Artillery: 163–65
  7th, 8th Artillery: 108
  7th, 9th Artillery: 111–17
  7th, 11th Artillery: 111–17, 161–63
  8th, 4th Artillery: 158–60, 219
  8th, 6th Artillery: 72, 107–10, 112–17, 166–67
  8th, 25th Artillery: 179
  8th, 26th Artillery: 179
Artillery Command, Republic of Vietnam Armed Forces: 204
Artillery Groups
  23d: 73, 87, 133, 146, 167, 169, 189, 200, 207
  41st: 133–34, 167, 169
  52d: 169, 190, 194–95, 213
  54th: 112, 147, 167, 169
  108th: 155, 167, 219–20
Artilllery and Missile School. See Artillery School.
Artillery raids. See Fire support.
Artillery School: 23, 25–26, 84, 134–36, 227, 233
Artillery schools, Republic of Vietnam Army: 191, 200–205, 220, 228–29
Artillery units. See also Artillery Battalions.
  in airlifts. See Airlifts of troops and supplies.
  in airmobile division: 54
  in army artillery: 42
  arrivals and departures: 3, 38, 81, 86–87, 110, 129, 167–68, 215, 217
  artillery assistance program: 190–205
  combat effectiveness and deficiencies: 231, 236–40

INDEX

Artillery units—Continued
  in corps artillery: 42, 44–45, 233
  critiques of operations: 129–36, 165–66, 231–36
  in division artillery: 40–44, 46–47, 86, 96–97, 233
  emplacement and displacement: 44–45, 50, 55, 101–04, 107–08, 118–20, 133, 212–13, 215, 226–27, 232. *See also* Airlifts of troops and supplies.
  enemy: 13
  exchange program: 199
  in Field Forces: 45–47, 87
  fourth battalion concept: 169–70
  group organization: 42, 87
  infantry, relations with: 43–44, 55
  Jungle Battery: 200
  losses. *See* Materiel losses.
  mobility of: 43, 51–55, 238
  nondivisional units: 46–47, 96–97
  organization and training: 3, 23–24, 38–39, 45, 81, 87, 96–97, 133–36, 168–73, 231, 233–34, 238–39
  in parachute assaults: 31, 117
  personnel problems. *See* Personnel management and turbulence.
  platoon program: 215–16
  proficiency tests: 134
  separate battalions: 86
  soldiers, demands on and accomplishments: 129–30, 239–40
  strength, periodic: 97, 136, 169
  task organizations: 170–71
Artillery warning control centers: 48, 116, 179, 211
Artillery weapons
  8-inch howitzer: 44, 50, 59, 61
  105-mm. howitzer: 35, 49–50, 59, 61, 70, 77–79, 235
  155-mm. howitzer: 44, 47, 49–50, 59, 61, 70, 116, 235
  175-mm. gun: 50, 59
  in airlifts. *See* Airlifts of troops and supplies.
  on barges: 77–80
  deficiencies and improvements: 133, 231, 235
  dispositions and emplacements: 55–59, 70–71, 76–80
  Duster 40-mm. weapon: 60, 97, 111, 163–65
  enemy types: 11, 227
  on landing craft: 76–77

Australian forces: 48, 83–84
Aviation Group, 11th: 159–60
Awards. *See* Decorations and awards.

Ba Ria: 145
Ban Me Thuot: 138
Barges, artillery use of: 77–80, 147, 238
Base camps: 17, 44, 73–75, 160
Base camps, enemy: 112, 205. *See also* Cambodia; Laos.
Bearcat: 110
Beehive round. *See* Ammunition.
Beiler, Captain John A.: 77
Ben Het: 118, 195, 230
Ben Tre: 138, 145
Bien Hoa: 81, 83, 108, 143, 145, 167–68, 179
Binh Dinh Province: 98–110
Binh Duong Province: 167
Binh Gia: 107
Binh Long Province: 221
BINH TAY I operation: 213–15
BIRMINGHAM operation: 106–10
BLACK HORSE operation: 100–10
Bon Tri: 141
Bong Son: 35, 100–106
Box fire, application of. *See* Fire support.
Bridge demolition, enemy: 188
Brown, Major General Charles P.: 19, 134
Bu Dop: 212
Bulldozers: 162–63
Bunker systems: 73
Bunker systems, enemy: 147, 154, 214

Ca Lu: 155
Caches, enemy. *See* Food losses, enemy; Materiel losses, enemy.
Calibration and registration. *See* Fire support.
Cam Ranh: 19
Cam Ranh Bay: 16
Cambodia: 5–6, 108, 120, 143, 165–66, 175, 182, 194–95, 205–15, 230
Camp, Brigadier General Marlin W.: 107
Camp Carroll: 12, 151, 153
Camp Enari: 73
Camp Evans: 156
Camp Holloway: 89
Camp Radcliff: 73, 92
Can Tho: 138
Canals. *See* Waterways.

Capital Military Assistance Command: 169
Capital Military District: 145, 167, 169
Casualties: 94–95, 110, 113, 121, 123–24, 129, 162–63, 166, 176, 182
 allied: 17, 38, 219
 enemy: 15, 30, 83–84, 89, 91, 94–95, 98, 106, 110, 112–13, 120, 129, 142, 146–48, 154–55, 157, 160, 162–63, 165–66, 182, 195, 214, 219
Cavalry Battalions and Squadrons
 1st, 4th Cavalry: 107
 1st, 5th Cavalry: 94–96
 1st, 7th Cavalry: 92–96, 157
 1st, 8th Cavalry: 90, 111–17
 1st, 9th Cavalry: 90, 155
 2d, 7th Cavalry: 94–96, 156–57
 2d, 8th Cavalry: 91
 2d, 12th Cavalry: 89–96, 108, 110, 140–42
 5th, 7th Cavalry: 140–41
Cay Giap Mountains: 101
Cease-fire agreements: 137, 229
Central Highlands: 5–6, 117–20
Central Office of South Vietnam: 111–12, 206
Charlton, Major Daniel P.: 77
Chemical agents: 174
China, People's Republic of: 6
Chu-Luc-Quan: 9
Chu Pong Massif: 92, 94
Chup Plantation: 207
Civic action programs: 188–89
Civil affairs: 44, 46
Civilian Irregular Defense Groups: 87, 89, 92, 112, 122–24, 148, 191, 193, 195, 200, 204–05, 213
Civilians, control of and support by: 20, 35, 44–45, 138, 174
Clearances, fire. *See* Fire support.
Climate: 7
Cluster bomb unit: 148
Coastal Lowlands area: 5, 7
Combat service support: 40, 73
Combat support: 40, 106
Command and control: 29, 42, 46–47, 55, 86–87, 112, 130, 237–38
Command and control, Republic of Vietnam Army: 19–20, 22, 29, 37, 43, 145, 169, 216
Communications systems and operations: 32–33, 40, 43, 83, 106, 125, 132, 155–56

Communications systems and operations, enemy: 143, 159, 228
Computers, tactical use of: 136
Congress of Unification: 8
Conscription programs, enemy: 10
Continental Army Command: 38
Convoys, supply and movement by: 52, 185, 237–38
Corps
 XXIV: 168–69, 179, 202, 216–17
 organization: 45
 Provisional Corps, Vietnam: 167, 169
Corps Artillery
 XXIV: 11, 201–02, 204, 216–17, 219
 XXX: 87
 Provisional Corps, Vietnam: 169
Corps Tactical Zones: 19
 I: 86, 118–24, 138–43, 147–48, 160, 167–68, 181
 II: 38, 87–96, 134, 138–57, 169, 190–91, 213
 III: 86, 110, 112, 140, 143–47, 157, 168–69, 198
 IV: 147, 168–69, 226
Counterbattery/countermortar fire. *See* Fire support.
Counterinsurgency, meeting: 7–8, 235–36
"Crachin": 7
Crain, Staff Sergeant Carrol V.: 110
Critiques of operations: 129–36, 165–66, 231–36. *See also* Lesssons learned.
Crittenberger, Brigadier General Willis D., Jr.: 111
Cu Chi: 143–44, 147
Cushman, Lieutenant General Robert E., USMC: 149

Da Lat: 18, 191
Da Nang: 11–12, 18, 81, 138, 179
Daisy Cutter bomb: 160
Dan Quan Du Kich: 9
Dan Quyen operation: 195
Dan Thang operation: 30
Dang Lao Dong: 8
Dang Tri Mountains: 148
Dau Tieng: 143, 182, 223
Davis, Private First Class Sammy L.: 127–29
Dean, Lieutenant Colonel Robert: 61
Decorations and awards: 110, 123, 128, 167
Defectors, enemy. *See* Repatriation program.

DELAWARE operation: 157–60
Demilitarized Zone: 13, 179, 181, 220–21
DEWEY CANYON operation: 219
Diem, Ngo Dinh: 18, 20, 22, 37
Dien Bien Phu: 21
Dinh Thong Province: 124
Direct fire. *See* Fire support.
Distinguished Service Cross award: 110
Districts and district chiefs: 19
Division Artillery
   1st Cavalry Division: 86, 142, 156–60
   1st Infantry Division: 86, 107–17, 172
   4th Infantry Division: 118–20, 188, 194
   9th Infantry Division: 110, 168
   25th Infantry Division: 111–17, 121, 161–63
Documents, capture and exploitation of: 15–17, 84, 137–38
Dong Ha: 167, 221–22, 224
Dong Nai River: 84
Dong Tam: 124
DONG TIEN operation: 198–200
Dong Xoai: 81–82
Drugs: 226
Duc Hoa: 144
Duc My: 25, 191
Duster 40-mm. weapon. *See* Artillery weapons.

EAGLE'S CLAW operation: 100–10
Engineer support: 107
ENHANCE project: 205, 216–17, 229
Equipment losses. *See* Materiel losses.

FADAC (field artillery digital computer): 136
Field Artillery School. *See* Artillery School.
Field expedients: 70
Field Forces, Vietnam: 42, 45
   I: 86–87, 190, 194
   II: 86–87, 110–17, 143, 147, 225
Field Forces, Vietnam, Artillery
   I: 133, 169, 190–94, 198, 200, 215–16, 226
   II: 87, 111–17, 134, 145, 169, 172, 198, 204, 206, 210–15
Field Front Headquarters, North Vietnamese Army: 92–93
Field Liaison Directorate, Republic of Vietnam Army: 229
Fire adjustment. *See* Aerial observers; Forward observers.

Fire Bases: 17, 55–72, 110, 121–24, 136, 161–67, 238
   5 and 6: 222–23
   BARBARA: 224–25
   BASTOGNE: 221
   BEAUREGARD: 120–21
   BUELL: 165
   BURT: 120–21
   CARROLL: 217
   CROOK: 166, 182
   CUDGEL: 124–29
   GOLD: 113
   MACE: 126–27
   MALONE: 182
   MAURY I: 161–63
   NANCY: 217
   PACE: 221
   PIKE VI: 163–65
Fire control, co-ordination and direction of: 18, 35, 41–44, 47–49, 55, 83–84, 96–97, 107, 112–13, 118–20, 132–35, 142, 151, 174, 195–96, 199–201, 210–15, 219, 230, 233–34, 237–38
Fire co-ordination. *See* Fire control, co-ordination and direction of.
FIRE CRACKER ammunition: 148
Fire direction. *See* Aerial observers; Fire control, co-ordination and direction of; Forward observers.
Fire direction centers: 30, 32, 39, 41, 59, 68–69, 72, 132–33, 136, 155–56, 238–39
Fire Direction Officer's School, Republic of Vietnam Army: 200
Fire support. *See also* Aerial rocket artillery; Tactics.
   from airmobile firing platform: 124, 147
   artillery raids: 184–88, 216
   from barges: 77–80, 147, 238
   in base camp defense: 73–75
   box fire: 151–53
   calibration and registration: 199–200, 228
   in Cambodia: 205–16
   clearances for: 48, 83–86, 142–43, 145, 151, 168, 173–79, 196, 215, 230, 237
   control, co-ordination, and direction: 18, 35, 41–44, 47–49, 55, 83–84, 96–97, 107, 112–13, 118–20, 132–35, 142, 151, 174, 195–96, 199–201, 210–15, 219, 230, **233–34**, 237–38

Fire support—Continued
  counterbattery/countermortar fire: 61–69, 85, 117, 120, 156, 227–28
  in counterguerrilla operations: 7–8, 235–36
  at Dak To: 117–20
  deficiencies and corrections: 18, 83–84, 231–32
  direct fire: 61, 73, 79, 153–54
  effectiveness: 95, 106, 116–18, 146–47
  enemy: 13, 149
  errors, investigating: 177
  fire plan: 68–69
  firing data, computing: 132–33, 175–76
  harassing and interdiction missions: 151, 187–88
  in Ia Drang campaign: 87–96
  indirect fire: 69–70, 238
  intelligence and interdiction fires: 188
  at Katum: 165
  at Khe Sanh: 148–57
  Killer Junior and Senior techniques: 61, 164
  in Laos: 218–19
  lessons learned: 3, 18, 31–37, 39, 84–86, 95–96, 113–16, 130–36, 161–65, 231–36
  mission assignment: 40–42, 45–47, 174–75, 231
  multiple volley missions: 151
  mutually supporting: 69, 96, 166, 238
  in parachute assaults: 31, 117
  by Republic of Vietnam Army: 26–33
  in riverine operations: 75–80, 238
  in Saigon area: 157
  at Thien Ngon: 165
  time-on-target fires: 41, 104, 151, 188, 195, 211
  types: 48
Fire support bases. See Fire bases.
Fire support co-ordination centers: 48, 83, 199–200
Fire support co-ordinator: 47
Fire support element: 48
Firing charts: 32, 72, 136
Firing data, computing. See Fire support.
Firing tables: 61
Fish Hook area: 206–07
FISH HOOK operation: 166–67
Flares, tactical use of: 33, 59, 73. See also Illumination, battlefield.
Food losses, enemy: 83–84, 92

Forward observers: 29–30, 43, 47–48, 68, 72, 83, 89, 96, 130–33, 179, 190–91, 214, 233–34, 236–37. See also Aerial observers.
Foster, Lieutenant Nathaniel: 72
Fourth battalion concept. See Artillery units.
France and French Army: 21–22, 25–27, 29–32, 83, 239
Free Wold Military Assistance Forces: 134, 200, 211. See also by name.

Gadsden Village: 189
Gavin, Lieutenant General James M.: 53–54
General Reserve, Republic of Vietnam Army: 169
Geneva Accords, 1954: 8, 10, 22
Geography. See Terrain features.
Gia Dinh Province: 145
Giap, General Vo Nguyen: 9, 17
Go Dau Ha: 207
Grenade assaults, enemy: 113, 122, 127, 161, 163
Grenade launchers: 60
Guerrilla units and operations, enemy: 9, 22, 30, 135–36
Gulf of Tonkin: 7, 38

Hamlet organization: 19–20
Harassing and interdiction fires. See Fire support.
Hay, Major General John H., Jr.: 167
Helgoland (hospital ship) : 189
Helicopters
  AH–1G Huey Cobra: 50
  CH–21 Shawnee: 35
  CH–34 Choctaw: 34
  CH–37 Mohave: 81–82
  CH–47 Chinook: 54–55, 75, 103–04, 107
  CH–54 Tarhe (Crane) : 54–55, 75, 104
  UH–1 Huey: 50, 54
  airlifts by. See Airlifts of troops and supplies.
  assaults by. See Tactical air support.
  fire support by. See Tactical air support.
  losses: 31, 159–60
  supply and transport by. See Airlifts of troops and supplies.
Highway 1: 100, 143, 224
Highway 9: 149, 155–57, 218–19
Highway 13: 144, 146, 221, 223

Highway 14: 194, 221
Highway 14N: 188
Highway 19: 38, 221
Highway 19E: 188
Highway 548: 159
Highway 555: 224
Hill 471: 155
Hill 758: 154
Hill 861: 149
Hill 875: 118
Hill 881S: 154
Ho Chi Minh: 8
Ho Chi Minh Trail: 221
Hoc Mon: 143
Hou Nghia Province: 167
Howze, General Hamilton H.: 53
Hue: 18, 138–43, 168, 221–22, 224–25

Ia Drang Valley: 87–96
Illumination, battlefield: 59–60, 94, 120, 127, 177
Improved conventional munitions. *See* Ammunition.
Improvement and Modernization Plan, Republic of Vietnam Armed Forces: 196–97, 202
Indirect fire. *See* Fire support.
Indochinese Communist Party: 8
Infantry
 artillery relationship with: 43–44, 55
 support of and by: 32, 43–44, 59–61, 107–08, 165, 236–38
Infantry Battalions
 1st, 503d Infantry: 83
 2d, 501st Infantry: 140, 142
 2d, 503d Infantry: 83
 3d, 60th Infantry: 168
 4th, 23d Infantry: 161–63
Infantry Brigades
 1st, 1st Cavalry Division: 89–96, 101–06, 118–20, 159–60
 1st, 4th Infantry Division: 117–20
 1st, 5th Mechanized Division: 50, 167, 220
 1st, 9th Infantry Division: 111–17
 1st, 101st Airborne Division: 86, 121–24, 167
 2d, 1st Cavalry Division: 95–96, 101–06, 155–57
 2d, 1st Infantry Division: 86
 2d, 9th Infantry Division: 76
 2d, 101st Airborne Division: 110

Infantry Brigades—Continued
 3d, 1st Cavalry Division: 92–96, 100–106, 138–42, 156–60, 212–15
 3d, 4th Infantry Division: 111–17
 3d, 9th Infantry Division: 168
 3d, 82d Airborne Division: 168
 3d, 101st Airborne Division: 110
 196th Light: 96, 111–17
 199th Light: 96, 111–17, 145, 147
Infantry Divisions
 Americal. *See* 23d (American) *below.*
 1st: 75, 106–17, 138, 144, 146, 167
 4th: 73, 96, 117–20, 213–15
 9th: 96, 124–29, 134, 168, 226
 23d (Americal): 110, 167, 172, 202
 25th: 96, 110–17, 120–21, 143, 147, 165, 182, 212–15
Infantry Regiments
 22d: 113, 120
 60th: 124–29
Infiltration, enemy: 8–10, 138, 148
Infrared devices: 73
Inspections: 176
Instructors, Republic of Vietnam Army: 201–02, 204, 229
Intelligence and interdiction fires. *See* Fire support.
Intelligence operations and reports: 44, 91, 98–101, 106, 117, 125, 132, 153–54, 157, 159, 195, 205–06, 218, 220–21
Intelligence operations and reports, enemy: 148
Iron Triangle area: 110–11
Irrigation canals. *See* Waterways.

Jennings, Sergeant Delbert O.: 110
JIM BOWIE operation: 104
Johnson, Lyndon B.: 38, 128
Joint Chiefs of Staff: 197
Joint General Staff, Republic of Vietnam Armed Forces: 19, 193, 218, 220
Joint operations. *See* Riverine operations.
JUNCTION CITY operation: 111–17, 136
Jungle Battery. *See* Artillery units.

Katum: 117, 165
KEN GIANG operation: 124–29
Kennedy, John F.: 22
Kentucky National Guard, 167–68
Khe Sanh: 148–57, 168, 182, 219, 231
Khe Sanh Plateau: 218

Killer Junior and Senior techniques. *See* Fire support.
Kim Son Valley: 101, 108
Kontum: 138, 192, 222–24
Kontum Pass: 221
Kontum Province: 117, 194–95, 223
Korean forces. *See* Republic of Korea forces.

La Vong: 224
Lai Khe: 107, 144, 146
LAM SON operations: 157–60, 218–19, 224, 230
Lan, Major General Lu Mong, Republic of Vietnam Army: 194
Landing craft, artillery fire from: 76–77
Landing Zones: 17, 31, 52, 90
  ALBANY: 94–95
  BIRD: 61, 108–10, 136
  BLACKHORSE: 116
  COLUMBUS: 93–96
  FALCON: 92–95
  NOLE: 142
  STADIUM: 92
  STUD: 155–57
  X-RAY: 92–94
Lang Vai: 148
Language barrier: 48, 134
Lao Dong Party: 8
Laos: 5, 7, 154, 181, 194–95, 218–19, 221
Leaflets, warning by: 174
Lessons learned: 3, 18, 31–37, 39, 84–86, 95–96, 113–16, 130–36, 161–65, 231–36
Liaison personnel and measures: 18, 21, 46, 48, 68, 83–84, 89, 106, 112–13, 120, 134–35, 142, 145, 179, 190, 192, 196, 201, 207, 213–15, 234
Liberation Army of the Front: 9
Lien-Viet: 8
Lines of communication: 27, 45
Loc Ninh: 117, 137, 221
Logistical systems and operations: 23, 43, 46, 185, 192, 198, 202, 216
Logistical systems and operations, enemy: 9, 205
Lon Nol: 205
Long Binh: 143–45
Loudspeakers, warning by: 174

MACARTHUR operation: 117–20
McGuire, Brigadier General Thomas J.: 215–16
Machine guns: 60

Machine guns, enemy: 13
McNamara, Robert S.: 196
McNamara Wall: 181–82
Maintenance and repair: 23, 44, 186–87, 198, 216, 239
Malaya: 20, 51
Map reading: 130–31
Marxist Study Club: 8
MASHER operation: 98–110
Materiel losses: 129, 149, 151, 161–63, 219
  enemy: 83, 91–92, 101, 112–13, 156–57, 159–60, 182, 214, 227
  Republic of Vietnam Army: 222–23
Medal of Honor awards: 110, 123, 128, 167
Medical Civic Action Program: 188–89
Medical evacuation and treatment: 121, 123
Medical supply losses, enemy: 92
Mekong River and Delta: 5–6, 30, 52, 75–80, 147, 221, 226, 236
Meteorological data: 30, 183–84, 199–200, 228
METRO MEDIA operation: 226
Midway conference: 197
Mil system: 32, 70, 72, 135–36
Mildren, Lieutenant General Frank T.: 187–88
Military Academy, Republic of Vietnam: 191
Military assistance programs: 21–22, 190–205
Military Assistance Training Agency: 23
Military Regions: 42
  I: 201, 204–05, 217–25, 229
  II: 204–05, 221–23, 226, 229
  III: 205, 207, 213, 221, 223, 229
  IV: 110, 205, 226
Militia units, enemy. *See* Paramilitary units, enemy.
Minh, Major General Nguyen Van: 221
Mining operations: 59, 73
Mining operations, enemy: 14–15, 107, 188, 238
Mission assignment. *See* Fire support.
Mobile Riverine Force: 147
Mobile Strike Force, 3d: 173, 200
Monsoons. *See* Weather, effect on operations.
Montagnards: 154
Morale problems: 226
Morale status, Republic of Vietnam Army: 27–28, 31, 35–37, 216

Mortar fire assaults: 237
Mortar fire assaults, enemy: 11, 15, 68, 89, 92, 95, 108, 113, 120, 122–26, 138, 145, 149, 156, 161, 163, 166, 180, 182
Mortars: 60
    enemy: 13
    Republic of Vietnam: 27–28, 34–35
Motor vehicles: 44
Multiple volley missions. See Fire support.
Murray, Private First Class William H.: 128
Mutually supporting fires. See Fire support.
My Chanh River: 223–24
My Tho: 138, 145, 147
My Tho River: 147

Napalm, tactical use of: 94
National Guard units: 97, 167–68, 172
National Liberation Front: 8–10, 137–38, 142, 144
National Police: 138, 144–45, 169
Naval air and gunfire support: 45, 47, 76–80, 100, 106, 141–42
Navarre, General Henri-Eugène: 21
Navigation, land: 43, 130, 237
New Hampshire National Guard: 167–68, 172
New Plei Djereng: 213
New Zealand forces: 48
Newport: 144
Newsmen: 82
Nguyen Hue offensive: 221–22, 227–28, 230
Nha Trang: 25, 86–87, 138
Night operations: 88
Night operations, enemy: 11, 60, 108, 122–24, 151
Nixon, Richard M.: 168, 190, 193, 197
Noncommissioned officers: 24, 136
Noncommissioned officers, Republic of Vietnam Army: 25
Nondivisional artillery. See Artillery units.
North Vietnamese Army: 9–14, 87–96, 111, 118, 137–57, 166, 182, 196, 205, 221–25, 228. See also Viet Cong.
    9th Division: 221
    304th Division: 156
    4th Regiment: 138
    6th Regiment: 138
    18th Regiment: 100–101, 106

North Vietnamese Army—Continued
    22d Regiment: 101, 108
    28th Regiment: 195
    32d Regiment: 91–92
    33d Regiment: 91–93
    40th Artillery Regiment: 195
    66th Regiment: 91–94, 195
    210th Regiment: 100
Northern Mountains area: 3–6
Northern Plains area: 3, 5, 7

O'Daniel, Lieutenant General John W.: 22. See also United States Military Assistance Advisory Group, Vietnam.
Officer Candidate School: 135
Officers, Republic of Vietnam Army: 25–26, 31, 203
Okinawa: 81
On-the-job training: 134, 199, 234
Operational control. See Command and control.
Operational readiness evaluations: 199
Operations procedures. See Fire support; Tactics.
OPORD 17–65: 83
Orientation training: 39, 133–35
Outposts: 17, 27, 32

Parachute assaults: 31, 117
Paramilitary units, enemy: 9–10
Paramilitary units, Republic of Vietnam. See Civilian Irregular Defense Groups; Popular Forces; Regional Forces.
Parrot's Beak area: 206
Patrol actions: 60, 73, 75, 81, 95, 113, 165, 182
Peers, Lieutenant General William R.: 118, 194
PEGASUS operation: 155–57
People's Army of Vietnam. See North Vietnamese Army.
People's Liberation Armed Force: 9–14. See also Viet Cong.
People's Revolutionary Party: 8, 20
Perimeter defense: 39, 54–61, 73–75, 90, 93–94, 120–29, 136, 148–57, 165–66
Personnel management and turbulence: 23, 226, 228, 239
Philippines Embassy: 144
Philippines forces: 48
Photogrammetric survey: 116
Photography, aerial: 116

Phu Chang: 145
Phu Loi: 73, 75, 106–07, 145–46, 189
Phuc Long Province: 108
Phuoc Vinh: 75
Physical training: 89
Pike, Douglas: 8
Piper, First Lieutenant John T.: 109–10
Platoon program. *See* Artillery units.
Plei Me: 87, 91–92
Pleiku: 87–96, 190, 194
Political crises: 37
Political structure
 enemy: 7–9
 Republic of Vietnam: 18–19
Popular Forces, Republic of Vietnam: 19–20, 169, 190–92, 196, 198, 202, 215
Population, control of. *See* Civilians, control of and support by.
Power plants: 144
Presidential Unit Citation award: 110
Press corps: 82
Prey Vang: 207
Prisoners of war, enemy: 30, 84, 89, 91, 100–101, 106, 113, 160, 195
Provinces and province chiefs: 18–19

Quan Da Special Zone: 201
Quan Loi: 12
Quang Nam Province: 17
Quang Nga Province: 98
Quang Tri: 138, 155, 222, 224
Quang Tri Province: 150, 218, 224
Quang Tri River: 148
Que Chu: 140–41
Qui Nhon: 108, 138, 222
Quirey, Brigadier General William O.: 190–91
QUYET TONG operation: 157

Racial tensions: 226
Radar systems: 179
 AN/MPQ–4 countermortar: 11, 116–17, 123, 180–81, 232
 AN/TPS–25 ground surveillance: 73, 180, 232
 AN/TPS–58 target-locating: 232
Radio communications. *See* Communications systems and operations.
Radio set AN/GRA–39: 176
Ranges, artillery pieces. *See* Artillery weapons, *by type*.
Recoilless rifle fire: 151

Recoilless rifle fire, enemy: 11, 89, 113, 122–24, 126– 29
Recoilless rifles: 60
Recoilless rifles, enemy: 13
Reconnaissance
 aerial: 68, 116, 124, 187
 enemy: 148, 165
 by fire: 96, 166
 ground: 75, 135–36, 148, 155, 160
 map: 187–88
Red River and Delta: 5–6
Reference points: 70
Refugees, assistance to: 189
Regional Development Program: 138
Regional forces, enemy. *See* Paramilitary units, enemy.
Regional Forces, Republic of Vietnam: 19–20, 169, 190–92, 196, 198, 202, 205, 215
Registration procedures: 199–200, 228
Reorganization Technique Plan, Republic of Vietnam: 204
Repair facilities and parts. *See* Maintenance and repair.
Repatriation programs: 110
Republic of Korea forces: 48, 98
Republic of Vietnam: 18–20, 138
Republic of Vietnam Air Force: 214, 218
Republic of Vietnam Armed Forces: 19, 138, 196–97, 203–04, 217, 225
Republic of Vietnam Army: 48, 82, 89, 98, 110, 140–45, 148, 169, 182
 V Area Logistical Command: 229
 24th Special Tactical Zone: 194–95
 3d Airborne Task Force: 155–57
 I Corps: 218–19, 227
 II Corps: 100, 190–205
 III Corps: 198–200, 206–15, 221
 IV Corps: 207, 226
 I Corps Artillery: 202, 219–20, 225
 III Corps Artillery: 200
 1st Airborne Division: 207, 219, 224
 1st Division: 138–43, 201, 228
 1st Division Artillery: 201
 3d Division: 220–22
 7th Division: 226
 18th Division: 145, 227
 21st Division: 227
 22d Division: 100–101, 227
 25th Division: 145, 228
 5th Ranger Group: 143, 145
 Airborne Brigade: 100, 107

INDEX

Republic of Vietnam Army—Continued
　Airborne Brigade Artillery: 100, 106
　　138, 196–97, 203–04, 217, 225
　1st Armored Brigade: 219
　3d Brigade, 1st Airborne Division: 210–15
　3d Regiment: 157–60
　9th Regiment: 212
　42d Regiment: 118, 194
　43d Regiment: 84
　3d Battalion, 2d Airborne Brigade: 83
　4th Battalion, 2d Airborne Brigade: 83
　25th Battalion: 35
　30th Artillery Battalion: 220–21
　31st Artillery Battalion: 222
　32d Artillery Battalion: 220
　33d Artillery Battalion: 220, 222
　37th Ranger Battalion: 156
　101st Artillery Battalion: 216
　104th Artillery Battalion: 229
　221st Artillery Battalion: 192
　advisers, relations with: 24–37, 190, 192, 219, 230, 239
　artillery organization and strength: 23, 97, 191, 216, 220
　artillery units expansion: 204–05, 218, 220, 229
　Associate Battery Program: 193
　combat effectiveness and deficiencies: 25, 35–39, 190–93, 195–96, 202–03, 214–15, 219–20, 223, 225, 227–28, 230, 239–40
　difficulties with commanders: 89
　exchanges, battery personnel: 199
　instructor training: 201–02, 204, 229
　leaders, lack of and training: 25–26, 31, 203
　organization and strength: 21
　self-sufficiency program: 215–19. *See also* Vietnamization program.
　training programs: 25–26, 134, 190–94, 198–205, 216–18, 220, 229
　weapons deliveries to: 197
Republic of Vietnam Marine Corps: 138, 224
Reserves, tactical use of: 40
Resupply. *See* Supply systems and operations.
Riot control agents: 174
River Assault Flotilla 1: 76
Riverine operations: 75–80, 238
Rivers: 6

Road system: 27, 107
Rocket artillery, aerial. *See* Aerial rocket artillery.
Rocket assaults, enemy: 11–13, 68, 70, 118, 122–24, 138, 145, 149, 156
Rockpile area (Khe Sanh): 150, 153, 155
Rogers, Lieutenant Colonel Charles S.: 166–67
Ruses: 100
Ruses, enemy: 138

Saigon area: 18, 21, 25, 37n, 81, 138, 143–47, 157, 163, 166–69
Saigon River: 144
Sanctuaries, enemy: 92, 205. *See also* Cambodia; Laos.
Sanitation measures: 39
Sapper assaults, enemy: 14–17, 122
Schaible, Captain Dennis J.: 124–29
Schlenker, Captain Leonard L.: 109
Seaman, Lieutenant General Jonathan O.: 111
Search and destroy operations: 81, 92, 101, 106–10, 112–17, 156–57. *See also* Patrol actions; Reconnaissance.
Searchlights: 73
Secretary of Defense. *See* McNamara, Robert S.
Section chiefs: 133, 136
Security measures and operations: 11, 19, 39–40, 80, 89, 100, 107–08, 112, 124, 143, 198, 204, 215, 217, 238
Security measures and operations, enemy: 15
Sensor devices: 179, 181–82, 233
Sentries: 39
Separate battalions: 86
Shelling reports: 85
Sihanouk, Prince: 205
Smith, Captain Theodore F.: 35
Smoke, tactical use of: 130, 175, 236
Snipers, enemy: 61, 91
Song Be: 108
Soui Cut: 120–21, 136
Soui Da: 107, 112
Soui Tre: 113
Sound-and-flash ranging: 179, 232
South China Sea: 98
South Vietnam. *See* Republic of Vietnam.
Southern Plains area: 5–7
Soviet Union: 11, 231
Spare parts. *See* Maintenance and repair.

Special Forces troops: 101, 148, 173, 191, 193, 200, 213
Special Warfare School: 23
State, Department of: 22
Storage depots: 17
Strategic air support: 45
Strategic hamlets program: 20
Supply systems and operations: 27, 44, 75, 185, 239. *See also* Airlifts of troops and supplies.
Supply systems and operations, enemy: 138, 159–60
Surut, Lieutenant Colonel Lee E.: 81, 83
Surveillance. *See* Reconnaissance.
Surveys and survey equipment: 106, 116, 183–84, 199–200, 228, 232
Survival training: 39
Svay Rieng: 207
Sweeps. *See* Search and destroy operations.

Tactical air support: 30, 45, 47, 83, 88, 90–96, 100–10, 117–20, 129, 145–47, 150–57, 160–61, 167, 210–12, 218–19, 223, 228. *See also* Aerial rocket artillery; Strategic air support.
Tactical Mobility Requirements Board: 53–54
Tactical operations center: 48
Tactics: 23, 39–47
 enemy: 7–8, 10–11, 14–15, 27, 30–31, 39, 42
 Republic of Vietnam Army: 26–27, 29
Tam Ky:° 121
Tan Son Nhut: 144–45, 179
Tanh Canh: 118, 222
Tank–gun support: 151
Target acquisition and designation: 32–33, 41, 48, 73, 75, 85, 96, 106, 179–84, 187, 198, 211, 214, 216, 219, 227–28, 231–33
Task Forces
 ALPHA: 86–87
 BAI BAC I (Cannon I): 192–93
 DEXTER: 82
 HAY: 169
 INGRAM: 89
 OREGON: 110. *See also* Infantry Divisions, 23d.
 SHOEMAKER: 207–12
 SURUT: 81
 WARE: 145, 169

Task organizations. *See* Artillery units.
Tay Ninh: 107, 112–13, 165, 182, 207, 221–22
Tay Ninh Province: 106–17
Tchepone: 218–19
Terrain, effect on operations: 3–7, 18, 20, 34, 56–59, 70, 75, 96, 98, 108, 124–25, 130, 132, 236
Tests, proficiency: 134
Tet offensive: 137–57, 168–69, 193
Thach Han River: 224
Thailand forces: 48, 134
Thien Ngon: 165
Thien Phuoc: 121
Thieu, Nguyen Van: 37*n*, 197
Thu Dau Mot: 25
Thu Duc: 144
Thua Thien Province: 159
Ti Ti woods: 142
Time-on-target fires. *See* Fire support.
Timmes, Major General Charles J.: 28. *See also* United States Military Assistance Advisory Group, Vietnam.
TOAN THANG operation: 157
TOAN THANG operation 42: 206–15
Tonle Sap: 6
Training programs: 3, 23–24, 38–39, 45, 81, 87, 96–97, 133–36, 168–73, 231, 233–34, 238–39
 enemy: 17
 Republic of Vietnam: 25–26, 134, 190–94, 198–205, 216–18, 220, 229
Training Relations and Instruction Mission: 22
Trang Sup: 200
Transportation systems: 51–53
Trien Phong: 224
Troop transport. *See* Airlifts of troops and supplies.
Troop units, artillery. *See* Artillery Battalions; Artillery units.
Troop units, general
 arrivals and departures: 38, 167–68, 201
 buildup and reduction: 81, 96, 217, 220, 225–30
 enemy: 9–10
 Republic of Vietnam: 21
Trucks. *See* Motor vehicles.
Tunnel systems, enemy: 214

INDEX

United States Air Force: 17, 45, 47, 52, 89–90, 94, 108, 113, 148, 179, 200, 228, 235. *See also* Strategic air support; Tactical air support.
United States Army, Vietnam: 45, 86, 143, 172, 177, 187, 228.
  See also Abrams, General Creighton W.; Westmoreland, General William C.
United States Army Support Command, Vietnam: 86
United States Embassy: 37n, 144
United States Marine Corps: 38, 48, 81, 86, 98, 101, 138–43, 148–57
  Fleet Marine Force, Pacific: 81
  III Marine Amphibious Force: 86, 149–50, 168–69, 201
  3d Division: 155, 201
  9th Expeditionary Brigade: 38
  1st Regiment: 155–57
  26th Rigment: 155–57
  1st Battalion, 135th Regiment: 151, 155
United States Military Assistance Advisory Group, Vietnam: 3, 21–22. *See also* O'Daniel, Lieutenant General John W.; Timmes, Major General Charles J.
United States Military Assistance Command, Vietnam: 106, 138, 169, 196–97, 202–05, 211, 215, 217–18, 220, 237. *See also* Abrams, General Creighton W.; Westmoreland, General William C.
United States Navy: 76, 200. *See also* Naval air and gunfire support; Riverine operations.
Unity of command. *See* Command and control.

Vegetation, effect on operations: 6–7, 85, 96, 116, 130, 236
Vessey, Lieutenant Colonel John W.: 113
Vien, General Cao Vah, Republic of Vietnam Army: 218
Viet Cong: 9, 30–31, 35, 82, 87–96, 106–11, 117, 120–29, 137, 142, 147, 166, 182, 188, 196, 198, 205. *See also* People's Liberation Armed Force.
  250th Training Division: 10
  320th Training Division: 10

Viet Cong—Continued
  350th Division: 10
  338th Brigade: 10
  22d Training Group: 10
  1st Regiment: 100
  272d Regiment: 113
  273d Regiment: 146
  V-25 Battalion: 17
  514th Battalion: 30
Viet Minh: 8, 10, 21, 27
Vietnamization program: 190, 196–206, 214–19, 225–30
Village Administrative Committee: 19
Village Citizen's Council: 19
Village organization: 19
Vinh Long: 147
Vung Tau: 19

Walker, Captain Edward G.: 108
War Zone C: 112–17, 166
War Zone D: 83, 85, 173
Ware, Major General Keith L.: 145
Warsaw Pact: 231
Washington conference, 1955: 22
Water transportation: 52, 76
Waterways: 6
Weapons. *See by type*.
Weapons losses. *See* Materiel losses.
Weather, effect on operations: 7, 34, 101, 123, 157–59, 224
Westmoreland, General William C.: 143, 145, 149, 169, 190. *See also* United States Army, Vietnam; United States Military Assistance Command, Vietnam.
Weyand, Lieutenant General Frederick C.: 143, 145–46
WHEELER operation: 121–24, 181
White phosphorous rounds: 85, 130
WHITE WING operation: 98–110
Williamson, Brigadier General Ellis W.: 81, 84–85
Wind cards: 136
Winfield, Colonel Richard M., Jr.: 142
Wire communications. *See* Communications systems and operations.
Wire obstacles: 59, 73
World War II experience: 151

Xuan Loc: 145, 147

www.ingramcontent.com/pod-product-compliance
Lightning Source LLC
Chambersburg PA
CBHW070547160426
43199CB00014B/2403